Literary Research: S
Series Editors: Peggy K

Every literary age presents scholars with both predictable and unique research challenges. This series fills a gap in the field of reference literature by featuring research strategies and by recommending the best tools for conducting specialized period and national literary research. Emphasizing research methodology, each series volume takes into account the unique challenges inherent in conducting research of that specific literary period and outlines the best practices for researching within it. Volumes place the research process within the period's historical context and use a narrative structure to analyze and compare print and electronic reference sources. Following an introduction to online searching, chapters will typically cover these types of resources: general literary reference materials; library catalogs; print and online bibliographies, indexes, and annual reviews; scholarly journals; contemporary reviews; period journals and newspapers; microform and digital collections; manuscripts and archives; and Web resources. Additional or alternative chapters might be included to highlight a particular research problem or to examine other pertinent period or national literary resources.

1. *Literary Research and the British Romantic Era* by Peggy Keeran and Jennifer Bowers, 2005.
2. *Literary Research and the Era of American Nationalism and Romanticism* by Angela Courtney, 2008.
3. *Literary Research and American Modernism Era* by Robert N. Matuozzi and Elizabeth B. Lindsay, 2008.
4. *Literary Research and the American Realism and Naturalism Period* by Linda L. Stein and Peter J. Lehu, 2009.
5. *Literary Research and Irish Literature* by J. Greg Matthews, 2009.
6. *Literary Research and the Literatures of Australia and New Zealand* by H. Faye Christenberry and Angela Courtney, 2011.
7. *Literary Research and British Modernism* by Alison M. Lewis, 2010.
8. *Literary Research and the British Renaissance and Early Modern Period* by Jennifer Bowers and Peggy Keeran, 2010.
9. *Literary Research and the Victorian and Edwardian Ages, 1830–1910* by Melissa S. Van Vuuren, 2011.

Literary Research and the Literatures of Australia and New Zealand

Strategies and Sources

H. Faye Christenberry
Angela Courtney

THE SCARECROW PRESS, INC.
Lanham • Toronto • Plymouth, UK
2011

Published by Scarecrow Press, Inc.
A wholly owned subsidiary of The Rowman & Littlefield Publishing Group, Inc.
4501 Forbes Boulevard, Suite 200, Lanham, Maryland 20706
http://www.scarecrowpress.com
Estover Road, Plymouth PL6 7PY, United Kingdom

Contents

Acknowledgments

We would like to thank the series editors, Jenny Bowers and Peggy Keeran, for their support and encouragement throughout the course of the project, which took a bit longer than expected! We would also like to acknowledge Martin Dillon at Scarecrow Press, whose editorial expertise was essential to the final shaping of the volume.

We are grateful to the University of Washington Libraries and the Indiana University Libraries in granting professional leave, which allowed time away from regular duties to write the book. Without the diligent efforts of the University of Washington Libraries' Interlibrary Loan Department to borrow many of the resources described in selected chapters, the completion of the book would not have been possible. Finally, the state of Washington must be recognized for providing financial assistance to travel to Canberra, allowing the exploration of essential resources housed in the National Library of Australia. Indiana University and the Indiana University Libraries have generously supported this endeavor with travel grants that allowed for research at the University of Western Australia, the University of Sydney, the University of Melbourne, the University of Auckland, and the University of Otago. The IU Libraries Interlibrary Loan Department has been vital to the project by quickly and efficiently supplementing this research. And, of course, endless thanks go to Mike, Carolyn, Geoff, Zach, and Homer.

We would like to dedicate this book to the late Albert Wertheim, who taught at Indiana University from 1969 until the time of his death in 2003. It is due to Professor Wertheim's enthusiasm and love for Australian and New Zealand drama, poetry, and fiction that other North American scholars are researching and teaching the literature of "down under" today. It is our hope this book will encourage current and future students to discover the rich and diverse body of creative works emanating from Australia and New Zealand. Perhaps it will also facilitate additional scholarship devoted to this important area of literature.

Introduction

Literary research can be a challenging yet rewarding endeavor. Certain authors, such as Shakespeare, have been heavily studied; the sheer amount of research material currently available constitutes its own problems for literary scholars or students. Conducting research on more obscure authors often results in the opposite quandary; the lack of secondary resources forces scholars to use more refined search strategies and seek out alternative avenues for identifying information. Moreover, studying literature can be enhanced by examining the historical context in which a particular author lived and wrote. For some periods, such as Victorian England, significant portions of the primary printed resources (newspapers and magazines published during the nineteenth century, for instance) have been indexed, and many are now accessible as digitized, full-text documents on the Internet. For other literary periods, the situation is problematic. Indexes might be lacking, or periodical content still under copyright might not be obtainable in full text on the Web. Those interested in the literature of Australia and New Zealand can expect to encounter a unique set of challenges, depending on the type of information that is desired and the researcher's physical location.

We hope that *Literary Research and the Literatures of Australia and New Zealand* will remedy some of the common barriers faced in the study of this body of literature, especially for students and scholars living outside these two countries. Obstacles to the identification of primary and secondary scholarly materials relating to Australian and New Zealand literature are examined throughout this book, along with strategies for negotiating them. For those living in North America, a fundamental issue will be one of access. Very few research libraries in the United States have extensive collections of Australian and New Zealand source material, including texts such as early newspapers and magazines that would significantly augment an exploration of the history and culture of these two nations. Fortunately, many of these periodicals are now being scanned and made freely available by cultural institutions like the National Library of Australia and the National Library of New Zealand. Digitized finding aids to manuscript and archive collections are increasingly available, allowing researchers to discover the location of original documents without leaving their home or office computers. Still important to research in the discipline, however, are specialized bibliographies and indexes that facilitate an in-depth examination of a particular author or work. How do you identify specialized bibliographies and indexes relating to Australian and New Zealand literature if they have not been digitized and are not available on your library's shelves? Even the most basic task—the location of a book review—can be difficult, as the inclusion of Australian and New Zealand books in standard sources like the *New York Times Book Review* and the *Times Literary Supplement* is at best minimal. What is the best strategy for identifying reviews of Australian and New Zealand fiction and poetry if they are not present in these traditional literary research tools? These questions and more will be addressed throughout this volume.

In the past, a more fundamental challenge to researching Australian and New Zealand literature has been access to the literary works themselves. Fortunately, the Internet has eliminated much of this problem for libraries and individual readers. Bookstores with online inventories like Gleebooks in Sydney and used-book aggregator sites like Addall have made the identification and purchase of books by Australian and New Zealand authors a relatively easy, though often expensive, proposition. Nonetheless, the use of particular titles remains problematic for scholars interested in teaching Australian and New Zealand literature to their students. Due to copyright restrictions and lack of profitability, most books published in Australia and New Zealand are not distributed outside the two countries. Works that are picked up by a U.S. publisher often are only available for a brief period of time before going out of print. Exceptions do exist, of course (authors like Peter Carey and David Malouf are still in print and hopefully will remain so in the future), but in the case of most Australian and New Zealand literary authors, it is extremely difficult for college bookstores to acquire enough copies to meet classroom demand. To illustrate this problem, consider the work of Australia's 1973 Nobel Prize laureate for literature, Patrick White. White's fiction was out of print in the United States from 1994 to 2002, when the *New York Review of Books Classics* reprinted *Riders in the Chariot*. Penguin U.S.A. reprinted *Voss* and *The Vivisector* only recently, in 2009. All of White's other fiction is currently out of print; thus, multiple copies of these texts are virtually impossible to get for college literature classes. A similar example in the American context is illustrated by Alexis Wright's novel *Carpentaria*. Even though Wright won Australia's most prestigious literary award in 2007, the Miles Franklin, readers in the United States had no choice but to order copies from Great Britain (published by Constable in 2008) or directly from Australia until 2009, when Atria Books published the first U.S. edition of *Carpentaria*. Had *Carpentaria* not won such an important literary award, it is unlikely the book would have been published in either the United Kingdom or the United States, making it even more difficult to introduce this amazingly creative and enjoyable work of fiction to students of literature. Hopefully, the emergence of print-on-demand initiatives like *Classic Australian Works* and *SETIS Texts* (www .sup.usyd.edu.au/projects_etexts.html) will make literary and historical works more accessible to students and scholars, regardless of their physical location.

The format of our volume emulates others in Scarecrow Press's *Literary Research: Strategies and Sources* series. It provides descriptions of selected research tools pertinent to the study of Australian and New Zealand literature, including chapters on the following topics: the basics of online searching; general literary reference sources; library catalogs; print and electronic bibliographies, indexes, and annual reviews; scholarly journals; literary reviews; magazines and newspapers; microform and digital collections; manuscript and archive collections; Web resources; researching a difficult subject in Australian and New Zealand literature (Aboriginal or Māori creative works); and an appendix of selected resources useful to the examination of topics in related disciplines. In addition to outlining and describing the variety of resources available, fundamental concepts of research methodology are emphasized throughout the book. Each chapter stresses context-specific skills and processes that will enable literary scholars and researchers both to identify and locate what they might need in their work on Australian and New Zealand literature.

Literary Research and the Literatures of Australia and New Zealand endeavors to be as inclusive as possible, examining essential tools and recommending alternatives for those who may not have access to the best resources. The scope of the book includes information on identifying primary and secondary materials in all literary genres, from the beginning of the European settlement of Australia and New Zealand to the present day. The intended audience is researchers in the field of Australian and New Zealand literary studies, ranging from advanced undergraduate students to graduate students, faculty, and professional scholars who may not be familiar with the full array of resources pertinent to this discipline. Further, the volume should assist reference librarians working with students involved in this field of literary research. Anyone seeking to learn more about the literature and culture of Australia and New Zealand will find something of interest in this book. Reference tools covered in the guide range from the general and more familiar (such as the *MLA International Bibliography* and *AustLit*) to highly specialized bibliographies and histories (James Burnes's *New Zealand Novels and Novelists 1861–1979: A Bibliography* and Bruce Bennett's *Australian Short Fiction: A History*, for example). Those unfamiliar with Australian and New Zealand literature who are seeking guidance on how and where to locate information beyond the library catalog and standard bibliographic databases will find a variety of tools with suggestions for searching and identifying desired content more effectively. Advanced researchers in need of specialized resources such as guides to archival and manuscript collections will also have a range of options to investigate. These users are encouraged to cherry-pick through particular chapters and peruse sections that focus on a specific topic of interest. Researchers at all levels should be aware that information is constantly changing and evolving. By the time this volume is published, new resources (both in print and online) will be available to augment your examination of Australian and New Zealand literature. It is the authors' hope that the following chapters provide a better understanding of the literary research process and best practices for identifying and evaluating various types of resources, so scholars can meet the evolving information landscape head-on. Further, we hope the existence of the book will spark new interest in the exploration and scholarly study of Australian and New Zealand literature.

Chapter One

Basics of Online Searching

Literary researchers today must understand the complexities associated with using the vast array of online resources that are pertinent to the humanities in general, and to literature in particular, in order to be able to maintain control over their own research projects. In recent years there has been a virtual explosion in the range of online resources available to researchers. From increasingly robust databases that libraries access via subscription or outright purchase, to the rapidly expanding number of open-access digital resources, to more than one hundred years of print publishing, the national literatures of Australia and New Zealand offer distinctly diverse and exciting arenas of potential research.

This chapter will serve as a basic introduction to online searching, but it should be of use to students and scholars who are experienced users of digital resources, as well as to those who see themselves as beginners. Importantly, the theories and practices of online research covered in this chapter will appear often in the chapters that follow. The chapter starts at the beginning of a research project, moving from a question (the importance of place in the poetry of New Zealand, for one) to using the question as inspiration to develop a research plan, to deciding on keywords, honing the search, and finally figuring out how best to read, evaluate, and use the research results.

This book is starting with online searching because this now tends to be the way most research projects begin. Online research tools employ a broad range of *types* of bibliographic records, depending on such factors as national bibliographic practices, academic level of the resource, developer goals, submission policies (is the resource a vendor-produced one, or is it created and developed by an academic or interest community?), and so on. In this section, you will be introduced to the MARC record in order to explain the arrangement and function of most electronic records. While not every electronic record uses the MARC format, this logically arranged standardized

1

record will serve as a guide that should help you to decipher other electronic record results that may not be as easily understood. Exploring the facets of the MARC record will also help make sense of various search techniques, including the use of Boolean operators, effective truncation of search terms, and field searching. With the recent rise of *Google Books* and *Google Scholar*, the electronic landscape has become at once more fertile and more frustrating. This chapter will discuss these resources and their many implications for literary research.

STEP 1: THE RESEARCH PROBLEM AND ITS TOPIC STATEMENT

It is natural that a research project will shift and change as you work your way through the process, so it is a good idea to start by summarizing your idea in a brief topic statement. This initial step is easy to bypass and to discount as unnecessary, because it is natural to think you can keep your focus mentally without writing down your ideas. However, this step will not only help you to develop a map of the direction you want for your project, but it also creates a starting point that you can return to at various junctures in your research when you need to refocus or feel that you are deviating from your initial goals.

A project about writing that deals with women in the literature of nineteenth-century Australian settlers, for example, might be laid out as "I plan to examine the role of women in the writing of emigrants to Australia in nineteenth-century literature." For this project, your main ideas would include women, literature, Australia, and settlers. Similarly, if you were interested in learning more about New Zealand national identity in that country's literature, you might craft your topic statement as: "I want to research the influence of and imagery of the national identity of New Zealanders as conveyed in their literary genres." Your main ideas are New Zealand, national identity, poetry, drama, fiction, and prose.

STEP 2: EXPANSION TO A LIST OF KEYWORDS

Now, if you look over your topic statement and the list of general concepts, you will likely notice that your main ideas, although broad, are also limiting. When you are using online resources, you have to remember that these tools will not interpret your broad concepts in any way other than how you choose to use them; the responsibility for the completeness of an idea is yours. Practically speaking, you need to think broadly at this point in order to develop a list of synonyms for the extensive concepts as previously delineated.

Table 1.1. Possible Keywords for Searching on the Topic of Home in Emigrant Literature from Nineteenth-Century Australia

Concept #1	Concept #2	Concept #3	Concept #4
Women	Emigrant	Australia	Nineteenth Century
Feminine	Colonist		Colonial
Female	Settler		
Woman	Immigrant		
	Pioneer		

Why do you want to take this step? The purposes here are at least twofold: it allows completeness in your search, and it also gives you the opportunity to better develop and understand your own nascent idea. The list of terms will provide you with options if your initial terms do not work as well as you hoped. Similarly, the resources that you search will often employ different vocabularies, so an expansive but accurate list will be useful as your research becomes more advanced. If you return to the first topic, you can see that it looks fairly simplistic, but when you start thinking about the possible synonyms for each major term, you will see how quickly your list of terms can expand, how some words are indefinite, and how some need further precision. Look at the word *emigrant*, for example, and consider the meanings a researcher could imply with this word. *Emigrant* can also be a colonist, settler, immigrant, pioneer, and so on.

Listing potential synonyms in a table is a practical exercise. This brief task will arm you with a strong and far-reaching list of pertinent terms. As you use this list to explore databases, you may well find that the databases present other keywords that could prove quite beneficial (see table 1.1).

STEP 3: ELECTRONIC RECORDS AS
SEEN THROUGH THE MARC RECORD

One of the most effective ways to understand *what* a database searches is to look at a few bibliographic records that are part of a database. The MARC (Machine Readable Cataloging) record is a standard and commonly used format for electronic bibliographic records. While it is certainly not the format that every database appropriate for your research will use, it is a good example of the type of information you can find in an online database. MARC is the current standard for the Library of Congress, and most U.S. libraries use this format for records in their catalogs. When you search an online library catalog, you are looking at a collection of the MARC records, created by librarians and representing the items a library owns. Librarians examine the physical, and increasingly the electronic, items and work within the structure of the MARC record to describe as accurately as possible the item for which they are creating a representation. Successful searches in online resources rely on these representational records, and understanding their structure will help you to better exploit electronic resources. You have the ability not only to search for words within an electronic record, but also to specify where in the record you want to find your search terms. If you know the author or title (or parts of the author's name or title), you can create a search in which the database searches for specific words in certain areas, or fields.

Because there is a noticeable and important difference between MARC records for monographs and periodicals, this section will look at each type of record. A MARC record comprises a number of fields that are tagged with numerical codes indicating the content that belongs in any one field (author, title, subject, and so on). The contents of each field are used to create a specific index, and within the field is information that describes the item represented by the MARC record; each descriptive phrase in the subject field appears in an order specified by rules that govern the creation of MARC records, or a *controlled vocabulary*. All the individual indexes, along with the set of complete records, combined form the database.

Figure 1.1 shows a MARC record for a book, *Imagining Australia: Literature and Culture in the New New World*. This record has been modified for length by removing some fields that are designed for technical library use, but it retains the most pertinent information for use by students and scholars. By looking carefully at the record, you will be able to put together an assessment of the contents of the book, enabling you to decide whether or not the book is appropriate for your research. The author's name usually will appear in the 100 field, but you will notice that in this record there is no 100 field. As you look through the record, you can discern the title and publication information in the 245 and 260 fields, respectively. The 245 field also has a subfield for a statement of responsibility where you can find the editors' names. The statement of responsibility can also comprise the names of individual authors, compilers, corporate bodies, and conference sponsors. The 500 field is for notes, the 504 field provides information on the presence of an index or bibliography, and the very useful 505 field creates a place for the table of contents. A keyword search for *Ned Kelly* or *stolen generations* would have returned this record, but because these phrases are in the table of contents and not in the subject fields, a subject search would not have returned this record. The table of contents field, however, will not always be included in a bibliography, especially in records that represent older items. In this record, the 650 field is where you will find subject headings that describe the resource. These fields as well as

020 |a 0674015738

082 04 |a 700.994 |2 22

090 |a PR9609.6 |b .I43 2004

245 00 |a Imagining Australia : |b literature and culture in the new new world / |c edited by Judith Ryan and Chris Wallace-Crabbe.

260 ___ |a Cambridge, Mass. ; |a London : |b Harvard University Committee on Australian Studies : |b Distributed by Harvard University Press, |c 2004.

300 ___ |a xvii, 382 p., [8] p. of ill. : |b ill. ; |c 24 cm.

500 ___ |a "The essays in this volume emerged from a conference sponsored by the Harvard Committee on Australian Studies in late 2002 ... to showcase the exciting work that is being done in Australian literature and culture ..."--Introd.

504 ___ |a Includes bibliographical references and index.

505 00 |g PART ONE: NARRATIVE -- |t Out of England: literary subjectivity in the Australian colonies, 1788-1867 / |r Simon During -- |t Dead white male heroes: Ludwig Leichhardt and Ned Kelly in Australian fiction / |r Susan Martin -- |t Escaping the Bush paradigm / |r Lucy Frost -- |t David Malouf, history, and an ethics of the body / |r Andrew Taylor -- |t Identity, play, imagination: David Malouf, Hossein Valamanesh, and I / |r Ihab Hassan -- |t "Inner experience" in Gerald Murnane's The plains / |r Andrew Zawaki -- |g PART TWO: CULTURE -- |t A chance to hear a Nyigina song / |r Stephen Muecke -- |t "The first white man born": miscegenation and identity in Kim Scott's Benang / |r Tony Birch -- |t Sorry-in-the-sky: empathetic unsettlement, mourning, and the stolen generations / |r Gail Jones -- |t The mystery of the missing middlebrow or the c(o)urse of good taste / |r David Carter -- |t A short while toward the sun: the golden years of internationalism / |r Frank Moorhouse -- |t Australia, America, and the changing face of nature documentary / |r Graham Huggan -- |t The man from Hong Kong in Sydney, 1975 / |r Meaghan Morris -- |g PART THREE: POETRY -- |t "Woeful shepherds": anti-pastoral in Australian poetry / |r Paul Kane -- |t Two versions of Australian pastoral: Les Murray, |r William Robinson / |r Robert Dixon -- |t Darkness and lostness: how to read a poem by Judith Wright / |r Kevin Hart -- |t The presentation and performance of self in the poetry of John Forbes / |r Brian Henry -- |t "Split belonging" in Les Murray's novel in verse, Fredy Neptune / |r Judith Ryan -- |t The end of the line / |r Chris Wallace-Crabbe.

650 ___ 0 |a Australian literature |y 20th century |x History and criticism |v Congresses.

650 ___ 0 |a Literature and society |z Australia |v Congresses.

650 ___ 0 |a Arts |z Australia |y 20th century |v Congresses.

650 ___ 0 |a National characteristics, Australian, in literature |v Congresses.

651 ___ 0 |a Australia |x In literature |v Congresses.

651 ___ 0 |a Australia |x Civilization |v Congresses.

651 ___ 0 |a Australia |x Intellectual life |y 20th century |v Congresses.

700 1_ |a Ryan, Judith, |d 1943-

700 1_ |a Wallace-Crabbe, Chris.

710 2 ___ |a Harvard University. |b Committee on Australian Studies.

Figure 1.1. Modified MARC record for *Imagining Australia: Literature and Culture in the New New World,* with tags 245, 260, 650s, and 700s highlighted. Source: Auburn University Library Catalog.

the 505 field are of primary importance for keyword searching, which will be discussed in some detail later in this chapter. If you look farther down in the record, you will see a 700 field. This is a personal name field, and here you will find the names of the editors of this volume. Based on the rules that apply to the creation of MARC records, the names of editors and compilers always appear in the 700 field.

Figure 1.2 represents a periodical titled *The Journal of the Polynesian Society*. It looks a lot like the record for the monograph in figure 1.1, but several distinct features are characteristic of a record that reflects a periodical. The 245 field is for the title, and the 246 field indicates a variant title. This record tells you that *The Journal of the Polynesian Society* may also be called *JPS, the journal of the Polynesian Society*—not a huge variant, but good to know regardless. The 500 fields are for informational notes. Here, the 510 field indicates external indexes—*Index to New Zealand Periodicals* and *Current Contents*—that cover this particular publication. So, by understanding this record, you will know that you can go to either *Current Contents* or *Index to New Zealand Periodicals* in order to search for citations to articles in this publication. The 600s are subject fields. The 650 field is a topical term, here explaining that this periodical is about Polynesian languages, and the 651 field adds a geographic subject heading. The 710 fields list corporate names responsible for the publication.

The preceding brief discussion of the structure and content of MARC records only begins to scratch the surface of the information that you will be able to discover in a single bibliographic record. For more information about the fields that compose a MARC record, you can use the Library of Congress's MARC Standards page (www.loc.gov/marc/). This resource explains

```
022    |a 0032-4000
035 __ |a (OCoLC)01762632

050 0  |a GN2 |b .P7
082 __ |a 996/.005
245 04 |a The Journal of the Polynesian Society.
246 14 |a JPS, the journal of the Polynesian Society.
260    |a Wellington, N.Z. : |b Polynesian Society, |c 1892-
300 __ |a v. : |b ill., ; |c 24-26 cm.
362 0  |a Vol. 1 (1892)- .
500 __ |a Quarterly.
510 0  |a Current contents/Behavioral, social and managerial sciences
510 0  |a Index to New Zealand periodicals.
520    |a Vols. for 1892-1941 contain the transactions and proceedings of the society.
520 __ |a Vocabularies of some of the languages of Polynesia are included. "A list of Polynesian
         languages" is given in v. 21, p. 67-71.
555 __ |a Vols. 1-50, 1892-1941. 1 v.; Author and title index. Vols. 1-20, 1892-1911, in v. 21, no. 1.
651  0 |a Polynesia.
650 _0 |a Polynesian languages.
710 20 |a Polynesian Society (N.Z.)
```

Figure 1.2. Modified MARC record for *The Journal of the Polynesian Society*, with tags 245, 246, 260, 510s, 650, 651, and 710s highlighted. Source: Auburn University Library Catalog.

in great detail the content for any given field. Armed with an understanding of bibliographic records that make up a database, you will be able to develop effective searches that will help you determine the existence of pertinent resources for your research.

STEP 4: SEARCH STRATEGIES

Field Searching

Once you have a basic understanding of the MARC record and other similar bibliographic records, you can use this familiarity with the structure to help you develop precise and practical search strategies. The fields that together build the bibliographic record are actually individual indexes that the database can search in a variety of combinations, depending in large part on what you as the user tell the database to do. You can tell the search engine that runs the database which of the indexes you want it to retrieve. As an illustration, you could stipulate a database search for *Quintus Servinton* in the title field of the records that form the database. You can also have the database list all records that have *Quintus Servinton* in the subject field and *convict* in a second subject field. Similarly, you could search for *Savery, Henry* as the author and *convict* as a subject. Using fields in combination gives the researcher the opportunity to create a pointedly directed search inquiry that will ideally retrieve a list that is not too large for you to explore, but also one that is not so narrow that it is useless. Because of the strict constraints that field searching places upon inquiries to a database, however, it will also be useful for you to understand the concept of *keyword searching*. Keyword searching allows you to cast your net widely, without designating a particular index that limits your scope too severely. Keyword searching allows you to operate across fields and can be a useful discovery tool as you work to develop a rewarding search strategy.

Boolean Searching

The vast majority of databases that you will use in literary research will employ Boolean logic. George Boole was an English mathematician in the nineteenth century who developed an algebraic logic based on the operational terms *AND*, *OR*, and *NOT*. Named for its developer, Boolean logic simply uses *AND*, *OR*, and *NOT* as they are commonly used in the English language so that they create a connection among the terms used in a search. This means that if you are using a database that functions with Boolean operators, you can use keyword searching to establish a complex relationship among the words you are looking for in bibliographic records. Similarly, if you ignore the Boolean logic, you risk developing a search that is either far too inclusive or far too exclusionary to be of any use to you. Using the list of keywords from Step 2, Boolean operators can be used easily and effectively to build a successful search string.

Boolean *AND* Searching

The Boolean operator *AND* allows you to narrow your search by telling the database that you want to retrieve a list of records that include all your search terms. Based on the keywords in table 1.1, you could construct a search for *domestic **and** settler **and** Australia*. Figure 1.3 is a Ven diagram that illustrates this search. The shaded section represents the records in which all three search terms are present. Figure 1.4 shows one of the several records from *Modern Language Association (MLA) International Bibliography*, an impor-

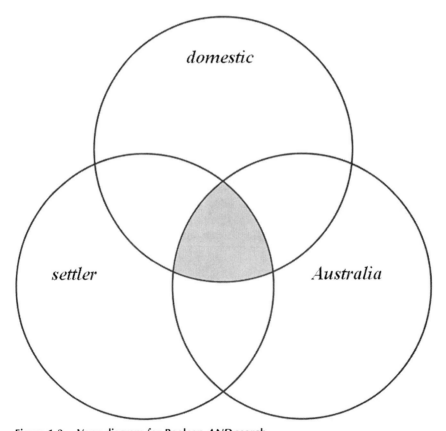

Figure 1.3. Venn diagram for Boolean *AND* search.

Title:	Convicts, Lunatics and Criminals: A Case Study of *Colonial Women* and the Contingent Nature of Marginality
Author(s):	Coleman, Jenny
Source:	Australasian Victorian Studies Journal (Queensland, Australia) (AVStJnl) 2005; 11: 8-22.
General Subject Areas:	General Subject Areas: *Subject Literature: Australian* literature; *Period:* 1800-1899; *Genre:* prose; Subject Terms: treatment of *women* criminals; mental illness; relationship to marginality
Document Information:	*Publication Type:* journal article *Language of Publication: English*

Figure 1.4. Modified record from the *MLA International Bibliography* using Boolean *AND* to combine keywords.

tant literary database that will be discussed in many sections of this book. The search terms are bold and italicized. Look at the fields in which the search terms appear. You can see that in using field searching for these terms you would have needed to look for *Australian* in the subject field and for *colonial* in the title field. *Women* appears in both of those fields.

Boolean *OR* Searching

The Boolean operator *OR* gives you the opportunity to broaden your search. Look at table 1.1 again, and you will see that each broad area has a variety of possible words, or synonyms, that you can use as potential keywords. You can construct a search for any of your list of synonyms by using the *OR* operator:

colonist **or** *settler* **or** *immigrant*

Boolean *NOT* Searching

The Boolean operator *NOT* will not return items that you designate as inappropriate to your search. If you want articles about colonial Australia, but not about postcolonial theory as applied to Australian colonial literature, you can use *NOT* to eliminate these articles:

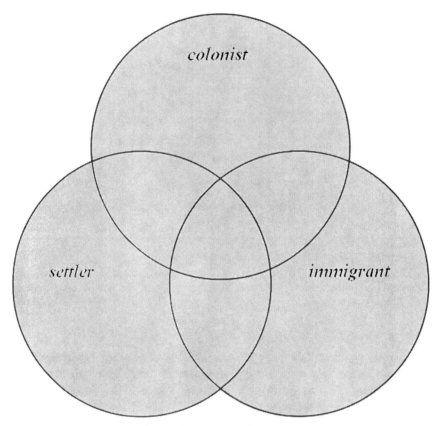

Figure 1.5.   Venn diagram for Boolean *OR* search.

*colonial **not** postcolonial*

This search will eliminate occurrences of postcolonial. You should be aware, however, that the *NOT* operator can either skew your results or lead you into a false sense of security when using it with words that are slippery in theoretical application or that have multiple meanings. For example, if you had told the *MLA International Bibliography* to eliminate the word "post," you could have removed articles written by someone with the last name Post, or articles in journals with "post" in the title. This approach, however, leaves you with "postcolonial" in the results list. If hyphenated, "post-colonial" will not appear in a search that eliminated the word "post." It is important to realize that database searching in the humanities can often be indefinite, because the written text is so often subjective. You also need to be aware that when trying to eliminate a particular theoretical approach from a search, you will run into trouble. Unless an article is

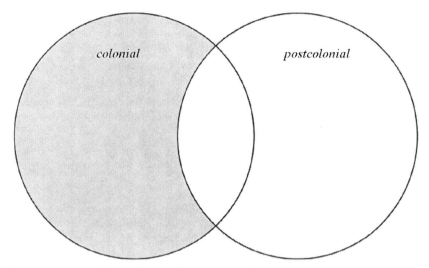

Figure 1.6.   Venn diagram for Boolean *NOT* search.

specifically about "postcolonialism" as a theory, for example, you may not find that word in the bibliographic record. The theoretical approach of an article is often only apparent when you read the article, not in a database record.

Truncation/Wildcards

If you look one more time at table 1.1, you will notice that *colonial* and *colonist* both appear in the list. Truncation will allow you to search for both of those words at the same time. By truncating a term, you broaden the search to include multiple variants. Depending on the database you are using, the method of truncation will differ. At a basic and largely standard level, you are removing the ending letter or letters of a word and putting in that place a truncation symbol. It is the symbol that will vary widely. Some of the most common truncation symbols in databases you may use are the asterisk (*) and the question mark (?); others, used less frequently, are the pound sign (#), the dollar sign ($), and the exclamation point (!). When you are using a database and are unsure of the truncation symbol, the database's help function will provide that information for you.

If you wanted to truncate *colonist* so that a search would return that term as well as *colonial*, you would want to truncate at the "i," by placing the appropriate symbol at that point: *coloni**. This search would retrieve *colonial*, *colonist, colonizer, colonization*, and so on. It will not return *colony*, but truncating further could return results that are not appropriate. You will have to decide how severely you want to truncate a term in order for the search to maintain its usefulness to your project.

Similar to truncation is wildcard searching, which allows you to substitute a symbol for a letter (or letters) within a word. Returning to the list in table 1.1, you can see that we may want to search for *woman* as well as *women*. To achieve this goal, you can replace the "e" with a wildcard symbol: *wom?n.* Check the database help pages to find what symbol performs this function.

Nesting

Another effective technique to employ while keyword searching is called nesting. This technique allows you to develop an advanced search while still using some of the other procedures discussed previously. Working from the same list of keywords pertaining to women settlers in Australia, you could develop an extensive series of searches in order to use all your important keywords:

*wom?n **and** colonist **and** Australia **and** nineteenth century*
*female **and** colonist **and** Australia **and** nineteenth century*
*wom?n **and** emigrant **and** Australia **and** colonial*
*wom?n **and** settler **and** Australia **and** colonial*
*wom?n **and** pioneer **and** Australia **and** nineteenth century*
. . . and so on . . .

An easier way to proceed is by employing the nesting technique. Nesting, most simply, is a series of Boolean constructions each within a set of parentheses, separated by Boolean operators. The strands within parentheses function as a search, and each parenthetical segment is connected to the other parts of the search with Boolean operators:

*(wom?n **or** female) **and** (emigrant **or** settler **or** pioneer) **and** (nineteenth century **or** 19th century **or** colonial)*

Nesting gives you the chance to include many synonyms in a single search and can make your work easier. Remember that with nesting, your search can become long and out of control. You will need to find a balance that works for you. If you are more comfortable not nesting, then you just need to remember which words you have used in individual searches. Most databases will have a search history function that will let you see what you have already searched, and they will give you the option to combine those searches. Also keep in mind that if you decide to forgo nesting, you will likely develop at least a few searches that will result in several duplicate records. Database searching can become overwhelming, so it is a good idea to keep track of what you have done.

Phrase Searching and Proximity Operators

In addition to searching for individual terms alone or connected by Boolean operators to other terms, you can also search for phrases. This type of search can be immensely useful, but it can also be confusing. Often, novice database users will instinctively type a phrase into a search bar—"the use of autobiography in the fiction of Janet Frame," for example. Such a search may indeed retrieve useful results, but for the apparent goal of this search, a complex keyword search not constrained by word order will likely work best. Phrase and proximity searching will be useful when looking for authors or titles, or when you need to locate words in specific proximity to each other.

Look through the series of *WorldCat* results in table 1.2 that reflect a variety of phrase and proximity searches for George French Angas (1822–1886), British-born author, artist, and naturalist known for recording in word and picture the Māori culture in mid-nineteenth-century New Zealand. Notice the variety in the number of results based on how his name is entered into a *WorldCat* search. This author is a good example of a writer who had considerable output (in spite of apparent concerns that he borrowed liberally from other authors and artists) but who has not often been the subject of secondary writing. He may, however, be mentioned in other books, and *WorldCat* is a useful resource both for locating books Angas wrote as well as books in which he is discussed. In *WorldCat* you can find Angas mentioned in the title of a book, as the author, as a subject, and sometimes in the table of contents if it is included in the bibliographic record. With this broad range of possible locations for your author's name within a record, particularly if you are uncertain of how he most regularly signed his work (all three names, first and last name only), phrase and proximity searches can be a very helpful way to figure out where your author has been mentioned and what he has written.

Just as you can use the database help section (sometimes called "search tips," "about the database," "frequently asked questions," and so on) for discovering truncation symbols, you can use this feature for specific guidelines for phrase and proximity searching. It is worth noting now, however, that many databases have help screens that are specifically designed for the point at which a user needs assistance. In other words, if you are starting a search and need support, the help screen that appears from the initial search screen will provide search help, but if you are looking at an overwhelming list of citations, the ensuing screens will be designed to help with interpreting results.

Table 1.2 is based on a series of searches performed in *WorldCat*, a database that is driven by the FirstSearch search engine. (The difference between search engines and databases will be discussed at the end of this chapter, and *WorldCat* will be discussed in detail in chapter 2). FirstSearch interprets a group of words surrounded by quotation marks as directions from the user that he or she wants only those words to appear in a phrase within the bibliographic record, in addition to using a range of other proximity operators. Many databases run on search engines that operate in the same way.

A search for "George French Angas" in *WorldCat* brings a results list of bibliographic records that include that phrase in the record. It will not retrieve records that do not include that specific phrase, so a record in which he is referenced only as "George Angas" will not appear in the list. FirstSearch does use other proximity operators in addition to the quotation marks:

w (with)—used between two words to indicate that the database should only return records that hold both terms in the order in which the user asks. Additionally, when the **w** is followed by a number between 1 and 25, the database will search for records that include both words, in order, separated by no more than the number of words indicated by the search.

n (near)—used between two terms to indicate the database should only return records containing both the terms next to each other in any order. When the **n** is followed by a number from 1 to 25, the database will search for records that include both words, in any order, separated by no more than the number of words indicated by the search.

- The first search looks for all the words neither in specific order nor in any definite proximity. It can be a quite broad search that risks returning records that are not appropriate.

Table 1.2. Results of Phrase and Proximity *WorldCat* Searches for "George French Angas"

Search Strategies	Retrieves	Number of Records
George French Angas	George and French and Angas	726
"George French Angas"	George French Angas	469
George w2 Angas	George Angas	486
	George French Angas	
George n2 Angas	George Angas	752
George French Angas	Angas George French	
George Angas	George and Angas	818
"George Angas"	George Angas	2

- The second search looks for the complete name as a phrase. Records in which the name is written in a different order will not be returned in this search.
- The third search specifies both order and proximity.
- The fourth search does not specify word order but does specify proximity.
- The fifth search looks for either word, and returns a high number.
- The last search yields only two records, an indication that George French Angas must have usually used his full name.

Based on these searches, it appears that the second and third are the most effective. They are neither too broad nor too narrow. The last search is narrow and is apparently not the way works are usually attributed to Angas. This type of searching can be particularly useful if you are looking for works by or about women from the nineteenth century or earlier, due in large part to the range of names that can be attributed to one woman.

Subject or Keyword Searches

Bibliographic records for books and articles that you find in databases will almost always include a subject heading or descriptor field. Indexers populate this field with descriptive words selected from a controlled vocabulary (a rule-bound descriptive scheme relying on specific selected words and a carefully developed and enforced syntax). One of the most frequently used controlled vocabularies is the *Library of Congress Subject Headings*, 26th edition (*LCSH*). A large, multivolume set that can be found in most American libraries, it is also used by the National Library of Australia and the National Library of New Zealand, as well as by Australian and New Zealand academic libraries, both with some enhancements to make the headings applicable to the respective countries. These volumes can be confusing and overwhelming to a researcher, but because databases tend to include a field for subjects, there is rarely a reason for you to consult this complex set. By running a keyword search to find items dealing with Māori literature using *Māori and literature* as the search string, one of the titles retrieved is *Dirty Silence: Aspects of Language and Literature in New Zealand*, edited by Graham McGregor and Mark Williams, displayed in figure 1.7.

The *LCSH* terms are bolded in the figure. It is always a good idea to look carefully at these subject terms in order to ascertain the words that the controlled vocabulary assigns to the particular resource. You can use those terms in other searches if you want to find similar titles. In this particular example, you may note that the *history and criticism* subheading could be of use in narrowing your search. You may also notice that the heading *Māori language* is important to your ideas. Because there are many catalogs available online

Dirty silence : aspects of language and literature in New Zealand
McGregor, Graham.
                    Title: Dirty silence : aspects of language and literature in New Zealand / edited by Graham McGregor and Mark Williams ; associate editor, Ray Harlow.
       Published: Auckland ; New York : Oxford University Press, 1991.
       Description: xvii, 179 p. : ill., map ; 21 cm.
Other contributors: McGregor, Graham.
Other contributors: Williams, Mark, 1951-
Other contributors: Harlow, Ray.
       Notes: "Essays arising from the University of Waikato Winter Lecture Series of 1990."
       Notes: Includes bibliographical references and index.
   Subject headings: English language--New Zealand.
   Subject headings: English language--Social aspects--New Zealand.
   Subject headings: Maori language.
   Subject headings: Maori language--Social aspects.
   Subject headings: New Zealand literature--History and criticism.
   Subject headings: Maori literature--History and criticism.
              ISBN: 0195582276

Figure 1.7. Modified record illustrating *LCSH* for *Dirty Silence: Aspects of Language and Literature in New Zealand* with subject headings bolded. Source: Indiana University Libraries catalog.

that include hyperlinked subject headings, you can move through a series of subject headings with relative ease. Be aware, however, that while subject headings can be pointedly narrow, they can also be quite broad. Following a subject link by clicking on it will start a completely new search. This search will look only for that particular subject, and it will ignore any other concepts on your original query. It can easily be a much wider search than is useful.

Remember also that the Library of Congress subject headings are not the only controlled vocabulary that you will encounter. Many databases have their own, frequently similar terms, so you may find that starting with a keyword search is a good way to discover the subject classification scheme of a particular database.

Relevancy Ranking

Now that you have an introduction to the structure of bibliographic records that make up a database, and to some basic search methodology, it is helpful to understand why a database arranges the results list as it does. Often a database will initially list the records in relevancy order, which means the database follows a set of criteria to determine what records most appropriately answer your query. These criteria include, but are not limited to the following:

- Presence of a matching term in the subject field
- Presence of a matching term in the title field
- Partial match in the subject field
- Frequency with which terms appear
- Proximity of terms to each other
- Location of terms (subject versus abstract, for example)

Even with an awareness of the logic behind relevancy ranking, you may likely find the ranking to be somewhat subjective. As such, many databases offer users the opportunity to select another arrangement in which the results appear. In *WorldCat* via FirstSearch, for example, you can use the *sort* function to have your results appear in order of publication date, by author, by title, and so on. Selecting a list order that makes logical sense to you can make exploring the results much more fruitful.

Limiting or Revising

If your search returns a list that looks potentially useful but far too large, you can limit or revise the search. Usually databases have one of two options for revision: your initial search may appear at the top of the screen for you to edit, or a simple *revise* button may appear on the screen. Similarly, databases will provide you with the option to limit your search by setting constraints around the search terms you use. Setting a limit for your search can remove a type of resource such as dissertations or book reviews. You can also limit by year(s) of publication, language of publication, type of document, peer review status, and so on.

STEP 5: UNDERSTANDING DATABASES, INDEXES, AND SEARCH ENGINES

There is a difference between search engines and databases. The search engine is the outward appearance of a database, and it is also the motor that controls the operational aspects of the database behind the scenes. The database, on the other hand, is the intellectual content that is searched and processed by the search engine. *Most* literary databases will function similarly, but it is important to remember that there are distinct differences. Some database content is offered by more than one vendor's interface, so you may use one version of the *MLA International Bibliography* at one institution and then find it looks completely different at another library.

Table 1.3 offers a summary of several literary databases and their corporate search engine providers. These and many other databases will be discussed in detail later in this book. If your library subscribes to several databases from the

Table 1.3.   Databases and Their Search Engines

Database Content	Search Engine Provider
MLA International Bibliography (MLAIB)	EbscHost
	CSA
	ProQuest
	Gale
Annual Bibliography of English Language and Literature (ABELL)	ProQuest
Eighteenth Century Collections Online (ECCO)	Gale
	Online
AustLit	Custom-built collaborative project

same vendor, you may be able to search them at the same time. For example, a library with a subscription to the *Annual Bibliography of English Language and Literature* (*ABELL*) and the *MLA International Bibliography* through ProQuest has the added bonus of being able to search both of those resources together. More often, however, you will find yourself moving among several search interfaces. When this is the case, it is important that you remember to use the help screens mentioned previously. Some important questions you may want to ask concerning features or limitations include the following:

- Does the search engine automatically use Boolean *AND* searching or phrase searching?
- How do you need to enter Boolean terms (capitalized, bold, etc.)?
- How do you tell the search engine that you are searching for a phrase?
- What are the wildcard and truncation symbols?
- In what order are the results returned?
- Can you limit by type of resource, language, etc.?

STEP 6: UNDERSTANDING INTERNET SEARCHES

Most databases that you will use for literary research will be accessed through the Internet. There are also countless library catalogs and open-access resources developed and maintained by libraries and other institutions that are easily accessible through the Internet.

You likely know that the Internet is full of wonderful repositories of resources, and it has as many if not more useless distractions. Google is quickly becoming synonymous with the Internet, since it has grown from one of many search engines into an unavoidable entity that pervades the Internet. Two particular developments within the Google empire are of particular note for literary research: *Google Books* and *Google Scholar*. *Google Books* (www.google.com/books) is a complicated endeavor, and agreements and activities behind the scenes remain, in general, a mystery. Important for literary research is that *Google Books* allows anyone to search the full text of books that Google has scanned. Because many of the scanned books are under copyright, you will not have access to read the complete text of all the titles, but you will be able to see the immediate context of the words or phrases you have searched. For a lengthy history of the program and some information about the agreements with various libraries and publishers, you can look at the informational pages Google provides (www.google.com/intl/en/googlebooks/about.html). As a caveat, you should be aware that in spite of the amazing ease with which you can use *Google Books*, there are indeed problems. Some pages scan very poorly, and you will often see the hand of the person who scanned the book on some page images. More importantly, you will see some resources incorrectly cited, and this can take valuable time from your research endeavors.

Google Scholar (scholar.google.com/schhp?hl=en) limits your search to scholarly resources. With literary topics, however, many of the resources that you retrieve will be digitized books rather than critical commentary on literature. *Google Scholar* includes a concise *About* page (scholar.google.com/intl/en/scholar/about.html) that explains how and what it searches. The advanced-search option lets you limit your search to quite broad subject areas, such as "Social Sciences, Arts, and Humanities." *Google Scholar* is frequently both a good starting point for research and a good place to look when your research is frustrating you. Remember, the Google environment is considerably more random than what you will find in a library database. Most importantly, you are relying only on keyword searching. There are no set fields, such as the subject descriptors that you will find in other databases. Google does, however, frequently allow libraries to place links to their resources in Google records.

CONCLUSION

This chapter has covered the basics of literary research. Any preceding section could be expanded exhaustively, but ideally this chapter has given you a solid understanding of the structure of databases and the records they comprise. Techniques in this chapter will be of use as you move through the research process. In the ensuing chapters, you will be introduced to general literary reference resources, as well as many resources that are specific to research in the literatures of Australia and New Zealand. All formats will be discussed—electronic, print, and the often dreaded microforms. The literatures of Australia and New Zealand are exciting areas that remain underexplored in American scholarship. This book will introduce you to an extensive array of resources that will lead you into these unique national literatures.

Chapter Two

General Literary Reference Sources

The primary goal of this chapter is to familiarize yourself with a range of literary reference sources that will be beneficial as you begin your research on the literature of Australia or New Zealand. It should be useful to take note of the types of resources in this chapter so you will know the type of information to expect a resource to provide. With these tools, you will be able to locate biographical information on an individual author and contextualize that author in his or her historical era. Similarly, you will be able to locate works within their eras and apply theoretical approaches to your developing area of research. Many of the resources discussed in this chapter will also serve as gateways to other, more pointed research tools.

Remember that if you find a title to be particularly useful, you can look it up in your library's online catalog. From the record for that item, you can see how it is classified and then follow those subject headings to other valuable titles.

RESEARCH GUIDES

Harner, James L. *Literary Research Guide: An Annotated Listing of Reference Sources in English Literary Studies*. 5th ed. New York: Modern Language Association of America, 2008.

Klarer, Mario. *An Introduction to Literary Studies*. 2nd ed. New York: Routledge, 2004.

Lock, Fred, and Alan Lawson. *Australian Literature: A Reference Guide*. 2nd ed. Melbourne: Oxford University Press, 1980.

Marcuse, Michael J. *A Reference Guide for English Studies*. Berkeley: University of California Press, 1990.

James L. Harner's ***Literary Research Guide*** is the standard by which others are measured. Designed primarily for graduate students, this source is ideal for literary-research methodology classes as well as collection-development librarians. It comprises more than 1,050 annotated citations to literary research tools and references to more than 1,500 other resources. The *Literary Research Guide* is divided into twenty-one chapters by resource type (such as "Research Methods"; "Guides to Reference Works"; "Literary Handbooks, Dictionaries, and Encyclopedias"; "Bibliographies of Bibliographies"; "Libraries and Library Catalogs"; "Guides to Manuscripts and Archives"; "Serial Bibliographies, Indexes, and Abstracts"; "Guides to Dissertations and Theses"; "Internet Resources"; "Biographical Resources"; "Periodicals"; and "Genres") as well as geography and language (English, Irish, Scottish, Welsh, and American). It also contains other literatures in English, foreign-language literatures, and comparative literature. Harner provides references to outside reviews of resources (more than 700 in this edition) and refers readers to more than 1,500 supplementary resources. Researchers at all levels will find Harner's work indispensable: his annotations should be read carefully, because within them lurk so many other suggestions of places a literary researcher will want to go. He helpfully notes earlier editions of works that may still be particularly valuable. Of primary importance is the section on other literature in English. Here you will find sections on both Australia and New Zealand, as well as a general introductory section that covers Anglophone literature. Remember, when using this resource, as well as other general tools, that in spite of the vast inclusiveness of Harner's selections, the work is not designed to go into any one area in extreme depth but rather to point researchers to tools that will enable them to move forward to more nuanced and targeted endeavors. New editions of Harner's *Guide* will be online.

Michael J. Marcuse's much larger ***Reference Guide for English Studies*** is a stellar complement to Harner's *Guide*. Although it is dated by its 1990 publication, many older resources in this guide remain useful. This well-annotated guide was a strong and thorough resource almost twenty years ago, and it is still one of a few standards in general literary reference tools. It is divided into the following sections: general works; libraries; retrospective and current national bibliography; serial publications; miscellany; history and ancilla to historical study; biography and biographical references; archives and manuscripts; language, linguistics, and philology; literary materials and contexts; literature; English literature; medieval literature; literature of the Renaissance and earlier seventeenth century; literature of the Restoration and eighteenth century; literature of the nineteenth century; literature of the twentieth century; American literature; poetry and versification; theater, drama, and film; prose fiction and nonfiction; theory, rhetoric, and composition; bibliography; and the profession of English.

Marcuse also offers several sections that explain abbreviations and codes, as well as the overall organization of the text. He accurately suggests that using the helpful eighty-eight page subject and author-as-subject organized index will be your best method for working through this text. While there are sections on Australia and New Zealand, you will also want to look at other areas, such as national bibliography and biography, for other potentially important resources. The annotated entries contain a concise explanation of the authority and scope of the resource, as well as tools such as indexes or chronologies that are included.

Mario Klarer's 2004 second edition of *An Introduction to Literary Studies* deserves comment. It is a solid example of a practical resource for a lower-level undergraduate student who is a novice writer and researcher of literature. This concise resource takes a student point by point through the process of writing a paper and also offers an introduction to historical, critical, and theoretical terms that are a significant part of literary research. A brief list of other resources is a practical addition to the book. While Klarer's book is not directed specifically to any era, national literature, or theme, it is a helpful tool if you are still unfamiliar or uncomfortable with writing about literature.

Although dated, *Australian Literature: A Reference Guide* nevertheless remains a beneficial, though not imperative, resource to consult. Its strength lies in its arrangement by the function of the resource and the succinct use instructions. This guide is a handy discovery tool for older resources that might otherwise remain unknown to a researcher. It features dated but still useful research tools such as the 1898 *Austral English: A Dictionary of Australasian Words, Phrases, and Usages*, which can help a researcher define early slang. Once a researcher knows this dictionary exists, a quick Internet search reveals that this book has been digitized by at least two different services. The 417 entries are concisely annotated, and most sections within chapters are accompanied by short introductions.

AUSTRALIAN AND NEW ZEALAND LITERARY ENCYCLOPEDIAS AND COMPANIONS

Bennett, Bruce, and Jennifer Strauss, eds. *The Oxford Literary History of Australia.* Melbourne: Oxford University Press, 1998.
Benson, Eugene, and L. W. Conolly, eds. *Encyclopedia of Post-Colonial Literatures in English.* 2nd ed. New York: Routledge, 2005.
Birns, Nicholas, and Rebecca McNeer, eds. *Companion to Australian Literature since 1900.* Rochester, N.Y.: Camden House, 2007.
Goodwin, K. L. *A History of Australian Literature.* New York: St. Martin's Press, 1986.

Green, H. M., revised by Dorothy Green. *A History of Australian Literature: Pure and Applied*. London: Angus and Robertson, 1984.

Hergenhan, Laurie, ed. *The Penguin New Literary History of Australia*. Ringwood, Victoria: Penguin Books, 1988.

James, Trevor. *An Introduction to Australian Literature*. Harlow, Essex, England: Longman, 1992.

Kramer, Leonie. *The Oxford History of Australian Literature*. Melbourne: Oxford University Press, 1981.

McCormick, E. H. *New Zealand Literature: A Survey*. London: Oxford University Press, 1959.

McLaren, John. *Australian Literature: An Historical Introduction*. Melbourne: Longman Cheshire, 1989.

Pierce, Peter, ed. *The Cambridge History of Australian Literature*. Melbourne: Cambridge University Press, 2009.

———, ed. *The Oxford Literary Guide to Australia*, rev. Melbourne: Oxford University Press, 1993.

Robinson, Roger, and Nelson Wattie, eds. *The Oxford Companion to New Zealand Literature*. Melbourne: Oxford University Press, 1998.

Schafer, William J. *Mapping the Godzone: A Primer on New Zealand Literature and Culture*. Honolulu: University of Hawaii Press, 1998.

Stevens, Joan. *The New Zealand Novel: 1860–1960*. Wellington: A. H. and A. W. Reed, 1961.

Sturm, Terry, ed. *The Oxford History of New Zealand Literatures in English*. Auckland: Oxford University Press, 1991.

Webby, Elizabeth. *The Cambridge Companion to Australian Literature*. Cambridge: Cambridge University Press, 2000.

Wilde, William H., Joy Hooton, and Barry Andrews. *The Oxford Companion to Australian Literature*. Melbourne: Oxford University Press, 1994.

"Encyclopedia" and "companion" are used to refer to the same type of resource. The encyclopedias in this section are usually one of two types: one comprises a series of short factual articles in alphabetical order, and the other is usually made of significantly longer articles that are not necessarily in alphabetical order and frequently read like a series of chapters all treating a larger topic. Articles are most often signed with authors' names, or initials refer to an appendix of contributors and credentials. Encyclopedias should have at least one index, and articles will provide cross-references to other sections. Articles will frequently close with a short bibliography or a list of further readings on the topic.

Most encyclopedias will be enhanced by useful appendixes and introductions to contextualize their themes. Chronologies or time lines present a temporal framework that connects the literary history, in this instance, to the development of these countries. Usually these types of resources include a larger bibliography at the end of the volume, one that is much more comprehensive than the short lists that follow individual articles. Frequently, a list of concepts arranged by theme precedes the main text and can be particularly accommodating by providing suggestions for keywords and helping to narrow a broad idea or vice versa.

The two-volume *History of Australian Literature: Pure and Applied* covers traditional literary genres such as poetry and fiction, but it also treats newspapers, magazines, philosophy, psychology, biography, education, economics, politics, and so on. Covering 1789 through 1950, this work represents an overarching history of Australian print media. The *History* follows a chronological and genre-based arrangement. The set closes with a series of appendixes, a select list of reprints and new editions, and an extensive author-title index. Although older, this resource remains useful, especially in light of its clear organization and its inclusive sweep of genres not traditionally covered in literary histories. In addition to chapters that discuss the novel, drama, poetry, and the short story, this history also treats criticism, scholarship, philosophy, psychology, magazine writing, biography, economics, politics, the sciences, and newspaper writing as genres.

Designed to fill a need with scholars, students, and other interested parties, Wilde, Hooton, and Andrews's *Oxford Companion to Australian Literature* is an indispensable source for concise, alphabetically arranged explanations and explorations of Australian authors, their works, and other concepts pertinent to the study of the literature. Entries range from the Aboriginal Arts Board, to Australian English, to *The Fortunes of Richard Mahoney*, to Queensland author Rosa Praed. For this resource, *author* comprises historians, critics, and journalists, as well as the more traditional purview of creative writers and essayists. Contemporary authors are included with the caveat that their writing portfolio is young and critical assessment will likely change over the years. Contemporary critics are not part of this resource. Author entries are bio-critical in approach and vary in length based on current reputation and perceived importance. Context entries cover the literary, historical, and cultural influences and backgrounds in which an author writes or a work is placed. These context entries comprise journals, awards, movements, associations, places, and events. Essays range from a few sentences to several pages in length. There is no index.

Bennett and Strauss's 1998 *Oxford Literary History of Australia* looks at Australian literature in its entirety, irrespective of current or past assessment of quality. Naturally, the classics do receive a great deal of space in the volume, but this attention is not singular. Treating the constituent literary movements, groups, authors, and works, the *History* looks at Australian literature as a part of the culture from which it emanates. Taking advantage of the relatively well-developed concept of Australian literature in the twentieth century, this volume sets out to present a new assessment of both the culture and the writing the culture has inspired.

Following the methodology of Sacvan Bercovitch's *Cambridge History of American Literature*, the editors charged scholars from across Australia to avoid imbalance geographically, institutionally, critically, and theoretically. Recognizing both the fluidity of critical opinion on literature historically and the blurring of the erudite and lowbrow, the editors encouraged a variety of perspectives and approaches. Essays in this volume feature commentary on traditional literary genres, but they also include discussions on such written genres as journals, diaries, letters, and even petitions, as well as oral literature and languages (of great importance in the early histories of both literatures), and film and television. Additionally, with a tendency toward cultural studies, this book explores the commoditization of Australian literature.

Although arranged chronologically, the individual essays move between any chronological prescription to create a sense of context and connection. Chronological divisions are subdivided into chapters that deal with literary culture and history, with extensive and thoroughly substantiated essays. The *History* features a bibliographic guide to other research material designed to help researchers with basic tools. It also features a detailed chronology that starts in 1605, as well as an extensive index.

Beginning with an eleven-page chronology that runs from 40,000 BC to the 2000 Olympic Games in Sydney, Elizabeth Webby's ***Cambridge Companion to Australian Literature*** is a collection of ten essays written by acknowledged experts in the field of Australian literature. Chapters are chronologically ordered, and many are also limited to a specific genre. They cover "Indigenous Texts and Narratives," "Colonial Writers and Readers," "Poetry from the 1890s to 1970," "Fiction from 1900 to 1970," "Theatre from 1788 to the 1960s," "Contemporary Poetry: Across Party Lines," "New Narratives: Contemporary Fiction," "New Stages: Contemporary Theatre," "From Biography to Autobiography," and "Critics, Writers, Intellectuals: Australian Literature and its Criticism." Contributors are listed at the front of the volume with their academic and publishing credits.

Webby's introduction is well worth reading as a strong overview of the history of Australian literature, offering a virtual literature review ranging from the development of the country to its creative literary output. Webby explains that her target audience includes people thoroughly familiar with Australia, as well as those who know little about the country and culture. She also takes time to explain her arrangement as primarily genre based but nevertheless tied inextricably to period. As such, after her traditional introduction in which she discusses the ensuing chapters, she delineates the major highlights of Australian literature since 1788 and the establishment of a penal colony by the British in New South Wales. Written from a variety of points of view, this companion should be within easy reach of both student and scholar when taking on a research project that involves Australian literature.

An older volume, Leonie Kramer's 1981 *Oxford History of Australian Literature* reflects its time. Divided into four sections—fiction, drama, poetry, and bibliography—this work is written by four reputable scholars: Adrian Mitchell, Terry Strum, Vivian Smith, and Joy Hooten. Large genre-centered sections are subdivided by era. The introduction is a critical overview of Australian literary history. It includes a bibliography that is useful for locating older resources dating to the late 1700s and comprising bibliographical and reference aids, general studies, and individual authors.

Published in 1989, the fifteen chapters in John McLaren's *Australian Literature: An Historical Introduction* cover Australian literature from European settlement to the waning years of the twentieth century. The book is based on the belief that the first Australian literature is indeed the texts resulting from the first records of the advent of European discovery of Australia and the events, encounters, and responses to the newly discovered land. Authors and works were selected based on their chronicling of the dynamic between the European settler and the new land and people. Predominately arranged chronologically, with author's birthday as the touchstone, this history treats all genres at the same time when that makes sense—although McLaren tends to discuss only published books, avoiding journals and newspapers (a decision that eliminates some potentially interesting explorations, especially in the context in which he places his work). Such inclusivity, however, in 1989 would have been considerably more difficult and time consuming that it would be now, with the electronic resources that allow for a much easier exploration of works published in the periodical press.

McLaren explains that the method of this book is to examine the structure, forms, and language of the works in order to determine the part they have played in the overall shaping of Australian literature, and to rediscover the social and cultural milieu in which the literature was created. More broadly, he places Australian literature next to Western literature and culture. With an unapologetic white point of view, this book limits mention of the Aboriginal population, an area where McLaren perhaps unintentionally creates an "us-them" binary that may be jarring to readers almost two decades later. This volume is well indexed and contains a handy list of further readings, as well as endnotes. It offers succinct introductory essays about authors and works as they relate to the development of a national literature.

Sponsored in part by the Australian Council for the Arts (supported by the Australian government), the *Companion to Australian Literature since 1900* devotes considerable space to the concept of identities, with a multicultural approach to Australian literature. With two chapters on Aboriginality, and chapters on multicultural authors, Jewish writers, Asian-Australian writers, women writers, and hoaxes in which authors assumed Aboriginal identity, the first section of the *Companion* takes a wide view of the varied landscape of Australian literature.

The second section takes a chronological and generic approach—beginning with the year 1900 and exploring genres in time. The third section explores the international reputation of six Australian authors, and the fourth treats five authors and regions of Australia. The final section looks outside the traditional canon to explore science fiction, popular fiction, film, children's literature, environmental literature, and gay and lesbian writing. This volume takes a markedly different approach to the traditional study of Australia's national writing. Prefaced by a useful chronology of major events in Australian history from 1900 to the 2005 Sydney beach riots, the *Companion to Australian Literature since 1900* notes that in the 1980s, Australian literature became noticed by the rest of the world, but also notes that the literature was good and warranted attention long before that time. In the introduction, the editors suggest that the interest surfaced in the 1980s and waned by 2006. They also boast of the diversity of this text, not only in the subjects treated but also in how they are covered—by scholars not necessarily reputed to be experts in the areas on which they are writing, bringing new eyes to the topics. This volume is an important resource for students and scholars with an interest in the diverse nature of Australian literature in the twentieth century.

Seven sections covering the Australian states and territories serve as the structure for Peter Pierce's **Oxford Literary Guide to Australia**, a hefty geographical compendium of Australian literary history. With scores of contributors from historical societies and various interest societies, as well as many libraries and universities, this volume represents a national collaborative effort to highlight the vast local literary kaleidoscope, privileging the importance of place in Australian writing. Supported by the Association for the Study of Australian Literature, the entries in this volume highlight a variety of literary impressions across the country. Entries are about areas, geographical and geological sites, cities, towns, and other features large and small. Exploring both the sublime and the beautiful, awe-inspiring and fear-inducing experiences are chronicled in this guide.

Essays range in length from less than half a page, to several pages for larger cities and their suburbs. While there is no bibliography, individual entries frequently contain many, often obscure, internal citations, from well-known novels to nineteenth-century poetry published in newspapers. An index of authors who are mentioned in the essays closes the volume. This is an excellent resource for a researcher who needs a primer on Australian geography. Finally, even though it is not a small book, it would be an excellent book to accompany a traveler with literary interests on a trip to Australia.

Pierce also edited *The Cambridge History of Australian Literature*, a new publication from 2009. He emphasizes the connection between Australian literature and nationalism and nation-making. In his introduction he explains that literature and a national identity have intersected in various ways and degrees for decades. Acknowledging the difficulties in discerning any sort of truly authoritative official literary history of Australia, Pierce explains that the contributors to the volume understand that they are participating in "the chequered larger history of Australian literary histories," while looking toward a crisis in Australian literature domestically in publishing and in incorporating the literature into curricula at all levels.[1]

Arranged in an overarching chronology, the book covers movements and contexts, as well as individual authors. The introduction should be read before delving into the text because it offers an interesting overview of the history of Australian scholarship on Australian literature. The text is divided into large sections: "From European Imaginings of Australia to the End of the Colonial Period," "From the Late Nineteenth Century to 1950," "Traverses," and "From 1950 to Nearly Now." Within this structure, topics such as Aboriginal literacy and writing, colonial literature, Australian literature in the world, children's literature, theater, and more are treated.

A thin, chronologically arranged book starting in 1788 and running through the early 1990s, *An Introduction to Australian Literature* by Trevor James is an extremely concise preface to Australian literature. Individual chapters feature a short overview of the historical events of the eras into which the text is segmented: "Contact and Conflict (1788–1850)," "Consolidation (1850–1875)," "The *Bulletin* Era (1875–1900)," "From Federation to the Second World War," and "From the Second World War to the Present Day." Historical contextualization is minimal, but for a newcomer to this national literature and history, James's book proves to be a combination of an introduction and a teaser to pique curiosity. Well footnoted, the book should motivate an interested novice reader to find adequate direction for the next steps. More experienced researchers may find this work less rewarding.

Chapters comprise historical information occasionally followed by a discussion of the literary events—issues and influences—of the period. Earlier chapters have sections on writers and works. Later eras divide writer sections into poets and prose writers. Discussions of individual works briefly place them in history and offer a very short synopsis and commentary. This book includes a bibliography and index.

Although now dated, the history provided in *A History of Australian Literature* by Ken Goodwin remains relevant, with clear intent to connect literature and authors to the time and cultural contexts in which they were created or were creating. The importance of the cultural connection is discussed in the introductory matter, and a history such as this one serves as encouragement, help, and guidance to students and other readers as they explore literature and the culture from which it emanates.

Beginning with a short chapter on the nature of Australian literature, Goodwin establishes a relationship between Australia's literature and the land and languages of the nation. He suggests that Australian literature is characterized by such polarities as colonialism and nationalism, hope and despair, and British and Irish heritage. Similarly, he establishes a number of themes that appear in Australian literature, including the wanderer's search for identity, the establishment of home, the quest for the past, violence, the outcast, and oppression. Following this brief opening chapter are several more extensive treatments of the following themes: the first one hundred years of colonization; the *Bulletin* school; national self-definition; the 1930s and 1940s; symbolism and realism in fiction; the 1960s; and new writing. There is a classified list of further reading, followed by a chronologically arranged table with parallel columns for date, author/title, and historical events. An index with names, titles, and subjects closes the book.

Laurie Hergenhan explains in his introduction to **The Penguin New Literary History of Australia** that this revisionary history was warranted because Australian writing has been aggressive and groundbreaking. Critical histories, however, have not paralleled the spirit evident in the literature, and Hergenhan points to an academic tradition that begins Australia's literary history based on its purported Western European roots, to such an extent that white writers work hard to incorporate indigenous influences. This volume, the editor suggests, seeks to discover and uncover at least some of what has been obscured by previous traditional Anglocentric explorations of Australian literary history.

Pointing to a duality existing between postcolonial/colonial nationalism and internationalist sensibility that looks to European literary standards, Hergenhan blames this duality for the stagnation in Australian literary criticism. The text of this book compiles a variety of contributors and hopes to raise questions about the concept of "Australian" literature. Structurally, the book uses both chronological and generic frameworks. Divided into five parts and thirty-four chapters, the broad chronological organization lends an overarching although not constricting structure to the narrative. An extensive index makes it easier to work within the relatively loose organizational arrangement. A lengthy bibliographic essay in a readable narrative style points to many other resources. *The Penguin New Literary History of Australia* provides a lively discussion of the still-unfolding history of Australia's literature, and it encourages its readers to make connections, discover the unexplored, and reevaluate the traditional.

Eleven scholars (professors, lecturers, and editors) contributed essays to the robust ***Oxford History of New Zealand Literatures in English***, which chronicles the growth of English literary output in New Zealand. Arranged primarily according to generic divisions (nonfiction, novel, short story, poetry, drama, literature for children, and popular fiction), this volume also features chapters such as an overview of Māori literature, publishing, and literary magazines. A bibliographic essay in four parts follows the genre chapters. Covering bibliographies and other reference works, literary history and criticism, anthologies, and periodicals, the essay ends with sections devoted to individual authors. An extensive and practical bibliography provides enough explanatory notes to enable researchers to decide which resources are potentially helpful while arming them with basic expectations of how to use the items discussed.

The introduction is worthy of a read; it explains that the writing teams understood the importance of original research to avoid falling into the comfortable reliance on earlier works and their tendency toward dependence on the traditional English literary canon. This endeavor, six years in the making, was designed for scholars as well as other interested readers. The introduction explains that New Zealand, due in large part to a smaller population, had a slower trajectory of development than Australia and Canada.

Literally and figuratively a dense volume, at more than seven hundred pages, it is a long read from cover to cover. Individual chapters are extensively footnoted, most boasting between thirty and two hundred notes. Suffice it to say that not only are the chapters diverse and inclusive, but they offer engagingly written explorations of genres. Additionally, the rich footnotes provide a wealth of other resources for your research. This volume should be nearby as you begin your research into New Zealand literature.

Robinson and Wattie explain in their introduction to ***The Oxford Companion to New Zealand Literature*** that their book is unique among reference resources for the literature of New Zealand, in large part due to the lack of an institutionalized body of scholarship around the national literature. They stress that they wanted the book to be both informative and fun to use, a standard that was conveyed to their numerous contributors. This volume features entries on short stories, novels, plays, poems, literary journals, institutions such as the Alexander Turnbull Library, and authors such as Rore Hapipi, Janet Frame, Ngaio Marsh, and Vincent O'Sullivan. Another useful inclusion is the explanation of terms such as *bullock-driver* and *Iwi*. Designed to complement *The Oxford History of New Zealand Literatures in English*, this volume treats many smaller ideas rather than the sweeping concepts covered in the *History*. Robinson and Wattie made a concerted effort to treat Māori writers and the language. Overall, this book represents an inclusive treatment of a developing area of literary scholarship.

E. H. McCormick's *New Zealand Literature: A Survey* is an older work, published in 1959. A good read, this book came from a 1940 survey, *Letters and Art in New Zealand*, published for the centennial of the country. Following the chronological development of the national literature, the volume observes the growth through the works of New Zealand's most prominent writers. Authors in this survey must have published at least one book. A combination of history, biography, and close reading, this book can serve as a handy introduction if you are not familiar with writing from New Zealand. Following on the heels of McCormick's work, and paying homage to it throughout the text, is Joan Stevens's *The New Zealand Novel: 1860–1960*. Acknowledging McCormick's space constraints, this book seeks to pay greater attention to the novel—in particular minor writers and early novels, such as Isabella Aylmer's *Distant Homes; or the Graham Family in New Zealand* and Lady Campbell's *Martin Tobin*. Designed for general readership, *The New Zealand Novel: 1860–1960* avoids an academic tone and reintroduces early novels while providing a detailed exploration of the national genre. With appendixes that cover in depth six individual novels, a section of topics for study and discussion, and references, this book offers an easily readable historical look at New Zealand literature.

William J. Schafer explains in *Mapping the Godzone: A Primer on New Zealand Literature and Culture* that the inspiration for his work came from a five-month trip through the North and South Islands of New Zealand. His goal was not a traditional history, but rather he wanted to capture firsthand the local characteristics that combine to inspire the culture of New Zealand. Discussing New Zealand novels that deal with important people and events in New Zealand history, Schafer characterizes his approach as neither exhaustive nor authoritative, but often quite individual and experiential.

Eschewing chronological and generic classification structure, Schafer instead presents a traveler's pathway through New Zealand via its literature. Starting with two chapters that provide an introduction to words and practices as the author sees them, the book proceeds through the pioneer era, Māori cultural mythology, religion, bildungsromans, horror stories, Janet Frame as a national and world author, and New Zealand cinema. *Mapping the Godzone: A Primer on New Zealand Literature and Culture* offers the reader a different way into a national culture and literature, one that is the result of traveling and discovering an interest in a place and then learning about that place through immersion in the culture and exploration of the literature. Certainly it is not a standard literary history like you would get from an Oxford or Cambridge University Press encyclopedia. This resource, rather, represents another type of approach that is much needed for this national literature, one that has yet to receive the full academic treatment that pervades most other Anglophone literatures of the former British Empire.

Originally published in 1994, the ***Encyclopedia of Post-Colonial Literatures in English*** is a three-volume text that comprises concise entries on a wide range of postcolonial authors, works, genres, regions, concepts, schools, movements, and more. The format remains the same as the first edition, and many of the entries have been updated. The editors tried to allow the original authors to update entries, but if that was not possible new authors were sought, and both authors are credited at the end of the entry. This second edition adds two hundred completely new entries to the original work.

The introduction to the 1994 volume, reprinted in the second edition, explains the difficulty with applying an efficient descriptive term to the broad-ranging literatures of countries as far-flung as Sri Lanka, Nigeria, Australia, New Zealand, Canada, and many others. Alphabetically arranged, the set is also prefaced by a lengthy table of contents for easy navigation. The third volume closes with an index of more than two hundred pages, which makes it possible to locate topics that may not have their own individual entries. Cross-references are incorporated, and most entries have short lists of further readings. When publications are mentioned in an entry, the date of first publication is given. Useful topical essays touch on such areas as anthologies of national literatures, literary awards, broadcasting, criticism, literature of exploration, and translation. This resource is a thorough and far-reaching compendium of postcolonial literature. While the individual entries are concise, they do deliver solid introductions to the topics treated. This is also an excellent resource to keep in mind if, in your research, you feel that you are encountering names and concepts with which you are unfamiliar.

LITERARY GENRE ENCYCLOPEDIAS, COMPANIONS, AND HISTORIES FOR AUSTRALIA AND NEW ZEALAND

Bennett, Bruce. *Australian Short Fiction: A History*. St. Lucia, Queensland. University of Queensland Press, 2002.

Clancy, Laurie. *A Reader's Guide to Australian Fiction*. Melbourne: Oxford University Press, 1992.

Collins, Paul, ed. *The MUP Encyclopaedia of Science Fiction and Fantasy*. Melbourne: Melbourne University Press, 1998.

Dutton, Geoffrey. *The Australian Collection: Australia's Greatest Books*. North Ryde, New South Wales: Angus and Robertson, 1985.

Jones, Joseph, and Johanna Jones. *Australian Fiction*. Twayne's World Author Series. Boston: Twayne, G. K. Hall, 1983.

———. *New Zealand Fiction*. Twayne's World Author Series. Boston: Twayne, G. K. Hall, 1983.

Lees, Stella, and Pam MacIntyre. *The Oxford Companion to Australian Children's Literature*. Melbourne: Oxford University Press, 1993.

McNaughton, Howard. *New Zealand Drama*. Twayne's World Author Series. Boston: Twayne, G. K. Hall, 1981.

Nolan, Maggie, and Carrie Dawson, eds. *Who's Who? Hoaxes, Imposture and Identity Crises in Australian Literature*. Queensland: University of Queensland Press, 2004.

Rees, Leslie A. *A History of Australian Drama*. rev. ed. 2 vols. Sydney: Angus and Robertson, 1978–1987.

Saxby, H. M. *A History of Australian Children's Literature (1841–1941 and 1941–1970)*. 2 vols. Sydney: Wentworth Books, 1969.

Wilde, William. *Australian Poets and Their Works: A Reader's Guide*. Melbourne: Oxford University Press, 1996.

This section will explore several encyclopedias of Australian and New Zealand literatures that cover the literary histories, various genres, and special readerships of both these countries. As encyclopedias and companions, these resources will logically appear structured similarly to the resources listed previously. Even though the titles here are narrowly focused, it is important to remember to consult the general resources discussed previously because their broader purview complements the limited coverage of the resources in this section. The following titles provide a more concentrated and exhaustive exploration of a particular type of literature.

The thin volume edited by Paul Collins (assisted by Steven Paulsen and Sean McMullen), ***The MUP Encyclopaedia of Science Fiction and Fantasy***, is deceptive in its outward appearance. Inside the covers lurk nearly two hundred double-columned, small-print pages of author and subject entries that cover the world of Australian science fiction and fantasy from 1950 through the late twentieth century. While refraining from providing a strict definition of either science fiction or fantasy, the editors delineate a series of eight basic tenets they tried to follow while compiling this resource: post-1950 entries only; horror works are included if they have substantial characteristics of science fiction or fantasy; children's books are part of the purview, but not picture books; stories published in fanzines and other amateur publications are not in the encyclopedia; educational publications are not part of the encyclopedia; authors must have more than three published works of science fiction or fantasy; film, television, and drama are included only as part of larger articles and author biographies; and only Australian authors (broadly defined as Australian-born living in Australia, Australian-born living abroad, or foreign-born living in Australia) are part of the encyclopedia. Authors include John Baxter, Stephan Dedman, Greg Egan, and Nevil Shute, to name a few.

Arranged alphabetically, *The MUP Encyclopaedia of Science Fiction and Fantasy* has entries on authors and on relatively broad subjects. Author entries can contain biographical essays in addition to bibliographies, or simple explanations of pseudonyms with cross-references. A lengthy entry on pseudonyms explains their use and is followed by an extensive list of pseudonyms and their corresponding real names. There are seventeen subject entries on topics such as awards, fandom, indigenous mythology, and magazines, easily located through a directory in the introductory material. A short list of common abbreviations precedes the body of the encyclopedia.

Another older title, ***A History of Australian Drama*** is a two-volume set that covers the development and growth of Australian drama from the colonial years through the mid-1980s. The author explains that the work is very much a revised and expanded edition of the author's own 1953 *Towards an Australian Drama*, with the notable additions of television, radio, and Aboriginal playwriting. Film resources are left out because the film industry was, at the time of writing, mature enough to have its own scholars and resources. This work assumes that an Australian play is either written by an Australian (Alfred Dampier, Sumner Locke-Elliot, Ray Lawler, and so on) or written about Australia regardless of national origin or location of the author, with the caveat that only the early years will allow discussion of non-Australian plays. Like many histories of Australian literature, this book is concerned with the development of "Australian" drama and identity, while trying to refrain from a distinctly nationalist tenor. Beginning in the colonial era, this set takes a chronological approach in organization, with chapters that deal with particular playwrights, genres within the drama, movements, and other topics. Several appendixes include, but are not limited to, the Playwrights Advisory Board and chronologies of radio and television plays. The volumes are indexed by names, titles, and topics, and the second volume contains a bibliography. This set was carefully developed and is characterized by a smooth integration of historical and critical approaches to the dramatic history of Australia. The chapters feature references to useful primary resources, such as newspaper articles, that can be otherwise difficult to locate or to determine that they even exist.

William Wilde's 1996 ***Australian Poets and Their Works: A Reader's Guide*** was developed as a way to expand poetry coverage in the editor's *Oxford Companion to Australian Literature* (1985, 1994) discussed previously. With alphabetically arranged entries on poets, the preface cites the contemporary spike in published poetry as a caveat that this volume cannot, even with the best intentions, treat poets and their poetry in a thorough manner. For the most part, in order to be discussed in this volume a poet needed to have published two collections. Some entries on poems, books, groups, movements, journals, and terms appear among the author entries. With measured critical assessment of both the critical record and the historical record in the case of historical figures, and of the author's own summary for the more contemporary poets (on which critical opinions are still forming), the entries present a varied look at poets and works.

An encouragingly readable introduction, though packed full of names and details, takes you chronologically through the history of Australian poetry, covering eras, schools, and movements, literary and otherwise. With over eight hundred entries, more than five hundred of which are devoted to poets (Barron Field, Charles Harpur, Christopher Brennan, John Tranter, and Gwen Harwood, to name a very few), this volume stands as a quick and thorough resource for brief biographies of poets and factual entries on publications, organizations, movements, and more.

Part of the University of Queensland Press series *Studies in Australian Literature*, Bruce Bennett's ***Australian Short Fiction: A History*** covers the colonial years through the end of the twentieth century. Beginning with a chronology of short fiction publications, the history takes a similarly chronological approach in its arrangement. Broadly titled chapters ("Unquiet Spirits: 1825–1880"; "Alternative Traditions: 1880–1930"; "Politics, Location and Storytelling: 1950"; "Home and Away: 1980–2000," for example) house much more narrowly defined sections on specific authors, publications, subgenres, or ideas. Indexed by author, title, and subject, this volume includes extensive endnotes and a handy bibliography of short fiction.

Comprising entries for nearly 150 authors of fiction, Laurie Clancy's biocritical reference work, ***A Reader's Guide to Australian Fiction***, asserts that it covers the major novelists and short-story writers from Australia in the 350-plus-page guide. Clancy concedes that *major* is a slippery and imprecise term, but he based his assessment in large part on literary excellence (another loaded term) and historical importance. Contemporary writers were the most difficult to assess, he acknowledges, conceding that his current assessment may not hold up as the years pass.

Clancy's essays, ranging from less than one page to more than six pages, with most near one thousand words, are based on his own readings of the authors' works. Eschewing biographical diversions and plot summaries, the essays offer the reader an overall assessment, stylistically and critically. Arranged chronologically by the author's birth date, most essays are not substantial enough to carry you very far in a major research project. They are useful, however, in providing a general introduction to and overview of many Australian authors, from the country's first novelist, Henry Savery, to those such as Peter Carey and Kate Grenville who are still writing in the twenty-first century.

Clancy also had to wrestle with the always looming elephant in the room: what is an Australian author? His struggle is well documented in the introduction, which includes a personal rehashing of the many issues he dealt with simply in the selection of authors. The book is indexed by author name, and unfortunately there are no references for further research.

For those interested in the "who is an Australian?" discussion, the 2004 University of Queensland Press publication *Who's Who?: Hoaxes, Imposture and Identity Crises in Australian Literature*, edited by Maggie Nolan and Carrie Dawson, features a series of essays that explore authors such as Norma Khouri and John O'Grady's Nino Culotta, who created fictional identities (Australian, Aboriginal, etc.) and were eventually exposed.

A collection of descriptive and critical essays on ninety-seven classic Australian books, Geoffrey Dutton's *The Australian Collection: Australia's Greatest Books* looks like more of a coffee table book than a research resource. For the novice, however, this book provides a helpful introduction to a varied national literature. Selections come from novels as well as children's books, histories, biographies, natural history, and humor. Entries begin with an excerpt from the original text and then proceed with Dutton's discussion of the work. Short biographies close the entries. Any one author is allowed to have only one book in this volume, and the books must be one coherent narrative (not a collection of poetry or short stories). While not a traditional reference source, this charmingly illustrated book offers an excellent overview of the books that have characterized Australian publishing from its colonial days onward, such as Francis Ratcliffe's *Flying Fox and Drafting Sand*, Donald Horne's *The Lucky Country*, and Joan Lindsay's *Picnic at Hanging Rock*.

Divided into six temporal areas ("Settlers, Convicts, and Early Narrative"; "Pre-Federation Fiction"; "From Federation to the 1930s"; "Through World War II"; "Postwar: Exile and Hope"; and "Postwar: The Moderns"), *Australian Fiction* covers such topics as short fiction, Aboriginal life, and convict communication. This book leaves out science fiction in the hope that it will be treated in a later publication (one such as the *MUP Encyclopaedia of Science Fiction and Fantasy*).

The authors note a sense of abandonment that Australia and New Zealand felt at the hand of the British literati who did not consider the literature of these antipodean former colonies as part of its own. More than twenty years later, there has been some improvement in international acceptance, but neither Australia nor New Zealand is yet on even ground with British or American literature.

Beginning with a chronology that starts in 1606 when explorers chronicled their experiences, the authors cover the publication of fifty books and novels, scholarly publications of particular significance, periodicals, and important dates in the political and cultural development of Australia (featuring a variety of natural disasters, weather-induced tribulations, and geological, geographical, and meteorological events). Essays quote extensively from primary and secondary resources. The notes and bibliography together become a solid starting point for further research. The bibliography is subdivided into general reference, historical and social resources, literary history and criticism, anthologies, and authors and their works. Indexed by name, title, and topic, this concise volume provides a wide range of resources and a strong historical exploration of fiction through the 1970s. A caveat: this volume is a decidedly white-centric literary survey, with little attention given to Aboriginal writers.

The two-volume *History of Australian Children's Literature (1841–1941 and 1941–1970)* covers the genre in Australia for 130 years, through the 1960s. Although it is somewhat dated, it remains a standard tool for parents, scholars, and librarians. With the rise in interest in children's literature from the mid-twentieth century, the author points to a clear curiosity within Australia but notes the lack of a real attempt at an academic study or critical assessment of Australian children's literature. Willing to undertake that task, H. M. Saxby limits himself to fiction, and he wrestles with the classification of "Australian" (as do many other authors and editors). For his work, "Australian" is a book published in Australia regardless of the nationality of the author, or a book published overseas that is set in Australia. William Howlitt's *A Boy's Adventures in Australia*, Mrs. Aneas Gunn's *The Little Black Princess*, and Helen Marey's *Stolen Voyage* are examples of texts and authors that Saxby chooses to discuss. Saxby also limits children's books to those primarily written for children, although those that have crossover interest to adult readers are allowed.

Offering a brief overview of criteria that have been used to assess children's literature, Saxby privileges books able to elicit joy from their child readers, in addition to style appropriateness and integrity of the author. The introduction is a useful assessment of the needs of children and offers some suggested surveys of children's literature. Arranged chronologically, each chapter is neatly subdivided within the table of contents, making this work easily negotiable for specific topics and eras. It includes a bibliography divided into Australian books for children and books that cover reading interests for children and young adults. An index facilitates author, book title, and genre access.

The second volume avoids chronological divisions and instead discusses genres of adventure, family stories, fantasy, animal stories, and Aboriginal and race relations. It also features chapters on books for the very young and for the "tween" reader. This volume closes with a chronology, bibliography, and index.

The Oxford Companion to Australian Children's Literature comprises one thousand six hundred entries that encompass 150 years of writing for children. Authors covered are predominantly Australian (with some who wrote about Australia), including Pamela Allen, Max Dann, and illustrator Pamela Lofts, to name a few. The alphabetically arranged main text includes authors, illustrators, works, and subjects such as awards, themes, settings, historical events, genres, and historical figures. Most books discussed won or were in contention for the Book of the Year Award, and a thorough list of these titles can be found in the appendix. Pseudonyms are cross-referenced, and entries range from one sentence to more than five pages in length. This volume contains generous black-and-white illustrations.

Beginning in 1840, Howard McNaughton's *New Zealand Drama* follows the development of the national genre through the 1970s. McNaughton's preface asserts that New Zealand drama and theater lack a self-awareness that would otherwise be apparent in a national genre that is connected to a national history. Covering over forty playwrights, such as Barry Marschel, Merton Hodge, Allen Curnow, Bruce Mason, and Roger Hall, this study resists the teleological tendency to try to establish a pattern of development for the body of New Zealand drama. The volume notes that *Act* (quarterly to 1975 and monthly after) is a useful resource for contemporary drama research. *New Zealand Drama* features a concise chronology of events (births, theater openings, journal beginnings), performances, and publications. Although it is dated, this resource provides a solid, concise overview of the first 140 years of New Zealand drama. The volume concludes with a helpful bibliographic overview of primary and secondary resources and an index of names, theaters, and works.

Similarly constructed is Joseph and Johanna Jones's *New Zealand Fiction* in the *Twayne's World Author Series*. They discuss the necessary differences between the development of New Zealand fiction and the genre that developed in Great Britain, North America, and Australia. This book looks to both the influence of the land and location as well as the distinct social and cultural influences on the literature. It begins with a brief introduction that explains the obvious but often misunderstood differences between the geography and culture of New Zealand and Australia.

Arranged chronologically, *New Zealand Fiction* starts with the fiction of emigrants to the newly settled New Zealand, through utopian/dystopian fiction at the turn of the century, moving to expatriate fiction in the early nineteenth century and the self-reflective fiction of the first half of the twentieth century. It discusses post–World War II fiction that brought with it a new third-world element, and moves through the midcentury into the 1980s with a look to the future. Prefaced with a chronology, this volume contains a concise yet broad overview of New Zealand fiction. For an advanced researcher or a scholar familiar with New Zealand, this book may prove too elementary but may nevertheless be worth a quick look. An index and classified bibliography close the work.

BIOGRAPHICAL SOURCES

Ackland, Michael. *Henry Handel Richardson*. Melbourne: Oxford University Press, 1996.
Australian Writers. Melbourne: Oxford University Press, 1992–.
Australian Writers and Their Work. Melbourne: Oxford University Press, 1963–.
Contemporary World Writers. Manchester: Manchester University Press, 1998–.
Dictionary of Literary Biography. Detroit: Gale Research Co., 1978–. Online at www.gale.cengage.com.
Dictionary of New Zealand Biography. 5 vols. Wellington: Allen & Unwin, with the Department of Internal Affairs, 1990–. Online at www.dnzb.govt.nz/dnzb/.
Jones, Jenny Robin. *Writers in Residence: A Journey with Pioneer New Zealand Writers*. Auckland: Auckland University Press, 2004.
Nesbitt, Bruce, and Susan Hadfield. *Australian Literary Pseudonyms: An Index with Selected New Zealand References*. Adelaide: Library Board of South Australia, 1972.
Oxford Dictionary of National Biography. Oxford University Press, at www.oxforddnb.com/.
Serle, Percival. *Dictionary of Australian Biography*. Sydney: Angus and Robertson, 1949.
Twayne's World Author Series. New York: Twayne Publishers, 1966–.
Who's Who of Australian Writers. Port Melbourne, Victoria: D. W. Thorpe, 1991.

Critical and biographical resources on authors frequently overlap and can be hard to distinguish from one another. Often biographical resources will consist of critical commentary, and likewise critical resources often turn to biographical information in order to explain or discuss an author's works.

Australian Writers and Their Work is an older series published by Oxford University Press, with most of its titles published in the 1960s (by Landsdowne Press) and 1970s (by Oxford). Thin volumes hover around fifty pages, and the narratives weave the authors' life, career, and works together in short essays. The volumes have brief bibliographies. Authors covered include, but are not limited to, Barcroft Boake, Martin Boyd, Miles Franklin, Xavier Herbert, James McAuley, Vance Palmer, Katharine Susannah Prichard, Christina Stead, Charles Harpur, and Joseph Furphy.

Contemporary World Writers is a series published by Manchester University Press. It is predominately devoted to writers from outside the United

Kingdom and the United States, or from minority backgrounds within those countries. While the emphasis of the volumes within the series is focused on the works in a postcolonial milieu, they also touch on the life of the author and on the influences on his or her writing as connected to the writers' cultural framework. Individual volumes offer a chronology of the author's life, an index, and a classified bibliography that features works by the author, interviews, manuscripts, websites, criticism, reviews, and general resources. Thus far, Peter Carey and Les Murray have been covered by this series. Similarly, *Twayne's World Author Series* is an extensive series of books on individual authors, and sometimes national genres. Volumes have chronologies, bibliographies, and indexes, and the main text connects each writer's life and works. Writers covered include Australians Price Warung, A. B. Paterson, and Henry Handel Richardson and New Zealanders Janet Frame, Jane Mander, and Frank Sargeson, to name a few.

Dictionary of Literary Biography is a running series now exceeding 350 volumes. Each volume is usually centered on a particular genre and/or national literature. Essays in these volumes explore the life of an author as it intertwines with his or her writings. An individual author may appear in more than one volume, and he or she may be covered in greatly different ways in each, depending on the purview of the volume. Volumes dedicated to Australian writers are *Australian Literature, 1788–1914* (vol. 230); *Australian Writers, 1915–1950* (vol. 260); *Australian Writers, 1950–1975* (vol. 289); and *Australian Writers, 1975–2000* (vol. 325). These four volumes have all been published in the twenty-first century, an indication of the growing interest in literature in English from countries other than the United States and the United Kingdom. It is good to know that both *Twayne's World Author Series* and the *Dictionary of Literary Biography* are indexed in the Cengage-Gale product *Literary Index* (www.galenet.com/servlet/LitIndex), a free resource that helps researchers navigate this company's many products.

The *Dictionary of New Zealand Biography* is a five-volume print set that is also available online. The online version of this core reference tool contains over three thousand biographies of important New Zealanders, all deceased. Biographies originally published in the print version, *Dictionary of New Zealand Biography*, the parallel Māori-language series, *Nga Tangata Taumata Rau*, and an additional 3,541 biographies on white and Māori New Zealanders are freely available to search online. New biographies will be added in the future.

Comprising more than twenty writers from the nineteenth century, *Writers in Residence: A Journey with Pioneer New Zealand Writers* sets as its goal to return those authors from the academic realm and in a sense humanize them for a regular reader. It seeks to treat the people rather than their works—the emphasis is on the humanness of the writers. Jenny Robin Jones discusses in her forward that the national literature that developed from Anglo settlers or visitors and their writing often had a utilitarian impetus—from a growing population of missionaries, farmers, teachers, merchants, and so on. Starting with guidebooks and similar products, New Zealand writing progressed into histories, poetry inspired by Māori songs, war stories, and women's writing. Selection is based on authors who had an influence on the development of New Zealand's literature, such as F. E. Maning, Alfred Domett, Lady Barker (later Mary Anne Broome), Jessie Mackay, and Blanche Baughan. This book presents a new and nontraditional scholarly/critical approach. It is an enchanting, and factual, introduction to the literary landscape of nineteenth-century New Zealand. Heavily endnoted, *Writers in Residence: A Journey with Pioneer New Zealand Writers* also features a lengthy classified bibliography of manuscript collections, articles, books, pamphlets, booklets, and unpublished works by the writers discussed in the main text.

A partnership between D. W. Thorpe and the National Centre for Australia Studies at Monash University, ***Who's Who of Australian Writers*** was sponsored by the Ideas for Australia 1991–1992 program. It lists authors active in a wide range of subjects, with the requirement for inclusion that the author be a published Australian author. Film, television, and radio scripts count as publications. With more than 5,200 entries arranged in alphabetical order, this represents the only published information for 90 percent of the authors in this volume. Entries include author's name, pseudonyms, date of birth, place of birth if available, employment history, periodical and anthology publications, awards, genres, memberships, recreational activities, family writers, availability for activities such as speaking engagements and commissioned writing, and contact information (lacking e-mail addresses due to the date of publication). *Who's Who in Australian Writers* concludes with a useful 120-category subject index. A guide to abbreviations closes the book.

Although it is now sixty years old, the ***Dictionary of Australian Biography*** remains an important tool for researchers (see chapter 8 for a discussion of the electronic version as it appears in *Project Gutenberg*). Not scintillating prose, the set nevertheless offers concise essays with citations for obscure further reading on 1,030 figures in Australian history—forty-two of whom are women and 137 of whom are literary authors. The latter is a narrow descriptor for today's literary researchers who frequently incorporate prose and other writing that does not fall into the earlier concept of "literature." People in this resource must have died before 1942. If you are interested, the introduction provides a statistical assessment of those authors in the dictionary, a discussion on the difficulty of deciding whom to include, and the requisite explanation of the concept of "Australian"—for example, being born in Australia, but those who leave only count where there is clear evidence of Australian heritage in the written works. Percival Serle spent twenty years collecting information for the book, which he published at the age of seventy-five.

Australian Literary Pseudonyms: An Index with Selected New Zealand References is a basic alphabetical list of pseudonyms that send you to an entry for the author's real name. The entries list all known pseudonyms. Those marked with an asterisk (*) indicate New Zealand authors. The compilers, Nesbitt and Hadfield, look to the nineteenth century as the era in which literary pseudonyms were actually quite necessary for authors—of convict origin and otherwise. A brief introduction explores the tendency toward pseudonyms in Australian writing, often used to protect writers who were critical of the government. The authors have one large caveat: this volume is intended as preliminary, a beginning attempt to connect literary pseudonyms with their historic owners. New Zealand authors are part of this compilation due to the tendency of people to move between the two countries—leaving aside the nationality discussion for those who undertake to compile national bibliographies.

Concise volumes of around one hundred pages comprise the *Australian Writers* series published by Oxford University Press. They provide a short overview of the authors' lives and writings, and they work well as solid introductions to select authors. Authors treated in this series include Henry Handel Richardson, Peter Carey, Patrick White, Bruce Dawe, Judith Wright, Kenneth Slessor, Gwen Harwood, Christina Stead, Gerald Murnane, David Malouf, A. D. Hope, James McAuley, and Peter Porter.

You may also look for biographies on individual authors. Using library catalogs covered in the next chapter, you can look for books about an author by using the *subject* search function. Often, a biography about an author will also offer critical discussions of his or her work, chronologies, and bibliographies. For example, a concise volume from the *Australian Writers* series, Michael Ackland's *Henry Handel Richardson* (née Ethel Florence Lindesay Richardson) provides an introductory overview on her life and writings. The first chapter treats her life, and the other chapters cover her novels and short fiction. The volume closes with a bibliography and notes, but no index.

One broad resource that includes many historical and contemporary figures from Australia and New Zealand is the *Oxford Dictionary of National Biography*. An online product with a print counterpart, this database is widely held among academic libraries. It comprises over fifty-seven thousand biographies of individuals who had an impact or influence on the British Isles, starting in the fourth century BC and running through the beginning of the twentieth century. Articles range from quite short to thirty-five thousand words and are often accompanied by illustrations. They include, when available, full names and name changes; places and dates of births, deaths, baptisms, marriages, and burials; parents' names, dates, and professions; other important family members; and education. Articles also feature a list of resources used by the author, archival repositories, images, and information pertaining to an individual's wealth at the time of death.

CHRONOLOGIES

Hooton, Joy W., and Harry Heseltine. *Annals of Australian Literature*. Melbourne: Oxford University Press, 1992.

Norburn, Roger. *A Katherine Mansfield Chronology*. Houndsmill, England: Palgrave Macmillan, 2008.

A chronology will provide you with a list of events in the order that they happened. You will often find chronologies as parts of other research publications, added as a way to help users contextualize their research and place literary works and figures in history. Chronologies will vary in detail and complexity and can cover the entire history of a national literature or the life and works of one specific author. These resources are particularly useful if you are starting to work in an area that is new to you. For the literature of Australia and New Zealand, there are few chronologies that are not part of other publications. The earlier annotations in this chapter should help you locate those published as part of a larger work.

An update to the original written by Grahame Johnston in 1970, **Annals of Australian Literature** is an extensive and detailed chronology of the development of Australian literature to 1988. It preserves, and occasionally enhances, the entries from the 1970 volume, which begins coverage in 1789. The newer volume revisits the earlier years in literary history and adds titles that Johnston had left out. The authors explain that they felt this expansion was important for two basic reasons: more works had been discovered as the years passed, and in the two decades since the original publication, the concept of *literature* had changed to be much more inclusive of a range of genres. This volume treats traditional literary genres such as drama, fiction, and poetry, but it also extends coverage to genres that are not always considered to be *literature* in its most strict interpretation, such as biography and autobiography, history, travel writing, and so on.

The body of Hooton and Heseltine's work is a straightforward chronology of books written by year. When they believed it was needed, the authors added a symbol following the title of a given work to indicate the genre. A guide to the abbreviations precedes the main text. Entries include authors' last names, birth years, and first initials or names if there are several authors that share the surname. Pseudonyms are used in the main text only if the author usually wrote under that name. Illustrations, date published if different from date written, editor, co-writer, and so on, are included when appropriate. A third column contains birth and death dates for authors, as well as dates for selected periodicals and newspapers. A substantial index covers both of the content columns. Because of the book's far-reaching nature, it should be of potential use at many points in your research, from early starting points at which you are trying to focus your topic, to more advanced stages when you are looking for specific authors, types of writing, or points in the development of a national literature.

One volume of a series titled *Author Chronologies*, *A **Katherine Mansfield** Chronology* is part of an eclectic collection. The series is designed such that it serves as a quick point of reference for dates and events, an excellent way to verify facts, and a useful supplement to a narrative biography. Based on letters, diaries, and other personal documents, as well as biographies and bibliographies, the Mansfield volume is prefaced by a legend of abbreviations and a family tree. This is a detailed chronology—almost one hundred pages for a life that lasted only thirty-four years. The main body is followed by a list of explanations of people in her life, a bibliography, and an index.

DOCUMENTARY VOLUMES
AND SCHOLARLY PUBLICATIONS

Eggert, Paul, ed. *The Academy Editions of Australian Literature*. University of Queensland Press, 1996–2007.

Barnes, John, ed. *The Writer in Australia: A Collection of Literary Documents, 1856 to 1964*. Melbourne: Oxford University Press, 1969.

The scholarship that surrounds the literatures of Australia and New Zealand is young and developing, and as a result you will have to rely on original resources to a greater extent than if you were working on a writer like Wordsworth, for example, who has a large body of scholarship that surrounds him. Documentary resources include the primary texts around which the ensuing theory and criticism form. If you use the word "documentary" or "sources" in a library catalog keyword search, you will frequently get these types of documentary resources, ones that provide primary works. Primary works are the original works you will study—poems, prose, diaries, communication, and so on—and in a still-young field of study these resources are invaluable.

Similarly, scholarly editions will prove to be of great value, when they exist. A scholarly edition will be one that comprises editorial explanations of people, places, things, and a range of authorial decisions that make the text as we know it. They are often the result of a scholar reading multiple versions of a text and making informed decisions on what the definitive text should look like. A thoroughly researched scholarly edition will include extensive footnotes that explain and give examples of the various incarnations a text endures before reaching its final published form.

The Writer in Australia: A Collection of Literary Documents, 1856 to 1964 delivers exactly what it purports to: a collection of twenty-some documents comprising articles, introductions, reviews, letters, and diaries from writers and critics. Broad in coverage, these documents capture the sense of Australian literature and authors spanning more than one hundred years, rather than presenting a study of authors. As many resources in this chapter tend to do, this one points to the Australian writer's search for what it means to be an Australian writer and how this Australian character began to emerge in local and regional writing. Individual chapters are prefaced by editor John Barnes, who provides helpful context for the documents. This book is an excellent selective overview of Australian literature through primary sources and can certainly be used as a stepping-off point for a researcher interested in the contemporary reception of and reaction to the literary output throughout a national history. As such, it will give you an idea of the types of primary documents that are available.

A series of scholarly critical editions of classic works in Australian literature, *The Academy Editions of Australian Literature* was started by the Australian Academy of the Humanities as a result of scholarly agreement that nineteenth- and early twentieth-century Australian literary reprints were of relatively low quality. With great attention paid to developing the most authoritative text, the titles in this series are also accompanied with rich contextualization, usually including a history of the publication and its editions and translations, its reception, and other useful information such as maps, information on currency, text collation, lengthy explanatory notes, and biography and chronology resources on the authors. Titles in the series include *The Collected Verse of Mary Gilmore: Volume 1, 1887–1929* and *Volume 2, 1930–1962*; *Australian Plays for the Colonial Stage: 1834–1899*; Rolf Boldrewood's *Robbery Under Arms*; Catherine Martin's *An Australian Girl*; Henry Handel Richardson's *The Getting of Wisdom*; Marcus Clarke's *His Natural Life*; Richardson's, *Maurice Guest*, *The Journal of Annie Baxter Dawbin: 1858–1868*; and Henry Kingsley's *The Recollections of Geoffry Hamlyn*.

CONCLUSION

This chapter provides you with a range of resources that will help you as you begin your research. Even if you are well versed in the area of research you are undertaking, you might want to look at the general reference tools as a way to refresh your memory. Remember that when you need to confirm factual information, these types of resources are the best place to look. It is easy to rely on Internet resources for basic facts, but the tools discussed in this chapter have been through many levels of fact-checking and are considerably more reliable than what you may find with a random Internet search.

It is important you also remember, however, that no matter how useful these resources are, they cannot give you all that you need in order to develop a substantial research project. The rest of this book will look carefully at a variety of resources—print and electronic—that will lead you into a wealth of more expansive resources, ones that will help you to augment your project as you progress through the research process.

NOTE

1. Peter Pierce, *The Cambridge History of Australian Literature* (Melbourne: Cambridge University Press, 2009), 2.

Chapter Three

Library Catalogs

This chapter encompasses the complexities and nuances of library catalogs. If you have a clear awareness of how a library catalog works, you will see that library catalogs as well as other databases usually operate on a logical and well-organized structure. This chapter also illustrates how to use union and national catalogs. While searching these catalogs is obviously important, so too is being able to effectively and accurately evaluate the list of results you retrieve and to best limit or otherwise enhance your initial search. This chapter will cover author, title, and subject searches, explaining the strengths and weaknesses of each and discussing their overall value and when and why you will want to use them. The catalogs of the national libraries of Australia and New Zealand will both be excellent resources for your research, and *World-Cat* will provide additional options you can use to search catalogs nationally and internationally.

The library catalog helps you discover what a particular library or library system owns in all formats (print, microform, electronic, archives, photographs, etc.). Catalogs now, however, are growing larger and more inclusive, and as such they are becoming increasingly complex. Your local library catalog will likely be one of the first sources you use to locate materials for your research. In addition to telling you what your library owns, it gives you location and availability information. Because most catalogs are online, they now include URLs for electronic resources so that the user can simply click and go to that resource (e-book, journal, reference source, Web page, and so on). Some catalogs still exist only in print form, but those are usually highly specialized catalogs that you will encounter when you are fairly advanced in your research. Online catalogs differ from library to library, and for a research project that deals with the literature of Australia and New Zealand, unless your library has a strong collection, you will have to use other catalogs in order to locate all the resources you need. A library catalog contains records that represent the holdings of a library. These records are created by librarians who use a descriptive controlled vocabulary to illustrate the resources held by their libraries. Like the relationship between databases and their search engines (see chapter 1), catalogs are the intellectual content that is delivered by the search engines that run them. The search engines behind library catalogs are usually one of a few major vendors such as Sirsi's *Unicorn* catalog, Endeavor's *Voyager* catalog, and Innovative Interface's *Millennium* catalog.

Regardless of the type of search engine that powers a catalog, there should be enough similarities across libraries so that you will be able to search a wide range of catalogs with relative ease. Most online catalogs find their structure in the MARC record that was discussed in chapter 1. Within this structure, the majority of academic and research libraries in the English-speaking world employ the principles outlined in the *Anglo-American Cataloguing Rules* (*AACR2R*), a set of rules that normalizes the methods applied to describe a book (or an audiovisual item, Web resource, etc.). Within the parameters of these rules, catalogers will apply the Library of Congress Subject Headings (LCSH), a comprehensive controlled vocabulary that classifies and describes items within a catalog, collection, database, and so on. The LCSH is used by the National Library of New Zealand. Libraries Australia, a cooperative service that is organized by the National Library of Australia for libraries across the country, uses a controlled vocabulary that starts with the LCSH but is enhanced by additional headings that apply to Australian bibliographic records and is approved by the Libraries Australia Headings Review Panel. These headings describe such characteristics as author name and subject descriptors. This chapter contains examples of subject headings from the Library of Congress as well as the specialized headings applicable to Australia and New Zealand. Catalogers use the LCSH to populate appropriate fields within the MARC record, which in turn gives library catalogs a common structure from one to the next. As a result, there is a great similarity between the catalogs for the researcher in the United States and in other English-speaking countries. It is important to remember, however, that no matter how closely a library or its catalogers adhere to these standards, nothing is perfect. As you explore more and more library catalogs from a variety of places with diverse historical practices, you will find divergent customs within systems that will produce differing bibliographic records for the same item. Records are created by people, and an individual's understanding of an item will color that bibliographic record. These differences are most evident in *WorldCat* (discussed in detail later in this chapter), where more than one record may exist for the same item, with only minute differences between the records.

With the almost daily changes, updates, and improvements (and despite the glitches) presented to students and scholars conducting research on the Internet, the amount of research you are able to pursue from the comfort of your own computer allows you to move much further along in your initial, and even more advanced, research than would have been possible only a few years ago. For the literature of Australia and New Zealand, the availability of academic, public, and national library catalogs online provides invaluable discovery tools. Naturally, this ability to determine the existence of a particular text, image, recording, and so on brings with it an often added difficulty of actually being able to use the resource. Luckily, as finding items has become easier, other library services such as reference and interlibrary loan have similarly become more accommodating and eager to help the increasingly physically removed research community. In short, do not be afraid to ask reference librarians for help when you run into a difficult situation.

Online catalogs also allow researchers freedom from adhering to the alphabetically ordered, controlled vocabularies of printed card catalogs. The keyword search function provides for a considerably more random user approach that accommodates the adept researcher's ability to manipulate the catalog. This chapter is designed to help you to better understand how to take advantage of the intricacies of developing keyword searches. It will explore the configuration of a bibliographic record, which should enable you to construct efficient searches within an online catalog; by understanding the construction of these records you will know how to tell the search engine to find what you need. It might be useful to look back briefly at chapter 1 for a refresher on the types of searches that most databases support. And do not forget to locate the search tips available to you in online catalogs. Librarians are instinctively helpful, and library catalogs usually have informative tips to searching the content.

AUTHOR SEARCHES AND EVALUATING THE RESOURCES

Sometimes searching for books by particular authors can be either very easy, or quite tricky. If, for example, you are looking for books by New Zealand author Witi Ihimaera, you will have little difficulty locating his works in a library catalog. He is a writer popular in the twentieth and twenty-first centuries, and his name as an author is standardized in library catalogs. In fact, even searching for "Witi" as an author keyword will return a list of works that he wrote, both in catalogs from libraries in the United States and in New Zealand. Figure 3.1 represents the bibliographic record for Ihimaera's *The Dream Swimmer*. The author field is populated with the official author heading for Ihimaera.

The dream swimmer

Author:	Ihimaera, Witi Tame, 1944-
Title:	The dream swimmer / Witi Ihimaera.
Published:	Auckland, N.Z. : Penguin, 1997.
Description:	423 p. ; 23 cm.
Notes:	"The sequel to The Matriarch"--Cover.
Subject headings:	Māori (New Zealand people)--Fiction.
Subject headings:	New Zealand--Fiction.
ISBN:	0140272402

Figure 3.1. Modified catalog record for *The Dream Swimmer*. Source: Indiana University Libraries catalog.

You will usually have good success looking for the works of a particular author simply by entering the author's name, last name first, in the author search field. Increasingly libraries are also facilitating access to digital collections through their online catalogs, due in large part to MARC records provided by vendors for the texts in databases such as *Eighteenth Century Collections Online* (*ECCO*). These additions to the library catalog make it easier to locate electronic versions of texts. Many of these digital collections contain works beyond traditionally published genres, extending to the journals and diaries of individuals, as well as works such as reports of government-commissioned explorations that may list several contributors as authors. With these types of works, a keyword search is usually recommended.

The "authority" heading in the author field is extremely useful, but it is helpful only if the particular person you are researching has a heading that appears in the author field in the searchable MARC record. If, for example, you were trying to find writings by a more obscure, noncanonical figure, maybe a nineteenth-century settler who often wrote with a deliberately obfuscated identity, the author field is not always reliable. If you are thwarted by searching by author, try searching for the writer's name as a keyword. This method will let you search all parts of a bibliographic record, so if the author is mentioned in the record in the contents, for example, the search should return that record. Similarly, if your author wrote with a pseudonym, it is possible the real name of the author may be successfully searched only as a keyword. Leon Carmen, for example, appropriated an Aboriginal female identity, calling himself Wanda Koolmatrie. Koolmatrie has a standardized author heading, but searching for Carmen as an author will not return his pseudonymous creations. Figure 3.2 represents a record of Koolmatrie's *My*

Title   My own sweet time / **Wanda Koolmatrie.**
Author   Koolmatrie, Wanda, 1949-
Published   Victoria, BC ; Crewe : Trafford Publishing, c2004.

LOCATION   CALL NO   STATUS
Bendigo Main Collection   A823.3 KOOL   AVAILABLE

Description: 189 p. ; 22 cm.

Summary: "Unavailable for seven years, this is the award-winning novel which
                triggered a furore in Australian literary circles. In 1997, it was
                revealed that Wanda Koolmatrie, the book's part-Aboriginal
                narrator and apparent author, was in fact the creation of **Leon
                Carmen**, a white male. In a fierce backlash, the book was
                immediately withdrawn from sale - some say burnt. The resilient
                Wanda, however, has now risen from the ashes..." -- Back cover.

Awards: This work won the Nita May Dobbie Award for women writers
                before being revealed as a hoax in March 1997.

Figure 3.2. Modified record of Wanda Koolmatrie's *My Own Sweet Time*. Source: La Trobe University Library catalog.

Own Sweet Time, with Carmen's name and pseudonym highlighted. Carmen appears only in a summary field.

Similarly tricky is locating a work for which your author is a contributor (he or she wrote a chapter, story, etc.) but for which he or she is not the primary author. If the book record has been enhanced with the table of contents for the collection or anthology, then a keyword search for the author will also locate the book. With this in mind, it is important to remember that in spite of the vast amount of material findable online, there will still be times when you need to consult a book before you are able to determine whether or not you need to use it. Even with Google's massive digitization efforts under way, it is impossible to see inside every print volume.

Figure 3.3 represents a book in which a Peter Carey short story is included, but he is not listed in the author field within the bibliographic record. If you did not already know that a Carey short story was in this collection, you would need to search for his name as a keyword. His name is in the record in the table of contents, but not as an author heading.

Sudden fiction international: sixty short-short stories
  Shapard, Robert, 1942-

Title: Sudden fiction international : sixty short-short stories / edited by Robert Shapard
        and James Thomas ; introduction by Charles Baxter.

Published: New York : Norton, c1989.

Description: 342 p. ; 22 cm.

Other contributors: Shapard, Robert, 1942-

Other contributors: Thomas, James, 1946-

Contents: The falling girl / Dino Buzzati -- On hope / Spencer Holst -- The grasshopper and the bell
        cricket / Yasunari Kawabata -- Girl / Jamaica Kincaid -- The other wife / Collette -- La Volpaia /
        Mark Helprin -- An insolvable problem of genetics / Josef Sékvoreckyâ -- House opposite / R.K.
        Narayan -- Love, Your Only Mother / David Michael Kaplan -- Homage for Isaac Babel / Doris
        Lessing -- Welcoming the board of directors / Peter Handke -- The boy / Joyce Carol Oates -- The
        weather in San Francisco / Richard Brautigan -- Blue / David Brooks -- The grass-eaters /
        Krishnan Varma -- Preparations / Kenneth Bernard -- At the river / Patricia Grace -- Disappearing
        / Monica Wood -- By the creek / Barry Yourgrau -- The book / Rodrigo Rey Rosa -- Facing the
        light / Talat Abbasi -- Lost keys / Paul Milenski -- Arrest me / Denis Hirson -- Orion / Jeanette
        Winterson -- The verb "to kill" / Luisa Valenzuela -- All at one point / Italo Calvino -- Bigfoot stole
        my wife / Ron Carlson -- Mr. and Mrs. Martins / Edla van Steen -- Di Grasso / Isaac Babel --
        Courtly vision / Bharati Mukherjee -- The model / Bernard Malamud -- Terminal / Nadine
        Gordimer -- There's a man in the habit of hitting me on the head with an umbrella / Fernano
        Sorrentino -- Family Album / Siv Cedering -- **The last days of a famous mime / Peter Carey** -- The
        shoe breaker / Daniel Boulanger -- Katya / Sergei Dovlatov -- Looking for a rain god / Bessie Head
        -- The school / Donald Barthelme -- The fifth story / Clarice Lispector -- Tancredi / Barbara
        Alberti -- Las Papas / Julio Ortega -- The black dog / J. Bernlef -- Snow / Ann Beattie

Subject headings: Short stories.

Figure 3.3. Modified author keyword record for *Sudden Fiction International: Sixty Short-Short Stories* with Peter Carey bolded. Source: Indiana University Libraries catalog.

TITLE SEARCHES

The title search, much like the author search, will find the various editions of a title owned by a library. Because a search for a title could retrieve several variant titles, you will need to be careful to assess the results of the search based on such basic bibliographic criteria as editor, publisher, date of publication, and format. Books that are traditional literary classics will tend to have many editions, particularly those that have entered the public domain and are available freely for reissue. It is common practice for library catalogs to list titles alphabetically.

Figure 3.4 is a list resulting from a title search for E. J. Banfield's *Confessions of a Beachcomber*. The database that runs the catalog has produced an alphabetical list of titles that begins one title ahead alphabetically of the one you are looking for. In this list of oddly interesting titles, the second and third items are the ones that match the initial search. The fact that only two titles

Browse Results   Browsing on: **"confessions of a beachcomber"**

No. of Recs	Entry
1	Confessions of a bad dog / by James Cattell and Dorelle Davidson
1	The confessions of a beachcomber / E.J. Banfield
1	The confessions of a beachcomber; scenes and incidents in the career of an unprofessional beachcomber in tropical Queensland, by E. J. Banfield. With introductions by Alec H. Chisholm
1	Confessions of a concierge : Madame Lucie's history of 20th century France / Bonnie G. Smith
1	Confessions of a confirmed extensionalist : and other essays / W.V. Quine ; edited by Dagfinn Føllesdal, Douglas B. Quine
1	Confessions of a corinthian : poems / by Julian Croft
1	Confessions of a counterfeit critic; a London theatre notebook, 1958-1971
1	Confessions of a cultist: on the cinema, 1955-1969
1	Confessions of a difficult woman : the Renée Geyer story / by Renée Geyer and Ed Nimmervoll
1	Confessions of a failed finance minister / Peter Walsh

Figure 3.4.   Title search results for *The Confessions of a Beachcomber*. Source: University of New South Wales Library catalog.

match this search makes the next steps easier, because with only two titles, you need only to examine the records for those items to decide which you want to use.

A tip: because a library can have a variety of locations or keep materials in storage, you cannot assume that items will be shelved together.

The book represented by the second record in the list, Banfield's *The Confessions of a Beachcomber*, is reflected in figure 3.5. The record tells you a great deal about this particular book. It is a facsimile of the original first printing, but it also includes an introduction by Michael Noonan. You can also see that it is published by the University of Queensland Press, important for

Author: Banfield, E. J. (Edmund James), 1852-1923.

Title: The confessions of a beachcomber / E.J. Banfield. Edition   Facsim. 1st ed. / with an introduction by Michael Noonan.

Publication Details: St. Lucia, Qld: University of Queensland Press, 1994.

Series: UQP nonfiction

Description: xvi, 336 p., [46] leaves of plates : ill., map ; 20 cm.

General Note: Facsim. reprint. First published: London : T. Fisher Unwin, 1908.

LC Subject(s): Natural history --Australia --Queensland.
          Dunk Island (Qld.) --Description and travel.

Figure 3.5.   Modified record for title search on *The Confessions of a Beachcomber*. Source: University of New South Wales Library catalog.

Primary Author(s): <u>Banfield, E.J. (Edmund James), 1852-1923.</u>
Title: The confessions of a beachcomber; scenes and incidents in the career of an unprofessional beachcomber in tropical Queensland, by E.J. Banfield. With introductions by Alec H. Chisholm.
Publication: [Sydney] Angus and Robertson [1968]
Description: Book
221 p. illus., map, ports. 22 cm.
Notes: First published 1908.
Subjects: Dunk Island (Qld.)

Figure 3.6. Record for title search on *The Confessions of a Beachcomber*. Source: University of New South Wales Library catalog.

at least two reasons: it is a university press, which usually indicates attention to academic quality, and the book itself is about Dunk Island, a Queensland island and source of pride. This record also tells you that this book is part of a University of Queensland Press series, *UQP Nonfiction*. So, with this choice you will get a text that looks just like the original publication, with the added benefit of an introduction that sets forth a history and context for the book.

You would find the item represented in figure 3.6, *The Confessions of a Beachcomber; Scenes and Incidents in the Career of an Unprofessional Beachcomber in Tropical Queensland*, if you had followed the link to the third item on the search list. Although this title is more complete than the one that precedes it, this one is nevertheless a less scholarly edition. In many ways, however, these books are quite similar. Both reprint the original text from 1908, and both include introductions. A quick search on the authors of the introductions should reveal their qualifications. Michael Noonan was a children's author, radio script writer, and also wrote a biography of E. J. Banfield. Alec H. Chisholm wrote fiction, Australian nature books, and encyclopedias. Truly, either of these books would be fine for research about the text. Because of the widely different publication dates, you may benefit from looking at both, as the introductions may provide different insights and diverse theoretical underpinnings.

SUBJECT SEARCHES

Look back to the first chapter to get a quick refresher on subject headings, particularly the controlled vocabulary endorsed by the Library of Congress that provides a standard structure and terminology by which catalogers classify bibliographic items. Subject headings, also called descriptors, are an important feature of most catalogs or databases. While catalogs do tend to make the subject field searchable as part of the keyword search feature, in many instances the keyword search is far too inclusive. For example, a keyword search in most catalogs will encompass the table of contents field. Look at the table of contents in figure 3.3 to see the extraordinarily broad collection of words from which a keyword search can pull. This book would appear in a keyword search for books about grasshoppers and crickets, genetics and iguanas, rivers and creeks, parlors, and bigfoot. A book of short stories is most likely an inappropriate resource for all of these topics. Remember to look at the catalog's help features in order to be certain what exactly a keyword search will comprise. Catalogs will vary in how they interpret the order in which words are entered, the fields searched, and the ability to limit to specific fields in keyword searches. Familiarity with subject headings will be of particular importance if you are using a catalog that lets you limit keyword searching to fields. If, for example, you are looking for works about the literature of Australia or New Zealand in a particular era, knowing the subdivisions for that era will be indispensable.

The Library of Congress subject headings include century subdivisions for Australian literature and New Zealand literature (for example, twentieth century), but the headings do not tend to be more specific as far as precision of time within a century. Within those headings, however, are other subheadings such as *awards*, *periodicals*, *social aspects*, and *bibliography*.

If you use a subject search, the database that runs the catalog will search for the LCSH that the library uses to describe particular items. If you wanted to find books *about* Janet Frame, rather than *by* her, you would want to type her name, *Frame, Janet*, in the subject search field. Figure 3.7 represents a record this search returned. Pay careful attention to other subject headings that describe a record that looks suitable for your project, because you can use those headings in future searches—in this situation particularly for books

The inward sun : celebrating the life and work of Janet Frame
    Alley, Elizabeth.

Title:	The inward sun : celebrating the life and work of Janet Frame / selected & edited by Elizabeth Alley.
Published:	Wellington, N.Z. : Daphne Brasell Associates Press, 1994.
Description:	214 p. : ports. ; 22 cm.
Other contributors:	Alley, Elizabeth.
Notes:	"Works by Janet Frame": p. 211-212.
Subject headings:	Frame, Janet.
Subject headings:	Women and literature--New Zealand--History--20th century.
Subject headings:	Women authors--20th century--Biography.

Figure 3.7. Record for search of author as subject. Source: Indiana University Libraries catalog.

about female authors in twentieth-century New Zealand, for example, to help to give you a stronger understanding of the national context. Note that the book represented in figure 3.7 is classified as being about Janet Frame as a New Zealand novelist, so you can expect that it will discuss her as a New Zealand writer, and what that means for her writing.

Following is a select list of germane examples of subject headings. Remember that parts of the subject headings can be used to construct keyword searches in addition to subject searches. The subheadings in particular are valuable when you are working to construct a strong keyword query. In spite of the accuracy and range of description that subject headings offer, not all items in a catalog will be enhanced with overly useful or specific headings. If you recall figure 3.2, you will see that, in spite of the summary and awards note, it had no subject headings at all. Also of note here are the differences between the subject headings used in figures 3.5 and 3.6. The record represented in figure 3.5 was created more than twenty-five years after the record in figure 3.6, and the recent cataloging practice employs more headings and greater detail in those headings.

The list following offers some suggested headings for research on the literatures of Australia and New Zealand. It also has some useful subdivisions. All of these words and phrases can be used in keyword searches as well. Note the syntax in the headings—for example, subject headings for *New Zealand Poetry* versus *Children's Literature, New Zealand*:

Australian prose literature
Gay men's writings, Australian
Soldiers' writings, Australian
Travelers' writings, Australian
Australian literature—19th century—History and criticism
Australian literature—21st century
Australian literature—Australia—Western Australia
Aboriginal Australian literature
New Zealand literature—19th century—History and criticism
New Zealand literature—20th century—History and criticism—Theory, etc.
Folk literature, New Zealand
New Zealand poetry
New Zealand literature—Māori authors—History and criticism

For topics that are unique to Australia and where the Library of Congress headings fall short, the Libraries Australia Subject Headings Review Panel has approved an extensive list of headings: the following are a few examples, reflective of Australian literature and culture:

Aboriginal Australian English
Anzac Day sermons
Corroborees
Nukunu (Australian people)
Sacred sites (Aboriginal Australian)
Schools of the air
Transportation of convicts
Warlpiri (Australian people)
Welcome Stranger (Gold nugget)

Ngā Ūpoko Tukutuku / Māori Subject Headings Project, sponsored by LIANZA (Library and Information Association of New Zealand Aotearoa), Te Rōpū Whakahau, and the National Library of New Zealand, provide more than one thousand Māori subject headings directed toward Māori library users. The complete list can be found at the National Library's Ngā Ūpoko Tukutuku / Māori Subject Headings page (mshupoko.natlib.govt.nz/mshupoko/). This page also explains in detail the process for developing these headings. Recently added headings include the following:

Ahumoana
Haurangitanga
Kōhungahunga
Mokopuna
Ngārara pī
Pūnaha arahau
Raweke tamariki
Tuakana-teina
Turi
Ūkaipō

Part of the Māori Subject Headings Project is the Iwi Hapū Names List, developed to ensure accuracy and consistency when libraries classify material by and about Māori peoples. The list and a thorough explanation of the development process can be found on the National Library of New Zealand's Web pages (iwihapu.natlib.govt.nz/iwi-hapu/).

A familiarity with the LCSH system and its syntax will be a huge help when you search specific library catalogs in addition to the union catalogs that will be discussed in the next section. Also, if you want books about an author, search for authors as subjects. Figure 3.8 shows you the beginning of the list of subject divisions for Janet Frame. Using words and phrases from the subheadings such as *history* and *criticism and interpretation* will help

Browse Results	Browsing on: "frame janet"

Frame houses, Wooden	
Frame, Janet	9
Frame, Janet, 1924-	1
Frame, Janet--Criticism and interpretation.	8
Frame, Janet--Criticism and interpretation--History.	1
Frame, Janet--Drama.	1
Frame, John, 1950- --Exhibitions.	1

Figure 3.8. Catalog list for Janet Frame as a Library of Congress Subject Heading. Source: Indiana University Libraries catalog.

you to develop a more directed and specific search. Remember that you will benefit from trying several searches, because a single search usually will not bring back the range of resources that a library holds.

UNION CATALOGS

Center for Research Libraries. Chicago: CRL. www.crl.edu.

Library of Congress and the National Union Catalog Subcommittee of the Resources Committee of the Resources and Technical Services Division, American Library Association. *National Union Catalog, Pre-1956 Imprints: A Cumulative Author List Representing Library of Congress Printed Cards and Titles Reported by Other American Libraries.* 754 vols. London: Mansell, 1968–1981.

WorldCat. Dublin, Ohio: OCLC. www.oclc.org/firstsearch.

WorldCat.org. Dublin, Ohio: OCLC. www.worldcat.org.

The benefits of knowing how to search a library catalog extend far beyond being able to use your own local library's resources. One of the easiest ways to extend your research outside of your library is to use a union catalog, the product of collaborative contributions of several libraries that serves as a discovery tool by which a user can ascertain the holdings of many libraries at the same time. The size and inclusivity of union catalogs will vary, from a few public libraries in a larger system, to hundreds of libraries participating in a national or international effort. Because you will tend to use union catalogs to determine the existence and/or location of an item not owned by your own library, once an item is found in a union catalog the next step is to get a copy for yourself. Logically, you will want to avail yourself of your interlibrary loan services. Talk to your librarians to get the details of policies and procedures for this service. When interlibrary loan is unable to borrow a copy of the item you want, travel may be necessary, or you may be able to speak to a librarian at the institution that owns the item in which you are interested—an endeavor that if successful will save both time and money. Often by speaking to someone at a library that owns the item of interest, you can decide if you really need to see the item.

OCLC's *WorldCat* is an international, collaboratively maintained subscription catalog that provides access to the bibliographic records of items shared by more than forty thousand participating libraries. While this is an extremely useful resource, you do need to remember that not all libraries have contributed all their records to the project. In particular, some special collections are not represented. Touting itself as the largest online library network in the world, this collaboration is not only a collection of records from thousands of libraries, but it has also developed a process by which libraries and librarians portion the actual cataloging of bibliographic items. Once a catalog record is created for an item and shared with OCLC (Online Computer Library Center), other librarians can attach their library's holdings information to that record, as well as import that record into their own local catalogs. Because libraries may choose to create their own records rather than share, there may be more than one record in *WorldCat* that represents exactly the same item, and the differences in the records can be as obvious as the subject headings selected or as obscure as differing punctuation, all depending on how the item was cataloged by a participating library. Therefore, it is important to examine the records to determine which source is best for your research needs.

WorldCat comprises over seventy million records. It is international in coverage, although holdings are still predominately American, Canadian, and English. Australia and New Zealand are nevertheless well represented, and the new records from the *Australian National Bibliographic Database* (*ANBD*) (see following section) appear virtually instantly in *WorldCat* once they are in the *ANBD*. When you retrieve a list from *WorldCat*, the default order of the items is by number of holding libraries, so the item held by the greatest number of libraries will be first on the list. This order is not often overly useful, but you can change it by using the sort button. Remember to look at the help screens for more detailed assistance. *WorldCat* records represent the spectrum of bibliographic resources: books, CDs, DVDs, microforms, periodicals, archives, and open-access and subscription online resources.

Figure 3.9 represents a *WorldCat* record for a 1981 edition of William Dampier's *A Voyage to New Holland: The English Voyage of Discovery to the South Seas in 1699*. In a *WorldCat* record you will find the same types of bibliographic information as you would in your local library catalog. *WorldCat* also provides additional access to holdings information, including a list

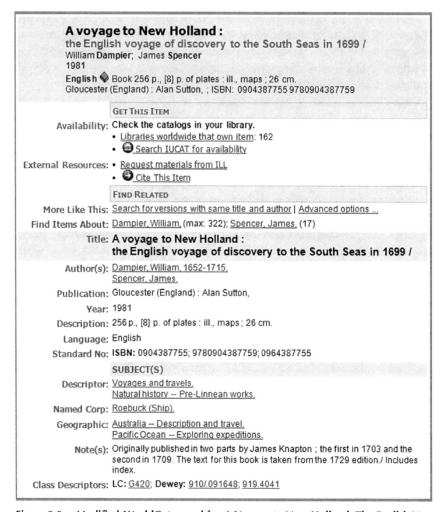

Figure 3.9. Modified *WorldCat* record for *A Voyage to New Holland: The English Voyage of Discovery to the South Seas in 1699*. Source: *WorldCat*.

of other libraries that own the item and a link to search your library catalog (to search the full database you must be logged in and authenticated as affiliated with a subscribing institution). There is a link to an interlibrary loan page, as long as your library has turned on that service. From the interlibrary loan page, you can submit a request for a resource quite easily. If your interlibrary loan options look slim (for example, the book is held by only one library, or by a few special collections), you may want to use the links to booksellers' Web interfaces. For this, the ISBN (International Standard Book Number, assigned to only one edition of a title) is included. Using that number will help ensure that you get the particular edition you want. Note the "class descriptor" field, in which you find LC and Dewey numbers. While helpful for catalog browsing, these are not complete call numbers. If you tried to find a book on the shelf with only these numbers, the best you would be able to do is to find a large section of books, in this case on travel and tourism. Look up the title in your institutional catalog to find the entire call number.

Also available from *WorldCat* is a product called ***WorldCat.org***, a freely available database that searches the contents of *WorldCat*. Figure 3.10 represents the same book as figure 3.9, but as it appears in *WorldCat.org*. *WorldCat.org* presents you with significantly less descriptive information than you would find in *WorldCat*. While the subject headings and the author information are the same, the record from *WorldCat.org* does not provide the notes on the original publication or the fact that Spencer edited and wrote the introduction for this item. From this record you can enter your zip code to generate a list of libraries subscribing to *WorldCat* that own the book, presented in order of nearest proximity.

While it is likely that you will often have access to a *WorldCat* subscription, the new *WorldCat Mobile*, a pilot as of fall 2009 (found by typing www .worldcat.org/m/ in your phone's browser) offers features of *WorldCat* that are potentially useful if you are using mobile technologies. You can search a library, locate it, call it, and find a map on your browser. As this is a pilot, you can find updates to this service as it grows at the previous address. There is also an iPhone application available for iPhone users.

The ***Center for Research Libraries*** (***CRL***) is a North American consortium of university, college, and research libraries. Armed with funds from member institutions, the *CRL* collects resources that are useful to researchers but that can be sometimes marginal or cost prohibitive. Pricey microform sets are a much-valued asset in the *CRL* collection. The newspaper holdings are of great potential use for research you may undertake, particularly those papers from Australia in the 1800s. The periodical press in early Australia acted as an outlet for a wide range of expressive writing. Poetry in particular can be found throughout many early newspapers. These publications also hold within their pages unparalleled primary contextualization of eras, areas, and people. Users of member libraries can borrow items for three months, and other users can borrow materials for four weeks.

The ***National Union Catalog, Pre-1956 Imprints: A Cumulative Author List Representing Library of Congress Printed Cards and Titles Reported by Other American Libraries***, a classic American publication also called the *NUC*, is the result of a joint effort of the Library of Congress and the National Union Catalog Subcommittee of the Resources and Technical Services Division of the

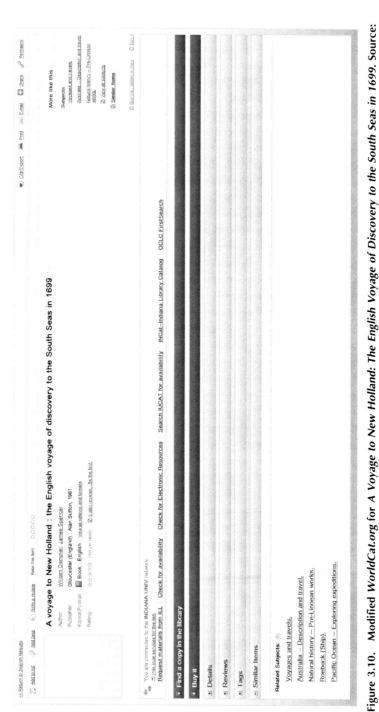

Figure 3.10. Modified *WorldCat.org* for *A Voyage to New Holland: The English Voyage of Discovery to the South Seas in 1699.* Source: *WorldCat.org.*

American Library Association. While it represents the holdings of libraries in the United States and Canada in print before 1956, it is not limited to publications that originated in North America. It provides a thorough pre-1956 snapshot of publications in libraries in the United States and Canada. This resource truly remains indispensable, in spite of the rather incongruous reality that it is over fifty years old and not available electronically. Importantly, you should be aware that there are indeed records in the *NUC* that have not made the transition to the electronic environment. In 2005 Jeffrey Beall and Karen Kafadar compared the *NUC* to holdings in *WorldCat* and discovered, based on a sample, that 27.8 percent of the records in the *NUC* were not in *WorldCat*.[1] This study was followed by a second by Christine DeZelar-Tiedman that confirmed, based on a sample, that 25 percent of the records from the *NUC* did not appear in *WorldCat* even after it merged with *RLIN*, a now-defunct collaborative union catalog.[2]

With 754 volumes, this set is often a victim of space constraints in libraries. Its pages are filled with copies of Library of Congress catalog cards reflecting the holdings of libraries between 1968 and 1982, the years in which this work was compiled. The cards are arranged alphabetically by author, or title if there is no author. Variant editions of one title are arranged by publication date, and library codes are included on the card to tell you what library owned the book at the time of publication.

NATIONAL LIBRARIES AND CATALOGS

Australian Libraries Gateway, n.d., at www.nla.gov.au/libraries/index.html (accessed 29 September 2009).

Australian National Bibliographic Database, November 23, 2007, at www.nla.gov.au/libraries/resource/nbd.html (accessed 29 September 2009).

Libraries Australia, n.d., at librariesaustralia.nla.gov.au (accessed 29 September 2009).

New Zealand Libraries' Catalogue, n.d., at nzlibrariescatalogue.natlib.govt.nz (accessed 29 September 2009).

Publications New Zealand, n.d., at publicationsnz.natlib.govt.nz/index.html (accessed 29 September 2009).

The National Library of Australia, located in Canberra, A.C.T., has a physical collection of more than nine million volumes, including serials and manuscripts. These holdings are the result of the library's primary function to develop holdings that comprehensively represent Australia, its citizenry, and their cultural heritage. The collections overview page (www.nla.gov.au/collect/) lists formats covered, with links to greater details on formats such as books, journals, electronic resources, manuscripts, maps, newspapers, oral histories, ephemera, photographs, and music. Nearly 90 percent of the library materials are searchable in the online catalog, and retrospective cataloging and conversion is under way. Operating hours for the library's seven reading rooms are available online.

In January 2009 the National Library of Australia's union catalog, *Australian National Bibliographic Database* (*ANBD*), discussed in greater detail in chapter 4, began to synchronize with OCLC's *WorldCat* to give nearly instantaneous access to new titles as they are entered into the *ANBD*. In 2008, older catalog records were entered into *WorldCat*. Although Australian libraries are now easily searched by using *WorldCat*, it is important to remember that not all records from all libraries are there. Many libraries will hold back their special collections, archives, and other ephemeral collections.

The *ANBD* is maintained as part of **Libraries Australia**, a collaborative endeavor that is organized by the National Library of Australia to serve Australian libraries and their communities. Representing the holdings of more than 850 libraries, the *ANBD* is available through a participating library's *Libraries Australia* membership. The National Library Web pages provide a statistical representation of libraries that have records in the *ANBD* and the percentages of the individual collections that are in the catalog. Access is available to *Libraries Australia* by subscription; at this writing the cost was $55 Australian annually. The subscription includes unlimited searching of *ANBD*, *Picture Australia*, *Singapore National Union Catalogue*, *Te Puna* (New Zealand), *Australian Research Online*, OCLC's *WorldCat*, and more.

Libraries Australia, however, offers users a basic free search through *Trove* (trove.nla.gov.au/). This option is a recent improvement over an older interface that allowed unsubscribed users to search by basic keyword methods. Please see chapter 9 for a more complete exploration of the richness of *Trove*.

The **Australian Libraries Gateway** (**ALG**), also a part of the National Library, is a free directory for information on more than five thousand Australian libraries. Libraries update their own information, and membership is free. Through this service, for example, a researcher who is planning a trip to Australia can find a link to museum information through the *Collections Australia Network* (*CAN*) (www.collectionsaustralia.net). The *ALG* is potentially extremely useful for access to uncataloged collections. It has brief descriptions of more than one hundred collections across the country. Additionally, the *ALG* helps users to find a library, locate a book within a library, and peruse numerous online exhibitions across the country, and it offers several subject portals for further online research. In summary, the *ALG* is a far-reaching national Web portal that provides information on collections and contacts that will help a researcher plan a potential research trip quite effectively. In addition to the National Library, individual states have their own library websites: State Library of New South Wales (www.al.nsw.gov.au); State Library of Queensland (www.slq.qld.gov.au); State Library of South Australia (www .slsa.sa.gov.au); State Library of Tasmania (www.library.tas.gov.au); State Library of Victoria (www.slv.vic.gov.au); State Library of Western Australia (www.liswa.wa.gov.au); Northern Territory Library (www.slq.qld.gov.au); and Australian Capital Territory Library Service (www.library.act.gov.au).

The National Library of New Zealand (Te Puna Mātauranga o Aotearoa) is charged by the national government in the National Library of New Zealand Act of 2003 to collect and make available to the citizens resources that document the history and heritage of the country and to work with other libraries and institutions toward those goals. The Alexander Turnbull Library, part of the National Library, cares for and makes accessible its collections to the New Zealand people, develops collections of New Zealand and Pacific studies interests, and collects documents pertaining to New Zealand. The 2003 act emphasized the library's responsibility for preservation of Māori knowledge (mātauranga Māori).

The National Library of New Zealand has an online catalog currently in a beta test version that is based on *Te Puna National Union Catalogue*, a subscription service that includes *ANBD*, *WorldCat*, the U.S. National Agricultural Library, and more. The free, Internet-based catalog is searchable in English and Māori languages, and it provides information about items held in New Zealand libraries. *Te Puna* is generally considered a resource for librarians and is available only to subscribers, and the **New Zealand Libraries' Catalogue** is the public version of this resource. As the beta project progresses, links from the catalog into individual libraries will be added.

Publications New Zealand, the updated version of the *New Zealand National Bibliography*, is available freely online. Use this resource to find publications by New Zealanders, or publications about New Zealand, or published in New Zealand. Searchable like other library catalogs, the records from this resource contain the same information you will find in other online catalogs. As a national bibliography, this catalog also provides for each record lists of libraries that hold individual titles.

CONCLUSION

Today, many library catalogs are available, at least in part, online. As you can see from the last section, union catalogs from Australia and New Zealand are available freely on the Internet in limited public versions, with the complete versions available by subscription. Even though the publicly accessible union catalogs are partial, they provide an excellent starting point for locating books on your topic that may not be available in U.S. libraries. Although the freely accessible national union catalogs may not include everything, the preponderance of online catalogs for individual libraries, as well as for cooperative library systems, are rewarding resources for research. While your local library may not have access to all the resources, by using these library catalogs in tandem with interlibrary loan services you will be able to find and access items you need. U.S. libraries such as those at the University of Texas, Pennsylvania State University, and the University of Washington have concentrated on developing collections that support research on literature from Australia and New Zealand, and they are often willing to share their resources.

NOTES

1. Jeffrey Beall and Karen Kafadar, "The Proportion of NUC Pre-56 Titles Represented in OCLC WorldCat," *College & Research Libraries* 66 (5) (2005): 431–35.

2. Christine DeZelar-Tiedman, "The Proportion of NUC Pre-56 Represented in the RLIN and OCLC Databases Compared: A Follow-up to the Beall/Kafadar Study," *College & Research Libraries* 69 (5) (2008): 401–6.

Chapter Four

Print and Electronic Bibliographies, Indexes, and Annual Reviews

This chapter presents an overview of bibliographies, indexes, and annual reviews that will lead you to resources on Australian and New Zealand literature. Bibliographies can vary greatly in terms of the sources they cover. Some list only secondary materials, such as scholarly journal articles and monographs, dissertations, or book reviews. Often, annotations are available to either describe or analyze the content of the sources included. Other bibliographies are designed to enable the discovery of primary resources—poems, short stories, and fiction—published in newspapers, journals, magazines, and literary anthologies. These resources can be especially useful when researching nineteenth-century Australian authors, who published much of their work in newspapers and magazines. Generally speaking, the goal of the print bibliography is to provide researchers with convenient access to topic-specific content that has not been previously collected in any one resource. Finding a bibliography on a particular author, literary work, literary genre, or movement can save considerable time and effort in gathering information vital to your research project.

Specialized print bibliographies are particularly useful when researching Australian and New Zealand literature, as standard literary bibliographies and indexes have failed to cover these areas comprehensively in the past. This lack of inclusion may be due to the scope of the tools themselves, as many focus primarily on British or American literature. The limited distribution of Australian and New Zealand literature outside the Pacific region may be another reason for the omission, as readers, reviewers, and scholars in other parts of the globe remain relatively unaware of the amazing variety and quality of creative works produced by authors in both countries. Fortunately, the emergence of *AustLit* has filled a large gap for those interested in the study of Australian literature. Researchers without access to *AustLit* must circumnavigate the limitations of the mainstream databases, and an important strategy will be locating a bibliography devoted to a specific author. Be sure to take a few minutes and review the introductory matter of a bibliography, as this is where the scope of the tool will be outlined. Some questions to ask include whether the bibliography attempts comprehensive coverage of the topic, or if it focuses on a specific type of resource, such as secondary materials. Also, it is essential to note the publication date of the bibliography. Many of the author-specific resources described in this chapter were published several years ago, so consulting additional tools may be necessary to identify current information.

Sections within this chapter outline a variety of resources with distinct goals. For example, national bibliographies cover a broad range of subjects on Australia and New Zealand, while online bibliographies like *AustLit* will include only materials pertaining to Australian literature. Many bibliographies and indexes began as print tools but now are available electronically. The advantage of using an online version is that a quick search can result in information about an author, a literary work, or topic from hundreds of resources that span a wide range of time. As more and more journals, books, and dissertations become available full-text online, the electronic bibliography will make literary research even more convenient for scholars. Keep in mind that most are available through subscription only, and some will be less accessible to researchers outside Australia and New Zealand. Thus, it is important to check your local library to determine if a particular resource is a viable option for your project. The goal of this chapter is to review these online tools, recommend search strategies for maximizing results, and offer alternative resources for those without access to the subscription-based resources.

By now you should be familiar with the process of locating bibliographies through your library's catalog. You can identify book-length bibliographies by performing a keyword search on the author or topic, along with the term *bibliograph**. Thus, a search for *bibliograph* and kate grenville* will produce book-length bibliographies or books that contain a bibliography on Kate Grenville. You may also use the appropriate Library of Congress subject headings to discover bibliographies on a specific topic. For Australian and New Zealand literature, monograph-length bibliographies are limited—these will be available only for well-established authors and core early writers of the nations' literary history. A more likely alternative is article-length bibliographies for Australian and New Zealand writers. The best tools to use for finding both book-length and article-length bibliographies devoted to a single author will be discussed in more detail toward the end of this chapter. If you need a refresher on the difference between searching by keyword versus searching by subject headings, please refer to the information in chapter 1.

NATIONAL BIBLIOGRAPHIES AND INDEXES

Australian National Bibliographic Database (ANBD). Canberra, A.C.T.: National Library of Australia, 1981–. www.nla.gov.au/librariesaustralia/anbd.html.

Australian National Bibliography (ANB). Canberra, A.C.T.: National Library of Australia, 1961–1996. Monthly with annual cumulations until the print version ceased in 1996. Continues online as the *Australian National Bibliographic Database (ANBD)*.

Australian Public Affairs Full Text (APAFT). Melbourne: RMIT Publishing. Available online from 1995 to present. www.informit.com.au/plustext_APAFT.html.

Australian Public Affairs Information Service (APAIS). Canberra, A.C.T.: Government Printer, 1945–2000. Monthly with annual cumulations. Available online from 1978 to present. www.informit.com.au/indexes_APAIS.html.

Bagnall, A. G. *New Zealand National Bibliography to the Year 1960*. 5 vols. Wellington: P. D. Hasselberg, Government Printer, 1969–1985.

findNZarticles. Wellington: National Library of New Zealand. findnzarticles.natlib.govt.nz.

Index New Zealand (INNZ). Wellington: National Library of New Zealand, 1987–. www.natlib.govt.nz/catalogues/innz.

Index to New Zealand Periodicals. Dunedin: Otago Branch New Zealand Library Association, 1941–1950; Continued by *Index to New Zealand Periodicals and Current National Bibliography of New Zealand Books and Pamphlets Published in . . .* Wellington: New Zealand Library Association, 1951–1966. Continued by *Index to New Zealand Periodicals*. Wellington: National Library of New Zealand, 1968–1987. Continues online as the *Index New Zealand (INNZ)*.

New Zealand National Bibliography / Te Rarangi Pukapuka Matua o Aotearoa (NZNB). Wellington: National Library of New Zealand, 1966–1999. 11 issues per year. Continues online as *Publications New Zealand*.

Publications New Zealand (PNZ). Wellington: National Library of New Zealand. find.natlib.govt.nz/primo_library/libweb/static_htmls/pubnz/.

The *Australian National Bibliography (ANB)*, previously issued as *Books Published in Australia* and *Annual Catalogue of Australian Publications*, is available in print from 1936 to 1996. Until 1973 the *ANB* listed only materials received and cataloged by the National Library of Australia. After 1973 the scope expanded to include all resources that contained a significant Australian focus, whether received by the National Library or not. The goal of the *ANB* was to be comprehensive; thus, it featured books, pamphlets of four or more pages, serials, printed music, microforms, and later, listed electronic publications as they become more prevalent. Items excluded from the *ANB* were individual pieces of legislation, technical standards, reprints, maps, video recordings, and sound recordings. Ultimately, the National Library decided to discontinue the print version of the national bibliography, and after 1996, the electronic version, the *Australian National Bibliographic Database (ANBD)*, became the sole publishing record for Australia. Hosted by the National Library of Australia, the *ANBD* serves as both the national bibliography of Australia and the national union catalog, representing the collections of more than 850 Australian libraries. The *ANBD* is accessible via the *Libraries Australia*, a fee-based service managed by the National Library. For more information on *Libraries Australia* see chapter 3. One feature of particular interest is RAP, or "Recent Australian Publications" (www.nla.gov.au/librariesaustralia/rap .html). RAP highlights materials from the current year and previous two years by Australian publishers and Australian authors, as well as items published elsewhere that contain significant Australian content. RAP is a free service, and researchers may browse the list alphabetically by title or by subject using the Dewey decimal classification system. For those unfamiliar with the Dewey decimal system, it is advisable to review its outline and become acquainted with its broad subject categories and their accompanying numeric classification. For literary research, it is important to know that the 800s pertain to literature and that within the 800s, Australian literature falls within the 820 range. In the *Libraries Australia* database, an "A" designates Australian literature from other literatures and separates genres by the following classification: A820— Australian literature; A821—Australian poetry; A822—Australian drama; A823—Australian fiction. RSS feeds are available on RAP for those who wish to be notified when new content is added.

Both the ***Australian Public Affairs Information Service (APAIS)*** and the ***Australian Public Affairs Full Text (APAFT)*** databases are produced by the National Library of Australia. *APAIS* indexes approximately 550 journals, and *APAFT* is an online collection of scanned articles from more than four hundred of these same journals.[1] Journal coverage in the online version of *APAIS* begins with 1978, but the print version goes back to 1945, if earlier content is needed for your research. The materials available in *APAIS* and *APAFT* derive from a wide range of mostly Australian periodicals, newspapers, scholarly journals, conference papers, and books dealing with topics in the social sciences and humanities. Selected overseas resources are also indexed, but only if the subject matter pertains to Australian economics, politics, or other social and cultural issues. Both *APAIS* and *APAFT* are available through paid subscription and will be accessible in most, if not all, Australian libraries. These two resources are less likely to be available outside Australia, which can present a challenge to researchers in the United States and Canada. To see a record of the journals indexed in *APAIS*, consult the following website (www.informit.com.au/journalsindexed_indexes_APAIS. html). Additionally, all full-text journals in *APAFT* may be viewed online (www.informit.com.au/plustext_APAFT.html). Journals of interest to topics pertaining to Australian literature and culture include *Antipodes*, *Art and*

Australia, Australian Aboriginal Studies, Australian Academic and Research Libraries, Australasian Drama Studies, Australian Feminist Studies, Australian Historical Studies, Australian Literary Studies, Australian and New Zealand Journal of Art, Journal of Australian Studies, Hecate, Meanjin, New Literatures Review, Overland, Quadrant, and *Westerly.*

In his introduction to volume 2 of the **New Zealand National Bibliography to the Year 1960**, A. G. Bagnall outlines the history of the bibliographical record of New Zealand. His five-volume set attempts to retrospectively document the years leading to the formation of the *New Zealand National Bibliography*, which existed in print from 1966 to 1999 (see following entry on *Publications New Zealand*). Volume 1 features publications that date from the very beginning of New Zealand as a British colony through the year 1889. Due to the extent of this coverage, volume 1 is available in two parts. Volumes 2 through 4 cover the years 1890 to 1960 and organize entries alphabetically as follows: volume 2, A through H; volume 3, I through O; and volume 4 concludes with P through Z. Volume 5 is the supplement and index to the entire set. Entries are arranged alphabetically by author, corporate author, or title, if the author is anonymous. Basic bibliographic information, such as title, imprint, pagination, and size, accompanies each item, along with a brief note describing content. The scope of the bibliography includes books and pamphlets, if they are published in New Zealand or contain some significant reference to it (this is defined by the author as a minimum of two to three pages). Monographs published overseas by New Zealanders are documented if the work pertains to local issues or themes. Items excluded are reprints, primary and secondary school texts, juvenile material, university theses, material in the Māori language, parliamentary papers, and series that are listed in the *Index New Zealand* (see following entry). Volume 5 furnishes access to the bibliography's content by subject, title, and names of joint authors or illustrators. Note that there is a separate index to volume 1, located in the back of the second part. For an alternative bibliography of New Zealand sources from 1643 to 1909 where entries are arranged chronologically, rather than alphabetically, see T. M. Hocken's *A Bibliography of the Literature Relating to New Zealand* (Wellington: John Mackay, Government Printer, 1909).

findNZarticles provides access to materials by or about New Zealanders, published within a wide range of New Zealand newspapers and journals. The project began as a collaboration between Christchurch City Libraries, Dunedin Public Libraries, Landcare Research NZ Ltd., and the National Library of New Zealand. Following a successful pilot period, *findNZarticles* extended its scope to include resources available at other New Zealand institutions. The list of resources indexed (find.natlib.govt.nz/primo_library/libweb/static_htmls/findnzarticles/contributors.jsp) features *Index New Zealand* (see following entry for more information), the University of Waikato's *Māori Bibliography*, and several regional indexes to local newspaper content. The basic search in *findNZarticles* allows limits by material type (book, magazine, articles, or all) and five separate fields of information, such as author, title, and subject. Thus, you can look for poems or essays written by C. K. Stead, or search for him as a subject to locate critical or biographical texts about him. The advanced search permits users to limit their queries to a particular resource within the database, such as *Index Auckland*, focus on a specific date range, and combine two different terms in one convenient step.

Index New Zealand (**INNZ**) offers abstracts and descriptions of articles from approximately one thousand publications from 1987 to the present. The index originally existed in print format and began publication in 1941 as the **Index to New Zealand Periodicals**. Between 1951 and 1966 it expanded its scope to include books and pamphlets, but when taken over by the National Library of New Zealand it once again became strictly a periodical index. Information from years prior to 1987 is being added to the online version retrospectively. The titles indexed range from popular magazines such as *North and South* and *Consumer* to academic journals such as *Art New Zealand*. *INNZ* is updated daily, and approximately 2,500 articles are added monthly. Subjects covered are general-interest materials, social research, current affairs, and all areas of the arts and humanities. Of particular note are substantial reviews of books, poetry, and short fiction by New Zealand and South Pacific authors. Also listed are feature articles about authors or literature from the following local newspapers: *Dominion Post*; the *New Zealand Herald*; the *Otago Daily Times*; *The Press*; and the *Sunday Star Times*. For those with access to the subscription database *Newztext Plus*, full texts of many newspapers and magazines indexed in *INNZ* are available and can be useful tools for locating book reviews of New Zealand literature. You can either look for the full text of references retrieved from *INNZ* or search by topic. Content in *Newztext Plus* is updated daily, and articles from the *New Zealand Herald* appear online within twenty-four hours of publication.

Publications New Zealand (**PNZ**) is the online-only successor to the **New Zealand National Bibliography / Te Rarangi Pukapuka Matua o Aotearoa**, which existed in print and microform from 1966 to 1999. The *New Zealand National Bibliography* started as two separate publications (*Index to New Zealand Periodicals and Current National Bibliography of New Zealand Books and Pamphlets Published in . . .* and *New Zealand General Assembly Library Copyright List*) before merging into one resource. In its current form, the national bibliography aggregates and describes books, periodicals, films, music, and other materials published in New Zealand. Items published elsewhere are added if they meet the following criteria: have at least one-fifth New Zealand content, use a New Zealand setting for fiction, or have a New Zealand author or editor. When using *PNZ*, you can browse a "new releases showcase" and search by title, media, subject, and author. The option of subscribing to an RSS feed for immediate notification of recent additions to the database is available. For additional information on *Publications New Zealand* see chapter 3.

GENERAL LITERATURE

Annual Bibliography of English Language and Literature (ABELL). Leeds: Maney Publishing for the Modern Humanities Research Association, 1921–. Annual. Available online through ProQuest. www.proquest.com/en-US/catalogs/databases/detail/abell.shtml.

Modern Language Association International Bibliography of Books and Articles on the Modern Languages and Literatures (MLA International Bibliography). New York: Modern Language Association of America, 1922–. Annual. Available online through various vendors. For a list of vendors check www.mla.org/bib_electronic.

Year's Work in English Studies (YWES). Oxford: Published for the English Association by Oxford University Press, 1921–. Annual. ywes.oxfordjournals.org/.

The ***Annual Bibliography of English Language and Literature (ABELL)*** is sponsored by the British Modern Humanities Research Association. *ABELL* is similar to the *MLA International Bibliography* in that it offers access to scholarly journals and books, critical editions, essay collections, and dissertations pertaining to literature and language studies. A notable difference between the two tools is that *ABELL* includes book reviews of secondary resources. *ABELL* focuses on materials written in English from 1920 onward. One major drawback to using *ABELL* for researching Australian and New Zealand literature is that there is no separate subject indexing available to identify authors by nationality. In the print version of *ABELL*, entries for Australian and New Zealand literature are located under the category "British literature." To find materials on a specific author or literary work, look by the author's name or by the title of the individual work. The online version of *ABELL*, available through ProQuest, is preferable to use, as some of the more recent entries contain additional indexing that reflect the nationality of authors covered. However, this feature is spotty for Australian and New Zealand authors, as illustrated in figure 4.1, a record for Paul Eggert's recent publication on Peter Carey's *True History of the Kelly Gang*. For best results when using the online version of *ABELL*, it is advisable to search by a specific author or literary work, rather than using the terms "Australian" or "New Zealand." Often you can identify unique content in *ABELL* that is not indexed by other resources, including the *MLA International Bibliography*.

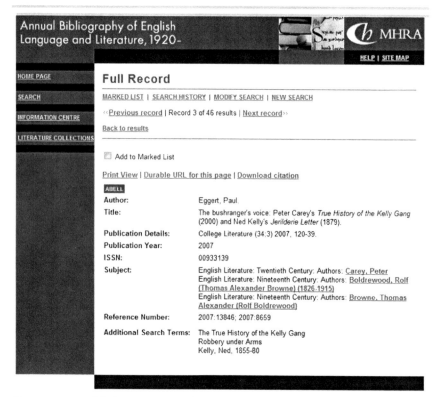

Figure 4.1. Modified *ABELL* record for "The Bushranger's Voice: Peter Carey's *True History of the Kelly Gang* (2000) and Ned Kelly's *Jerilderie Letter* (1879)." Source: *ABELL* via ProQuest.

The most widely used and referenced database for the study of literature in the United States is the **Modern Language Association International Bibliography** (**MLA International Bibliography**). The *MLA International Bibliography* indexes print and electronic journals, books, chapters of books, series, working papers, conference papers and proceedings, dissertations, and scholarly websites that focus on literature, modern languages, folklore, and linguistics. Appropriate reference tools such as dictionaries, catalogs, handbooks, and bibliographies are also included. Exclusions to note are primary works (unless accompanied by a new critical or bibliographic apparatus) and reviews of literary and scholarly materials. Most periodical publications in the database are covered from 1926 to the present. Journals in the *JSTOR* collection are indexed from the first issue, and in some cases coverage goes back to 1884. While there is some overlap of content between the *MLA International Bibliography* and *ABELL*, the Modern Language Association indexing system requires that all material on fiction, poetry, or drama is described by the national literature to which it belongs. Thus, you can search the database by "Australian literature" or "New Zealand literature" and locate relevant citations quickly. The record in figure 4.2, from the *MLA International Bibliography*, is of the same article on Peter Carey's novel shown in figure 4.1. Note that, in addition to designating authors by nationality, the *MLA International Bibliography* also provides more subject indexing for the item, which makes it easier to determine whether or not the content is suitable for your research needs. Most entries in the bibliography do not include abstracts, but the MLA is in the process of adding them when available.

If you are interested in locating information on indigenous authors, it is possible to limit your search by a specific group such as "Aboriginal writers" or "Māori writers." Keep in mind this indexing term will only be present in some circumstances—authors are not assigned to a group unless they are specifically identified as such by the author of the article or book cited. More information on the scope and indexing specifications of the *MLA International Bibliography* may be found on the Modern Language Association website under "Scope of the Bibliography" (www.mla.org/publications/bib_scope). When researching Australian and New Zealand literature, it is important to be aware that there is very little content available on these literatures prior to 1955. From the beginning of the database to 1970, there are fewer than eight hundred results on "Australian literature" as a subject. Perhaps this can be explained by the original scope of the *MLA International Bibliography*. From 1921 to 1955 the bibliography was published annually in the Modern Language Association's affiliated journal, *Publications of the Modern Language Association*. The "American Bibliography" strived to present a complete record of American scholarship for the previous year and was heavily focused on British and American literature, along with Romance and Germanic languages and literatures. In 1969 the bibliography became a separate publication and expanded its scope to include additional international materials. From 1970 to 2008 almost seven thousand results appear for the same subject search on "Australian literature." Clearly, the *MLA International Bibliography* is a significant resource for locating scholarship on contemporary Australian literary studies, and its indexing system enables the discovery of information by nationality as well as many other points of access. The *MLA International Bibliography* is available only through subscription, but most college and university libraries in North America have access to the database. It should be noted that due to dwindling subscriptions to the print version of the bibliography, the MLA decided to discontinue its publication after the 2008 edition.

The *Year's Work in English Studies* (*YWES*) is a publication of the English Association of the United Kingdom and is the only annual review source described in this chapter. Annual reviews offer an overview of resources that

Title: *The Bushranger's Voice: Peter Carey's True History of the Kelly Gang (2000) and Ned Kelly's Jerilderie Letter (1879)*

Authors: Eggert, Paul

Source: College Literature (ColL) 2007 Summer; 34 (3): 120-39. [Journal Detail]

Peer Reviewed: Yes

ISSN: 0093-3139
1542-4286 (electronic)

General Subject Areas: Subject Literatures: Australian literature
Period: 1900-1999
Primary Subject Author: Carey, Peter (1943-)
Primary Subject Work: The True History of the Kelly Gang (2000)
Genre: novel; historical novel

Subject Terms: narrative voice; treatment of outlaws; relationship to postmodernism; sources in letters; by Kelly, Ned (1854-1880)

Document Information: Publication Type: journal article
Language of Publication: English
Update Code: 200701
Sequence Numbers: 2007-1-9887

Electronic Access: http://muse.jhu.edu/journals/college_literature/v034/34.3eggert.html
DOI: 10.1353/lit.2007.0030

Abstract: There is an umbilical cord of outlaw folkloric tradition that joins Rolf Boldrewood's 1880s bushranger novel Robbery Under Arms and *Peter Carey's* Booker Prize-winning novel *True History of the Kelly Gang* (2000). Carey has done again what Boldrewood so innovatively achieved: *the* invention, or reinvention, *of the bushranger's voice*. But *the* more tantalising manifestation *of the* common outlaw tradition, for Carey, was *the* real-life bushranger *Ned Kelly's Jerilderie Letter* (1879). *The* relationship between *the Letter* and *Carey's* novel interrupts an easy postmodern take on his work: this interruption is *the* subject *of the* essay. It teases out *the* paradox of *the* novel's being simultaneously both postmodern=quotational and, in *the* old-fashioned sense, an act *of* imaginative engagement with a significant past, a historical tale in fact.

Accession Number: 2007300886

Persistent link to this record (Permalink): http://bert.lib.indiana.edu:2048/login?url=http://search.ebscohost.com/login.aspx?direct=true&db=mzh&AN=2007300886 [BOOKMARK] 🔖 ✉ ≡

Database: MLA International Bibliography

View Links: IU-Link | Check for availability

Figure 4.2. Modified *MLA International Bibliography* record for "The Bushranger's Voice: Peter Carey's *True History of the Kelly Gang* (2000) and Ned Kelly's *Jerilderie Letter* (1879)." Source: *MLA International Bibliography* via ProQuest.

have been published during the course of a given year and typically focus on secondary or critical resources. *YWES* is a narrative bibliography that highlights important scholarship in all areas of English studies, including Australian and New Zealand literature. Even though *YWES* began its coverage in 1919, the first addition of Australian and New Zealand literature does not appear until volume 64 (1983). Content is arranged by literary period, and materials on Australia and New Zealand are located in the chapter titled "New Literatures." Materials are subdivided further by the categories "general," "fiction," "poetry," and "drama." Each section features a narrative that analyzes recent publications about Australian and New Zealand authors, including books, book chapters, journal articles, critical editions, reviews, and relevant reference works. Journal issues devoted to a special topic or theme are also discussed. Each volume contains a separate index to critics, authors, and subjects. *YWES* is a valuable resource to consult—not only are the overviews of recent publications of interest, but students or researchers new to the discipline can use it to identify important scholars in the field. Further, since the popularity of Australian and New Zealand literature in academia has waxed and waned over the years, the essays in *YWES* can document trends in literary scholarship over time. Be sure to note that *YWES* is selective in its coverage, and publication is typically behind two years. Thus, the most recent volume will cover scholarship published two to three years prior to the copyright date. Full-text access to *YWES* is available online through Oxford University Press, if your library subscribes. Subscribers to the online version also have advanced access to essays online after they have been accepted for publication.

AUSTRALIA AND NEW ZEALAND

Arnold, John, and John Hay, eds. *Bibliography of Australian Literature (BAL)*. Kew, Vic.: Australian Scholarly Publishing, 2001–.
AustLit: The Australian Literature Resource. Canberra, A.C.T.: University of New South Wales at Australian Defense Force Academy, 1999–. Available online at www.austlit.edu.au.
Duwell, Martin, Marianne Ehrhardt, and Carol Hetherington, eds. *The ALS Guide to Australian Writers: A Bibliography 1963–1995*. 2nd ed. St. Lucia: University of Queensland Press, 1997.
Macartney, Frederick T. *Australian Literature: A Bibliography to 1938, Extended to 1950*. Sydney: Angus and Robertson, 1956.
Miller, Morris. *Australian Literature from Its Beginnings to 1935: A Descriptive and Bibliographical Survey of Books by Australian Authors in Poetry, Drama, Fiction, Criticism and Anthology with Subsidiary Entries to 1938*. 2 vols. Melbourne: Melbourne University Press, 1940. Revised and extended edition by Frederick T.

Macartney. *Australian Literature: A Bibliography to 1938, Extended to 1950*. Sydney: Angus and Robertson, 1956.

New Zealand Literature File. Auckland: University of Auckland Library. Available online at www.nzlf.auckland.ac.nz/.

Ross, Robert L. *Australian Literary Criticism—1945–1988: An Annotated Bibliography*. New York: Garland, 1989.

The ***Bibliography of Australian Literature*** (***BAL***), a long-term project sponsored by the National Centre for Australian Studies at Monash University and the University of Queensland, represents the result of more than a decade of collaborative research into the publication history of Australian authors. One of the basic goals of *BAL* is to update two core bibliographies devoted to Australian literature: Morris Miller's *Australian Literature from Its Beginnings to 1935: A Descriptive and Bibliographical Survey*, and a revised and condensed edition, *Australian Literature: A Bibliography to 1938, Extended to 1950*, by Frederick Macartney. For more information on Miller's and Macartney's work, see the separate entries following here. *BAL* documents all separately published creative works by Australian authors from 1788 to 1992. Entries feature the following information about each author: the name by which he or she is best known (pseudonyms are noted); gender; place of birth and death; and full bibliographic information for all books published, arranged chronologically and categorized by genre. Each volume contains a separate alphabetical index of pseudonyms and variant names for authors, as well as an alphabetical list of works published by title. The first volume appeared in 2001 and presents information on authors A through E, followed by authors F through J in 2004, and authors K through O in 2007. The fourth and final volume of the *Bibliography*, published in 2008, includes information on authors P through Z.

AustLit: The Australian Literature Resource is the result of a collaborative effort between twelve Australian universities and the National Library of Australia to provide authoritative information on hundreds of thousands of creative and critical Australian literary works relating to more than one hundred thousand Australian authors and literary organizations. Quite simply, there is no comparable resource to *AustLit*. The goal of the database is to index all relevant materials, regardless of format, by or about Australian authors from 1780 to the present. Biographical information, including pseudonyms and alternative names, is available for each author. One unique feature of *AustLit* is the detailed subject indexing assigned to most works of literature, enabling users to search for fiction or poetry about a certain theme, such as the outback or Aboriginal-white relations. It is useful to note that the majority of *AustLit* records relating to primary works contain library holdings information, rather than access to full text. *AustLit* is primarily an index, citing and describing Australian literature published in a range of print and electronic information sources. However, there are more than twelve thousand full-text works available. Links to content in *PANDORA*, the National Library's electronic archive of relevant Australian Web-based publications and websites of organizations and individuals, and selective creative and critical material in Australian literature digitized by *SETIS* (*Sydney Electronic Text and Image Service*) at the University of Sydney are examples of full-text resources in *AustLit*. More information on *PANDORA* may be found in chapter 8. Library holdings information in *AustLit* is available via *Libraries Australia*, the *Register of Australian Archives and Manuscripts*, and the *Guide to Australian Literary Manuscripts*.[2]

AustLit features several different ways to search for content, including the ability to focus on specialized subsets for targeted searching. A few of the subsets currently available are "Australian Children's Literature," "Australian Drama," "Australian Literary Responses to 'Asia,'" "Australian Magazines," "*The Bibliography of Australian Literature*," "Australian Multicultural Writers," "Australian Popular Theatre," "Black Words," "Literature of Tasmania," "South Australian Women Writers," "Western Australian Literature," "Writers of Tropical Queensland," and "Banned in Australia." More information about these specialized subsets may be found on the *AustLit* site (www.austlit.edu.au/specialistDatasets/index). Subscribers to *AustLit* have the ability to search the entire database by a quick search, a guided search, and an advanced search. The quick search offers a single search box to find information by or about a particular author, or title, or to use keywords to search across all fields available in the database. The quick search also allows the use of wildcards to truncate terms, phrase searching (by using quotation marks), and the automatic use of the Boolean term *and* to combine multiple terms. Results are listed by relevance, but it is possible to sort by date, title, and by "electronic format," which indicates that the source is available full-text online. The guided search may be used to find information by a selection of possible fields, such as language, gender and/or heritage of author, and type of work by genre. Thus, if you wanted to find information on Aboriginal authors from Darwin who wrote children's literature, you could do so with a guided search, as illustrated in figure 4.3.

The advanced search should be used for more complex queries or to search for more unusual combinations of information. It allows you to search on the full range of fields available in the database and select more than thirty different author and work search options. To use the advanced search, simply check the appropriate boxes that fit the type of information you seek from the categories "author," "work," and "subject," as illustrated by figure 4.4. The result is another screen with a customized form for selecting and searching by those preselected fields of interest.

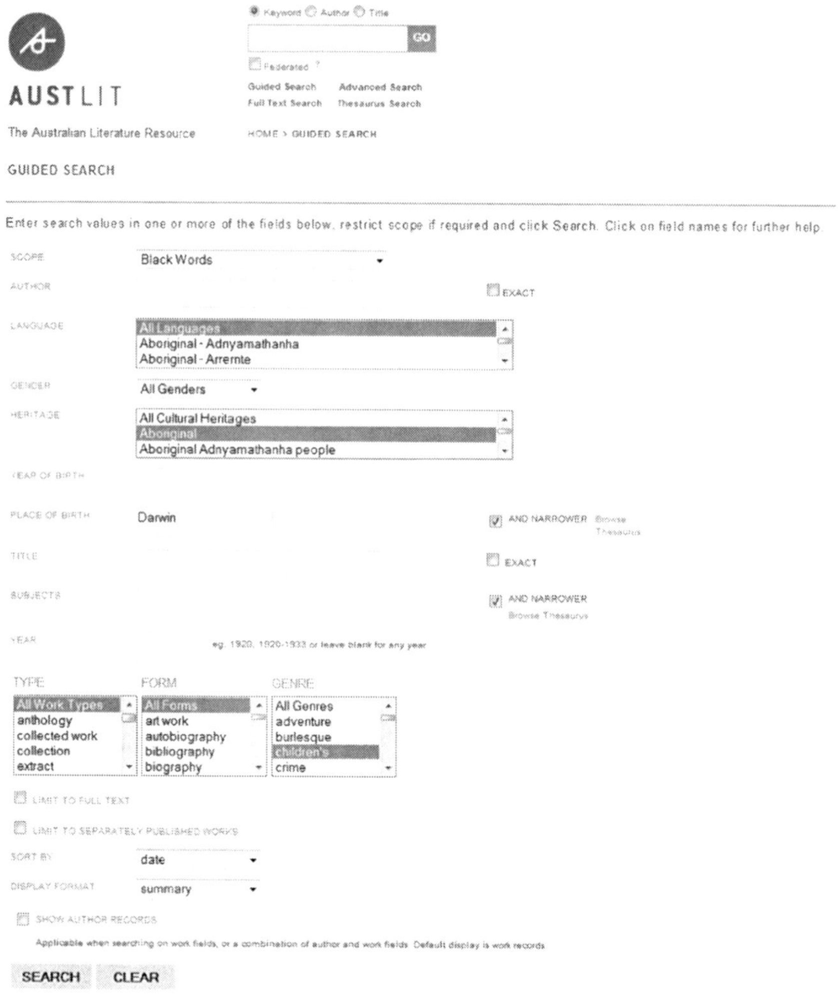

Figure 4.3. Modified record for *AustLit* guided search on Aboriginal authors from Darwin writing children's literature. Source: *AustLit.*

AustLit results may be printed, saved, or e-mailed, and the option to export information to citation management software such as EndNote or RefWorks is available. Finally, *AustLit* provides a comprehensive thesaurus to words and phrases used to index items in the database. Use the thesaurus to find broader, narrower, or related terms to target your search for better or more accurate results. For instance, a thesaurus search on "Ayers Rock" indicates that the Aboriginal term "Uluru" should be used instead to locate information about the sandstone rock formation in the southern part of the Northern

QUICK SEARCH

● Keyword ○ Author ○ Title

□ Federated ?

Guided Search   Advanced Search
Full Text Search Thesaurus Search

HOME > ADVANCED SEARCH

AUST LIT

The Australian Literature Resource

ADVANCED SEARCH

GO TO GUIDED SEARCH

Enter search values in one or more of the fields below, restrict scope if required and click Search. Click on field names for further help. To select other search options scroll to bottom of this page and choose required attributes.

Scope **Black Words**

Author
☑ Name
+ Birth/Death details
+ Residency
+ Personal details
+ Roles/Awards/Notes

Work
☑ Title
☑ Place of composition
☑ Publication details
+ Type/Form/Genre
+ Award details
+ Source details
+ First Line/Notes/Roles

Subject
☑ General Subject Terms
☑ Author's Work/s as Subject
+ Criticised Work's Characteristics

SELECT

Copyright

Figure 4.4.   Modified record for *AustLit* advanced-search screen. Source: *AustLit*.

Territory. Also, narrower terms for the subject heading "Australian poetry" are "Aboriginal poetry" or "Ern Malley Hoax." Access to the thesaurus is available for all search options. Because *AustLit* contains so much material, with an amazing amount of detail for each item, searching the database can be overwhelming. Fortunately, there are several options from which to chose, based on an individual's knowledge of the literature and the specificity of information desired. Help screens and search tips are available and should be consulted, if necessary.

The ALS Guide to Australian Writers: A Bibliography 1963–1995 compiles and integrates all the materials listed in the *Australian Literary Studies* annual bibliographies (see entry under "Serial Bibliographies" in this chapter for more information). Publications associated with each author are arranged by genre, such as collections, fiction, poetry, and critical materials. The scope of inclusion in the guide is the same as that used for the *ALS* annual bibliography—selected authors that "should have attracted substantial critical discussion [and] as many 'emerging' writers as space permits" (vii). It is not intended to be a comprehensive bibliography. *The ALS Guide* is a valuable source for the discovery of new publications and also reflects the changing interests and critical values of scholars in the field. Critical, biographical, historical, and bibliographical materials are featured, as well as selected reviews of primary works and interviews. For those without access to back issues of *Australian Literary Studies*, this one-volume collection is an essential tool, convenient to use, and readily accessible through most college and university library collections.

Even though Morris Miller's *Australian Literature from Its Beginnings to 1935: A Descriptive and Bibliographical Survey of Books by Australian Authors in Poetry, Drama, Fiction, Criticism and Anthology with Subsidiary Entries to 1938* was published almost seventy years ago, it is still considered a standard tool for researching Australian literary history. The two-volume set lists biographical and genre details on all Australian authors, which was approximately 9,500 at the time of publication in 1940. The organization is somewhat unorthodox, making the resource a bit more difficult to use than other bibliographies. However, Miller's work identifies core works by Australian authors, as well as important book reviews and literary criticism about them. Volume 1 covers poets and poetry, drama, and novelists from 1829 to 1899. Volume 2 is in two parts and features novelists and novels from 1900 to 1935, a bibliography of fiction from 1829 to 1938, and a bibliography of criticism from 1833 to 1938. The second part of volume 2 includes a number of useful indexes, such as an alphabetical list of non-Australian authors of novels associated with Australia. One notable example from this section is D. H. Lawrence's *Kangaroo*. A subject index for Australian fiction is also available, so if you were interested in novels about Aborigines in Victoria, you could easily locate them through Miller's work. The general index of Australian authors is especially helpful to researchers new to the field of Australian literature, as it identifies the genres for which each author is known, and pseudonyms used, when applicable. Frederick T. Macartney's *Australian Literature: A Bibliography to 1938, Extended to 1950* is designed to both update and condense Miller's bibliography. The primary goal of the volume was to make the original content easier to use, while also adding and updating information when possible. For instance, commentaries on selected individual writers are available to contextualize the lists of primary works. The result of strategically reorganizing content and deleting selected features in Miller's work is successful. The arrangement of content within Macartney's volume is straightforward. Historical background of each major genre is presented first, followed by the bibliography itself, which is arranged alphabetically by author, regardless of the genres in which he or she wrote. No additional indexes are provided, and for the most part they are not needed. However, the subject index for fiction and general index of authors still have purpose for the novice researcher of Australian literature. For those without access to *AustLit*, these two works by Miller and Macartney are essential to identifying information on early Australian authors and their literary works.

The *New Zealand Literature File* is a freely available tool that features bibliographies of works by New Zealand and Pacific authors, as well as references to biographical and critical materials about them. Initially, the bibliography was compiled by staff in the New Zealand and Pacific Collection of the University of Auckland's General Library to assist students enrolled in courses on New Zealand literature. The resource is easy to use and is organized alphabetically by author. Most entries contain lists of books written by the author, followed by citations to reviews and literary criticism on individual works. In addition to monographs, primary works published in periodicals are also documented. Information available in the *New Zealand Literature File* is not intended to be comprehensive, but to record core resources only. As a result, this is an excellent place to begin looking for secondary sources on a New Zealand literary work. Keep in mind that the majority of resources are published in New Zealand periodicals, which can present a challenge for researchers in North America. Interlibrary loan may be necessary to get the full text of items cited in the *New Zealand Literature File*.

Robert Ross was one the first American scholars to publish research on Australian literature and founded the only North American journal to focus on the subject, *Antipodes*. One of his books devoted to Australian literature, *Australian Literary Criticism—1945–1988: An Annotated Bibliography*, is an essential guide for those interested in Australian literary scholarship. The content is arranged in a unique way that lends itself to the research needs of both the beginning and advanced scholar of Australian literature. Categories for criticism include "General Materials" (anthologies, periodicals, bibliographies, and reference works); "International Views" (reports and opinions, comparative studies, and international journals with special issues on Australia); "Special Topics" (Aborigines, history, culture, and encounters with Western civilization); "Fiction about the Convict Period"; "Film"; "History and Culture" (bush myth, war, and national identity); "Language, Media and Publishing"; "Multicultural Writing"; "Women's Studies"; and "Universities and Australian Literary Study." Additional categories arrange works by genre and major writers. Indexes by author and subject are available to further expedite use of the guide. Because the book is designed to cover important criticism written during a specific time period, researchers will need to locate more recent information using other tools, such as Lever, Wieland, and Findlay's bibliography (see entry under "Research Guides and Bibliographies," in this chapter), *AustLit*, or the *MLA International Bibliography*.

AUSTRALIA AND NEW ZEALAND: SERIAL BIBLIOGRAPHIES

"Annual Bibliography of Commonwealth Literature." *Journal of Commonwealth Literature*. Annual.

Christenberry, Faye, comp. "Bibliography of Australian Literature and Criticism Published in North America." *Antipodes*. Annual.

Hetherington, Carol, and Irmtraud Petersson, comp. "Annual Bibliography of Studies in Australian Literature." *Australian Literary Studies*. Annual.

There are four serial bibliographies published each year devoted to Australian and New Zealand literature. Consult these bibliographies on a regular basis to maintain awareness of recently published fiction, poetry, and drama, as well as current scholarship on all aspects of Australian and New Zealand literature. The journals that publish these bibliographies are usually accessible in North American libraries, and all are available electronically through subscription services. Check your local library catalog to see if they are an option for your research project. More information about the individual journals, *Antipodes, Journal of Commonwealth Literature*, and *Australian Literary Studies*, may be found in chapter 5.

The *Journal of Commonwealth Literature* was created to promote information about creative writing in English from all Commonwealth countries. The **"Annual Bibliography of Commonwealth Literature"** has been published since the first issue of the journal appeared in 1965. The bibliography features resources published within a particular year and includes an introductory essay summarizing the major accomplishments, publications, and news pertaining to each country's literature from the previous year. Separate bibliographies are published for Australia and New Zealand, making it easy to concentrate on authors or works from a particular country. The arrangement of the bibliography has remained consistent since 1965. Categories for the following types of resources are available: bibliographies published serially; research aids; new titles arranged alphabetically by author and subdivided by genre (poetry, drama, fiction, letters and autobiography, anthologies); and literary criticism, which is further subdivided into "General Studies" and "Studies on Individual Authors." New works of nonfiction complete the bibliography. Because the *Journal of Commonwealth Literature* has changed publication frequency over the years, it is impossible to provide information on the specific issue in which the bibliography appears. However, with the aid of an indexing tool, such as the *MLA International Bibliography*, it is relatively easy to locate the exact citation information for a particular year.

The first **"Bibliography of Australian Literature and Criticism Published in North America"** appeared in the third volume of *Antipodes* in 1989 and covered the years 1985 to 1988. Since then the bibliography has been published annually and usually appears in the December issue. The *Antipodes* bibliography "attempts to provide a thorough listing of resources either published or distributed in North America" during a given year that pertain to Australian literature or Australian authors.[3] Although the title indicates Australia is the focus, New Zealand literature is also included. Because the bibliography concentrates on resources published in the United States and Canada, it may be more useful to North American researchers, as the materials should be readily available in local libraries. However, if a comprehensive examination of a particular author and/or work is required, it is advisable to consult additional research tools. Note that the *Antipodes* bibliography strives to feature works by or about new and emerging Australian authors, along with the more established writers. Authors who specialize in children's literature, romance fiction, or fantasy fiction are excluded. The *Antipodes* bibliography is divided into two main sections. Section 1 is devoted to individual Australian and New Zealand authors who have either had works published in North America during a given year or, if published elsewhere, have been reviewed in current North American periodicals. Section 2 is restricted to secondary sources on cultural issues such as Aboriginal, historical, language, and film studies, or general literary criticism on Australian, New Zealand, Commonwealth, or postcolonial literature. For all items in the bibliography, pertinent reviews and commentaries will follow the main entry. Annotations are not available.

Australian Literary Studies is the first journal to begin publishing an annual bibliography focusing on Australian literature. The first **"Annual Bibliography of Studies in Australian Literature"** was published in 1964 and was compiled by renowned scholar Brian Kiernan. Primarily devoted to commentaries useful to criticism and scholarship, the bibliography strives to compile a complete list of books and articles on Australian literature for a given year. Selected materials on Australian studies and the more important reviews and introductions of Australian language studies are available as well. New books by contemporary writers whose work has attracted substantial attention and discussion among scholars are cited, along with key reviews of each item. Most of the reviews are from scholarly resources, but a few newspapers are examined as well. Reviews from newspapers are restricted to the weekend issues of the *Sydney Morning Herald*, the *Age*, and the *Australian*. Feature articles on authors and interviews from newspaper sources are excluded, and coverage of overseas reviews is restricted by accessibility. For materials that are outside the scope of the bibliography, researchers are advised to consult *AustLit* or other bibliographies, such as the two mentioned previously from *Antipodes* and the *Journal of Commonwealth Literature*. The *Australian Literary Studies* bibliography is divided into two sections. The second section is arranged alphabetically by author and lists both primary and secondary sources published by and about individual authors within the past year. Occasionally, older materials may be included with the newer content, but only if they have not appeared in previous bibliographies. The first section is devoted to publications on more general topics, such as Australian studies, film studies, language studies, and Aboriginal culture.

RESEARCH GUIDES AND BIBLIOGRAPHIES

Andrews, Barry G., and William H. Wilde. *Australian Literature to 1900: A Guide to Information Resources*. American Literature, English Literature, and World Literatures in English: An Information Guide Series 22. Detroit, Mich.: Gale, 1980.

Day, A. Grove. *Modern Australian Prose, 1901–1975: A Guide to Information Sources*. American Literature, English Literature, and World Literatures in English: An Information Guide Series 29. Detroit, Mich.: Gale, 1980.

Jaffa, Herbert C. *Modern Australian Poetry, 1920–1970: A Guide to Information Sources*. American Literature, English Literature, and World Literatures in English: An Information Guide Series 24. Detroit, Mich.: Gale, 1979.

Lever, Richard, James Wieland, and Scott Findlay, eds. *Post-Colonial Literatures in English: Australia 1970–1992*. New York: G. K. Hall, 1996.

Thomson, John. *New Zealand Literature to 1977: A Guide to Information Sources*. American Literature, English Literature, and World Literatures in English: An Information Guide Series 30. Detroit, Mich.: Gale, 1980.

Andrews and Wilde's *Australian Literature to 1900: A Guide to Information Resources* is an annotated bibliography to the literature "that emerged from the Australian colonial experience between 1788 and 1900" (xi). Part 1 consists of bibliographies, bibliographical guides, and reference works devoted to the historical, biographical, social, and cultural background of Australian literature to 1900. In addition, this section features works of criticism and literary history relating to the period, organized within the following subcategories: anthologies, essay collections of individual critics, histories and surveys, works on specific genres, children's literature, publishing history, theater history, and common themes in Australian literature. Part 2 of *Australian Literature to 1900: A Guide to Information Resources* is committed to resources on individual authors. Each entry contains a brief biography, followed by a bibliography of works published about the author (biographies and critical commentaries), as well as citations to selected works by the author and important collections of his or her works. The lists of primary works are especially helpful, as many nineteenth-century writers published in newspapers and magazines, which can be more difficult to track down than monographs. The final section of the bibliography outlines nonfiction prose, such as early travel narratives, convicts' memoirs, and settlers' accounts that provide historical context important for the study of colonial Australian literature. All entries are numbered to facilitate the use of a separate name index and a title index. For those interested in early Australian literature, this guide is an essential tool for beginning research. *Australian Literature to 1900: A Guide to Information Resources* represents a gold mine of information on all aspects of early Australian literature and culture.

A. Grove Day's efforts continue the work completed by Andrews and Wilde, representing an annotated guide to "the prose literature published as a result of the Australian experience between 1901 and 1975" (xiii). Materials in *Modern Australian Prose, 1901–1975: A Guide to Information Sources* are organized similarly to those in *Australian Literature to 1900: A Guide to Information Resources*. Entries are numbered consecutively and organized within four main sections. Part 1, "General Bibliography," records works about Australian literature, including a variety of reference tools, such as bibliographies, bibliographical guides, and dictionaries. Also featured are citations to literary criticism, anthologies, and materials on Australian English. Part 2 is dedicated to approximately fifty-two individual authors of fiction. For each author, primary works are listed chronologically, with information on later editions and reprints. Translations are excluded. Following primary sources is a selection of critical commentaries taken from books and articles in scholarly journals. Unfortunately, book reviews have been omitted from this category. Part 3 pertains to works of nonfiction, such as biographies, essays, travel narratives, and a selection of publications on Aboriginal people and their culture. The final section is dedicated to Australian drama, offering sources on the history and criticism, and a two-page list of plays arranged alphabetically by author. There are three separate indexes available to the content in *Modern Australian Prose, 1901–1975: A Guide to Information Sources*—an author index, a title index, and a subject index, making this an easy-to-use and extremely valuable tool for the discovery of information on early twentieth-century Australian literature.

Herbert C. Jaffa's guide to modern Australian poetry covers poets who were born after 1901 and whose work was published through the early years of the 1970s. ***Modern Australian Poetry, 1920–1970: A Guide to Information Sources*** is arranged in ten sections. Section 1 concerns bibliographical aids and reference materials that are useful to the study of Australian literature. Most of the content duplicates the first section of Day's work, but some of the materials pertain strictly to poetry, such as significant anthologies and periodicals devoted to publishing poetry and poetry criticism. Section 2 lists major books on poetry—critical surveys by single authors, criticism by several authors in a collection, and histories. The bulk of Jaffa's work is dedicated to furnishing information on individual poets of Australia. An entry on James McAuley supplies a list of his published poetry, related prose, editorial work, critical responses to his poetry, and notes on available bibliographies about him. The guide is extremely useful in that it categorizes content by specific movements important to the study of Australian poetry. Thus, researchers can identify poets within groups such as the Jindyworobaks or Angry Penguins, and locate essential criticism on them. Additional categories featured are expatriate poets, poets by decade, and younger poets. Of particular note are Jaffa's excellent and informative abstracts on each item described. This work is very well organized and is the best guide to Australian poetry available today.

Lever, Wieland, and Findlay's bibliography focuses specifically on scholarly criticism of Australian literature. Entries in ***Post-Colonial Literatures in English: Australia 1970–1992*** have been selected and annotated "to show the ways in which critics have responded to Australian writing and to provide a guide to a literary critical culture that has undergone remarkable expansion and diversification" in recent history (ix). The introduction features an informative overview of critical history and developments in Australian literary studies. For the most part, reviews and newspaper articles have been omitted, along with dissertations. (For information on locating Australian university theses, see the entry on the *Australasian Digital Theses Program* in chapter 8.) The bibliography is organized chronologically by year and is separated into the following sections: "Reference Aids," "Survey & Overview," "Nonfiction," "Drama," "Fiction," "Poetry," and "Author." Annotations are descriptive, rather than analytical. A separate subject and author index is available. Even though the authors of *Post-Colonial Literatures in English* have been selective in scope, this is a very important tool for identifying literary criticism. For a similar resource that overlaps to some degree, but mostly complements in highlighting older materials, see entry on Robert Ross's *Australian Literary Criticism—1945–1988: An Annotated Bibliography.*

Similar to other volumes in Gale's *American Literature, English Literature, and World Literatures in English* guide series, John Thomson's book provides an excellent introduction to both primary and secondary works pertaining to New Zealand literature. ***New Zealand Literature to 1977: A Guide to Information Sources*** is divided into seven sections. The first is dedicated to reference sources—bibliographies, biographical dictionaries, indexes to serial publications, and guides to special collections. The bibliographies portion of section 1 is nicely organized by genre and contains a separate section on Māori writing. Section 2 is devoted to literary histories and criticism and is also organized by genre. Section 3 outlines important anthologies of New Zealand literature. Similar to Jaffa's work on Australian poetry, most of the content in Thomson's work is committed to individual authors. Each entry presents a brief introduction to the author, followed by serial and monographic bibliographies on the author, works by the author (listed by genre, when appropriate), and criticism written on the author's works (both periodical and monographic). Major authors are separated from those considered less significant. Similar categories are used to present core materials by and about these less significant authors. Unfortunately, a separate subject index is not available; however, indexes by author and title are present. Annotations accompany most entries, but many are brief—one or two sentences—and not as helpful as those available in the other Gale series. Still, as there are few bibliographies available on New Zealand literature, Thomson's book is an important tool for those beginning research in the field.

AUTHOR-SPECIFIC BIBLIOGRAPHIES

Gunton, Elizabeth J. *Bibliography of Catherine Helen Spence.* Bibliographies of Australian Writers. Adelaide: Libraries Board of South Australia, 1966.

Lawson, Alan. *Patrick White.* Australian Bibliographies. Melbourne: Oxford University Press, 1974.

Simmons, Samuel Rowe. *Marcus Clarke: An Annotated Checklist 1963–1972.* Studies in Australian Bibliography 22. Sydney: Wentworth Press, 1975.

Sussex, Lucy, and Elizabeth Gibson. *Mary Fortune ("Waif Wander"/"W.W." c. 1833–1910): A Bibliography.* Victorian Fiction Research Guide 27. St. Lucia: Department of English, University of Queensland, 1998.

Few book-length bibliographies have been published on Australian and New Zealand authors. This selected list should be readily accessible to all researchers, regardless of location. Check your local library catalog to see if a particular title is available. If not, consider borrowing a copy from another library through interlibrary loan. If you do not find a bibliography on your author, a strategy for locating one is to search OCLC *WorldCat* using the name of the author and the truncated term *bibliography**. You can also search more generally by using the appropriate Library of Congress subject headings. Some useful headings for this purpose are the following: *Australia—In literature—Bibliography*; *Australian literature—Women authors—Bibliography*; or *New Zealand fiction—Bibliography*. Often, author biographies will include a bibliography. Thus, it may prove useful to locate a biography on your author and check to see if a bibliography is available. For a list of core biographical series and resources on Australian and New Zealand writers, see chapter 2. Keep in mind that you may have more success finding author-specific bibliographies in journal literature. Article-length bibliographies may not be as extensive as a monograph, but they are just as useful and will often contain more current information. The best way to locate bibliographies in journals is to use an index that focuses on literature, such as *AustLit* or the *MLA International Bibliography*. Once again, use the author's name and the truncated term *bibliograph** to identify these resources.

Over the years, a few monographic bibliographical series devoted to Australian authors have been published. Unfortunately, most of these series are no longer active, but the extant volumes are extremely useful and should be consulted, if one is available on your author. For those researching early Australian and New Zealand authors, these book-length bibliographies are invaluable for their lists of primary sources alone. Because early authors published most of their creative works in periodical sources, identifying specific works can be a challenge, as most nineteenth-century and early twentieth-century magazines and newspapers have either selective indexing or none at all. Four series that are especially important are the *Australian Bibliographies* (Oxford University Press), *Bibliographies of Australian Writers* (the Libraries Board of South Australia), *Studies in Australian Bibliography* (Wentworth Press), and the *Victorian Fiction Research Guides* (University of Queensland). A few specific examples of each will be discussed in more detail.

The Libraries Board of South Australia made the decision to create the *Bibliographies of Australian Writers* series due to a perceived lack of documentation available on Australian authors. One of the early volumes in the series is Elizabeth J. Gunton's ***Bibliography of Catherine Helen Spence,*** published in 1966. Content includes works by Spence, which are further subdivided by genre. Articles and letters written for newspapers and other periodicals are also listed. Another section of the bibliography is devoted to materials housed in various archives around Australia. Finally, there is a section on biographical resources that were published during Spence's lifetime and after her death in 1910. An index provides additional access to material in the bibliography by author, title, and subject. It is noted in the preface of each volume in the *Bibliographies of Australian Writers* series that although much has been published by and about Australian authors, the materials were scattered and difficult to locate. The goal of the Research Service division of the Public Library of South Australia was to compile as much information as possible on individual authors, in hopes that the series would stimulate further interest and research on Australian literature. In addition to the volume on Catherine Helen Spence, other authors available are Hal Porter, Patrick White, Randolph Stow, A. D. Hope, Judith Wright, and R. D. Fitzgerald. The series concluded in 1970 with the publication on Ian Mudie, by Jennifer Tonkin and Jennifer Van Wageningen.

Oxford University Press began the *Australian Bibliographies* series in 1974 with the publication of Alan Lawson's work, **Patrick White**. Lawson's bibliography on the Australian Nobel Prize winner features works by White, published and unpublished, as well as all references to him and his work in books, theses, magazines, newspapers, and radio broadcasts from 1929 to 1973. Annotations indicate the subject scope and length of each item. The book is divided into seven categories, two of which are devoted to primary works by White. The rest of the volume comprises lists of secondary materials. Interviews and articles on White's abundant literary awards are available in the section on biographical material. Critical materials are categorized by genre. Finally, two indexes support additional access to content—an author index and a periodical index. The value of this bibliography on White, as is the case with all authors in the series, lies in the comprehensive scope of the work. Unfortunately, the series did not survive a full decade, and by the time the last book was published in 1981, only six volumes were available. These are some of the best single-volume bibliographies on Australian authors in existence today. Other titles in the series are Brenda Niall's work on Martin Boyd, Joy Hooton on A. D. Hope, and Shirley Walker's volume on Judith Wright. Finally, the reference guide on Australian literature that was published and later revised by Fred Lock and Alan Lawson is a must for anyone researching the literature. For more information on this source, see the entry in chapter 2 under "Research Guides."

Samuel Rowe Simmons's **Marcus Clarke: An Annotated Checklist 1963–1972** is an essential tool for locating this important author's contributions to journals, newspapers, and anthologies. Publications are arranged chronologically, and Simmons provides informative background notes for many of the entries. Also featured is a checklist of Clarke's books, including later editions and reprints. Critical and biographical sources from 1867 to 1972 are available in chronological order and contain reviews from newspapers and other periodicals. Simmons's bibliography on Marcus Clarke is part of a series published by Wentworth Press during the years 1954 to 1993. There are approximately thirty-six titles in the *Studies in Australian Bibliography* series, but only a handful are devoted to Australian literature. Most of the volumes pertain to Australian printing history or to special collections in Australian libraries. The Book Collectors' Society of Australia continued the series in 1994 under a new title, *Studies in Australian Bibliophily*, and these publications do not focus on Australian literature. To see all the items in the series, consult *Libraries Australia* on the National Library of Australia's home page. In addition to the volume on Clarke, other literature-related titles in the original series are Walter Stone's work on Joseph Furphy and Harry Chaplin's volume on Henry Lawson.

Sussex and Gibson's **Mary Fortune ("Waif Wander"/"W.W." c. 1833–1910): A Bibliography** is part of a series published by the Department of English at the University of Queensland. Not all the volumes in the *Victorian Fiction Research Guides* series are devoted to Australian literature, but Meg Tasker's bibliography on Francis Adams and Chris Tiffin's work on Rosa Praed are two that are of interest to the literary scholar. The goal of the series is to highlight minor novelists who were active during the Victorian period between 1860 and 1910, and on fiction published in journals during the same time frame. For the title on Mary Fortune, content includes books, serialized novels, series, short fiction, autobiographical writings and journalism, poetry, and miscellaneous writings. Critical resources are listed separately. There are approximately thirty-two volumes in this series, which began in 1979. Most are indexed in the *MLA International Bibliography* or *AustLit*, so you can search in either database to identify additional titles.

BIBLIOGRAPHIES ON WOMEN
AND MINORITY/ETHNIC WRITERS

Adelaide, Debra. *Bibliography of Australian Women's Literature, 1795–1990: A Listing of Fiction, Poetry, Drama and Non-Fiction Published in Monograph Form Arranged Alphabetically by Author*. Port Melbourne: Thorpe in association with National Centre for Australian Studies, 1991.

Gajer, Ewa, comp. *Australian Women Short Story Writers: A Selective Bibliography*. Armidale: Centre for Australian Language & Literature Studies at the University of New England, 1995.

Goetzfridt, Nicholas J. *Indigenous Literature of Oceania: A Survey of Criticism and Interpretation.* Westport, Conn.: Greenwood Press, 1995.

Gunew, Sneja. *Bibliography of Australian Multicultural Writers.* Geelong, Vic.: Centre for Studies in Literary Education, Humanities, Deakin University, 1992.

Murphy, Margaret. *Women Writers and Australia: A Bibliography of Fiction, 19th Century to 1987.* Parkville, Vic.: University of Melbourne Library, 1988.

Schürmann-Zeggel, Heinz. *Black Australian Literature: A Bibliography of Fiction, Poetry, Drama, Oral Traditions and Non-Fiction, Including Critical Commentary, 1900–1991.* Bern, Switzerland: Peter Lang, 1997.

Arranged alphabetically by author, Debra Adelaide's ***Bibliography of Australian Women's Literature 1795–1990: A Listing of Fiction, Poetry, Drama and Non-Fiction Published in Monograph Form Arranged Alphabetically by Author*** records primary works by women authors from the very beginning of Australian literature to the late twentieth century. Works are subdivided further by genre for writers who explored multiple styles of writing. One unique feature of the bibliography is the inclusion of manuscript locations, which can be important if your research requires the examination of a writer's original texts. (For more information on identifying manuscript collections see chapter 9.) Following each entry is a brief list of secondary resources about the author, including bibliographies, interviews, and selected literary criticism. The *Bibliography of Australian Women's Literature 1795–1990* is an extremely useful tool for identifying women writers and their publications. Because it was not Adelaide's goal to comprehensively document secondary resources, researchers should be prepared to consult other tools for literary criticism. The *Bibliography* is an updated and expanded version of Adelaide's earlier work, *Australian Women Writers: A Bibliographic Guide* (London: Pandora, 1988), which presents brief biographical snapshots of each author in addition to the creative works.

Ewa Gajer's ***Australian Women Short Story Writers: A Selective Bibliography*** is a list of stories written by women authors from 1846 to 1987. The short stories indexed appeared primarily in literary collections, anthologies, and magazines. Full publication information for these resources is available for further consultation. Stories written for children are not included unless printed in an adult anthology or magazine. In her introduction Gajer states that the work represents an important advancement in furthering literary scholarship, as the "short story has always been a powerful mode of literary expression in Australia" and more importantly, it has "a long tradition among Australian women writers" (v). Since few indexing tools to primary literature from the nineteenth and early twentieth centuries exist, this bibliography is an essential tool for the discovery of short fiction written by Australian women writers. Gajer did not intend for the bibliography to feature secondary resources, although a brief bibliography is available at the end of the book.

Nicholas Goetzfridt's *Indigenous Literature of Oceania: A Survey of Criticism and Interpretation* is an annotated bibliography of literary criticism on the fiction, poetry, and drama written by native people of the Pacific Islands, including Aboriginal authors from Australia and Māori writers from New Zealand. Content is arranged by the following categories: "Oceania, General," "Pacific Islands," "Aotearoa—New Zealand," and "Australia." Detailed and often lengthy annotations describe each work of criticism, enabling the identification of items that pertain to scholars' research interests. There is a separate title and author index, an index to critics, and a subject index. Goetzfridt's bibliography is the best single-volume collection of secondary sources available on Aboriginal and Māori literature. For an equally important companion tool that focuses on primary sources rather than secondary, see Heinz Schürmann-Zeggel's *Black Australian Literature*, which is described in more detail later in this section.

Sneja Gunew's *Bibliography of Australian Multicultural Writers* is an attempt to both update and expand two separate resources—Lolo Houbein's *Ethnic Writing in English from Australia: A Bibliography* (3rd revised and extended ed., Adelaide: Department of English Language and Literature, University of Adelaide, 1984) and Alexandra Karakostas-Seda's *Creative Writing in Languages Other Than English in Australia 1945–1987* (M.A. thesis, Monash University, 1988). The author's goal in compiling the bibliography was an attempt to "raise questions and encourage research and thinking around the issue of cultural difference" (viii). To be part of the bibliography, authors must fit within the following two categories: first-generation, non-Anglo-Celtic immigrant writers who have published in English or a language other than English; and second- or third-generation non-Anglo-Celtic writers who have access to languages/cultures other than English and have published in English or a language other than English. Thus, Aboriginal writers are excluded from the scope of the bibliography. Those who migrated to Australia after World War II make up the majority of writers, but the nineteenth century is represented as well. All genres of literature from monographs and periodical sources are featured, including autobiography, biography, essays, fiction, short fiction, and poetry. Dramatic works performed on stage or produced for radio, television, or film are also available. Gunew's bibliography is arranged alphabetically by author. A brief biographical essay accompanies each entry, followed by lists of primary works by genre. In addition to the information on each author, there are three appendixes that may supplement research on multicultural writers: a record of sources used to compile the *Bibliography of Australian Multicultural Writers*, names of writers grouped by languages of publication (pseudonyms are available where applicable), and selected critical writings on multicultural literature and Australian multiculturalism. A similar tool for identifying multicultural literature is Peter Lumb and Anne Hazell's *Diversity and Diversion: An Annotated Bibliography of Australian Ethnic Minority Literature* (Richmond, Vic.: Hodja Educational Resources Cooperative, 1983). To be included authors must be born outside Australia and in a country where English is not the first language. Lumb and Hazell's work should be used as a supplement to the more comprehensive work by Gunew and may be of particular use to those interested in children's literature, a genre excluded from *A Bibliography of Australian Multicultural Writers.*

Similar to Adelaide's *Bibliography of Australian Women's Literature 1795–1990*, Margaret Murphy's **Women Writers and Australia: A Bibliography of Fiction, 19th Century to 1987** is a valuable tool for locating primary sources written by Australian women authors. The advantage to using Murphy's resource is that the arrangement of entries is chronological, rather than alphabetical. Authors are separated into three different time frames— nineteenth century, 1900 to 1945, and 1946 to 1987. If you are interested in browsing a list of early women authors and their works, this is an ideal resource. Access to information by a specific author or title of a work is possible through a separate name index and a title index. Additional features of Murphy's work include pseudonyms used by women authors, literary award winners, and authors whose novels have been made into films.

Heinz Schürmann-Zeggel's **Black Australian Literature: A Bibliography of Fiction, Poetry, Drama, Oral Traditions and Non-Fiction, Including Critical Commentary, 1900–1991** is the best single source available for identifying primary literature in English by Aboriginal and Torres Strait Islanders. The work builds upon two of the earliest bibliographies published on Aboriginal writing, Adam Shoemaker's "A Checklist of Black Australian Literature"[4] and Wesley Horton's "Australian Aboriginal Writers: Partially Annotated Bibliography of Australian Aboriginal Writers 1924–1987."[5] Schürmann-Zeggel's work comprises primary literature in anthologies and collections, traditional narratives and texts, song cycles and lyrics, fiction, poetry, drama, children's literature, and life writing. The two final sections, "Remembered History" and "Political and Social Issues," present Aboriginal films, television programs, and literature commenting on Australian history and political and social issues. Within each section, entries are listed alphabetically by author. Most have annotations that provide context for the item. The second part of Schürmann-Zeggel's book focuses on secondary materials about Aboriginal literature and features sections on general bibliographies, literary studies and reviews, works on individual authors, interviews, book reviews, performance reviews, and biographical materials. Manuscripts, dissertations, and theses have been excluded from the scope of the bibliography.

BIBLIOGRAPHIES BY GENRE

Bedson, Jack, and Julian Croft. *The Campbell Howard Annotated Index of Australian Plays 1920–1955*. University of New England: Armidale, N.S.W., 1993.

Burnes, James. *New Zealand Novels and Novelists, 1861–1979: An Annotated Bibliography*. Auckland: Heinemann, 1981.

Cuthbert, Eleonora Isabel. *Index of Australian and New Zealand Poetry*. New York: Scarecrow Press, 1963.

McNaughton, Howard. *New Zealand Drama: A Bibliographical Guide*. Canterbury, N.Z.: Library, University of Canterbury, 1974.

Muir, Marcie, and Kerry White. *Australian Children's Books: A Bibliography*. 3 vols. *1774–1972*; *1973–1988*; *1989–2000*. Carlton, Vic.: Melbourne University Press, 1992–.

Murray, Sue. *Bibliography of Australian Poetry 1935–1955*. Melbourne: D. W. Thorpe in association with National Centre for Australian Studies, 1991.

Smith, E. M. *A History of New Zealand Fiction*. Wellington: A. W. Reed, 1939.

Torre, Stephen. *The Australian Short Story: 1940–1980*. Sydney: Hale & Iremonger, 1984.

A number of specialized bibliographies are available to assist researchers in locating primary source materials and secondary source materials pertaining to a specific genre within Australian and New Zealand literature. Examples of these resources are discussed in the following pages. No single-volume work on Australian fiction from its beginning to the present exists, likely because it is too large of a category to cover in any one resource. For those interested in fiction, a good place to start is Morris Miller's *Australian Literature: From Its Beginning to 1935*. If there is a specific category of fiction you would like to investigate, check for bibliographies that focus on it, such as Graham Stone's *Australian Science Fiction Index, 1925–1967* (Canberra, A.C.T: Australian Science Fiction Association, 1967) or Loder and Batten's bibliography on Australian crime fiction (*Australian Crime Fiction: A Bibliography, 1857–1993*. Clayton, Vic.: Thorpe in association with the National Centre for Australian Studies, 1994). Scholarly works that analyze a particular genre can also lead you to additional resources, as illustrated by David McCooey's book *Artful Histories: Modern Australian Autobiography* (Melbourne: Cambridge University Press, 1996). McCooey documents important Australian autobiographies and secondary works pertaining to the genre in a bibliography on pages 220 to 231. Finally, bibliographies typically accompany entries within specialized encyclopedias, companions, and histories. Check the list within the section on Australian and New Zealand literary genres located in chapter 2 to see if a source is available on your subject.

Specialized bibliographies that target the literature of a specific region of Australia are also available. Some of the more prominent resources in this category are Bennett, Hay, and Ashford's *Western Australian Literature:*

A Bibliography (Melbourne: Longman Cheshire, 1981), J. H. Hornibrook's *Bibliography of Queensland Verse* (Melbourne: Longman Cheshire, 1981), and John Fletcher's *Poetry Books and Poetry Broadsheets Published in New South Wales: A Catalogue* (Sydney: Book Collectors' Society of Australia, 1989). If you are interested in the literature of a particular region, search your library catalog or one of the appropriate indexes described earlier in this chapter to locate a bibliography.

The Campbell Howard Annotated Index of Australian Plays 1920–1955 is a unique resource that documents more than three hundred plays housed in the Dixon Library at the University of New England. The Campbell Howard collection comprises manuscripts and published plays that were performed by reputable companies between 1920 and 1955. Works by lesser-known authors are available, as well as those written by major figures of the time, such as Katharine Susannah Prichard, Dymphna Cusak, and Patrick White. The purpose of the index is to highlight and publicize the existence of the plays—their history, subject content, and availability—to interested researchers and theater producers. Information for each entry includes the author, title, date first performed/reviewed/published, length, setting, names of characters, cast lists, and a summary of the play's content. For plays that were performed on stage, additional information is available, such as production notes, performances, awards, and critical reviews. The editors of the index have assigned broad subject terms to each play in an attempt to indicate theme. Sample headings are "Aborigines," "Bush Life," "Convicts," and "Family Relations." The main section of the index is arranged alphabetically by author name. Separate title and subject indexes are available to assist researchers in accessing content.

James Burnes's work is a chronology of works by New Zealand authors, designed to present a visual pattern of the growth of New Zealand fiction over time. **New Zealand Novels and Novelists, 1861–1979: An Annotated Bibliography** is an updated version of *A Century of New Zealand Novels: A Bibliography of the Period 1861–1960*, also compiled by Burnes (Auckland: Whitcombe & Tombs, 1961). Authors in the bibliography must be from New Zealand, even if their works do not focus on the country itself. Annotations accompany each entry and consist of a brief description of content, rather than a critical assessment of the work. Two separate indexes facilitate access to material, either by title or by author. For a similar tool that highlights Australian authors, see Hooton and Heseltine's *Annals of Australian Literature* (Melbourne: Oxford University Press, 1992). More information is available on this title in chapter 2 under "Biographical Sources."

Eleonora Isabel Cuthbert's **Index of Australian and New Zealand Poetry** allows researchers to identify specific poems within twenty-two separate publications by author, title, and first line. Many of the publications examined by Cuthbert are anthologies, but a few annual resources are indexed, such as the *New Zealand Poetry Yearbook*, *Australian Poetry*, and *Verse in Australia*. Although limited in the scope of materials covered, the *Index of Australian and New Zealand Poetry* is still a useful tool for identifying early-to-mid-nineteenth-century poetry. However, one flaw of the tool is its lack of a geographical index. Author entries are arranged alphabetically, so there is no easy way to determine nationality. The best way to identify whether an author is from Australia or New Zealand is to consult the list of resources in which the author's poems were published. Since most of the anthologies focus on either Australian verse or New Zealand verse, this will provide an indication of the author's nationality. If you do not have access to Cuthbert's work, a similar, although less comprehensive, source to consult is *A Bibliography of Australasian Poetry and Verse: Australia and New Zealand* by Percival Serles (Melbourne: Melbourne University Press, 1925).

Howard McNaughton's ***New Zealand Drama: A Bibliographical Guide*** attempts "to list every New Zealand play, published or unpublished, of which a copy can be traced, and to record details of its publication or first production" (3). Entries are arranged alphabetically by author and include production details, along with the production society and date of performance. In cases where no production details were available, McNaughton provides information on the length and number of sets for each play. This guide will be of limited use to most scholars outside New Zealand, since few of the libraries with copies of scripts lend them through interlibrary loan. However, because it is one of the most comprehensive bibliographies of plays and playwrights available, it serves as a valuable source of information to anyone interested in the history of New Zealand drama. The guide also offers an index of plays by title, and a subject index that is limited to children's and religious plays only.

Marcie Muir and Kerry White's three-volume set, ***Australian Children's Books: A Bibliography***, is a valuable tool for the study of an important genre within Australian literature. This set offers the most comprehensive list of authors, their books, and publishing histories available. Muir notes in the introduction that because very few books were actually published in the Australian colonies, early children's books written, illustrated, and published overseas relating to Australia are available in the first volume (1774–1972). For Muir's second volume, covering 1973 to 1988, and for White's volume covering 1989 to 2000, non-Australian-published titles are included only if the content is about Australia on a significant scale. Entries are arranged alphabetically by author. Works are arranged chronologically by publication date. Every attempt has been made to incorporate all editions and translations of each title. Anonymous books are arranged alphabetically by title. Bibliographical descriptions are provided for each item, showing the physical dimensions, number of pages, illustrations, and artist's name, if available. Two separate indexes supplement the use of this work—a title index and an illustrator index.

Sue Murray's *Bibliography of Australian Poetry 1935–1955* includes more than one thousand two hundred books of poetry and attempts to create a comprehensive listing of more than thirty-five thousand individual titles written by more than seven thousand authors. Individuals featured must have either been born in Australia, spent his or her formative years there, or written works with an Australian setting or theme using experience gained while living in Australia. Murray selected the time frame based on her sense that Australian poetry changed significantly after World War II to reflect an "implied acceptance of the idea that an Australian literature had a place amongst world literatures" (vi). The bibliography also seeks to bring to attention the diversity and range of work published during the period and further demonstrates the changes in marketing and publishing history for Australian poetry during that time. The bibliography is arranged alphabetically by author. For each poem Murray provides publishing details, reviews, and dates of birth and death for the author, as well as miscellaneous information such as illustrations, dedications, number of signed editions, limited editions, and holdings within seven Australian libraries. Single publications in journals, magazines, and newspapers are not covered—only monographs and pamphlets have been examined.

For those interested in learning more about the history of New Zealand fiction, E. M. Smith's work is an excellent resource to consult. *A History of New Zealand Fiction* covers 1862 through the early part of the twentieth century and is especially useful for its alphabetically arranged "Bibliography of New Zealand Fiction, 1862–1939," located on pages 77 to 96. A complementary source to Smith's work is James Burnes's *A Century of New Zealand Novels: A Bibliography of the Period 1861–1960* (Auckland: Whitcombe & Tombs, 1961). Burnes covers early works that were omitted by Smith and offers information on more recent authors and their fiction.

Stephen Torre's *The Australian Short Story: 1940–1980* is an important index to short stories published in periodicals, anthologies, miscellanies, and collections. It also includes a selective list of interviews, commentary by short story writers, criticism about their works, and works relevant to the short story in general. Torre concentrates on this particular time period because he considers it "a time of development and innovation in Australian short story writing" and hoped the book would serve as a guide to these innovative developments in Australian short story writing (iii). Excluded are oral narratives (such as yarns and fables), children's stories, and stories written in languages other than English. Content in Torre's bibliography is arranged alphabetically by author. Primary sources and secondary materials are listed together. Torre provides separate lists of the resources used to compose his work, including periodicals, anthologies, single-author collections, and miscellanies. A final list records Australian periodicals that typically published short stories. A section devoted to works on the short story as a genre is also available, featuring critical and evaluative works, works on theory, methodology, special editions of journals, and letters devoted to genre. A similar tool, but one narrower in scope than Torre's work, is Keith Darling's *Guidelines to Australian Short Stories: An Index to Australian Short Stories Published in Anthologies and in Certain Periodicals* (Mount Waverley, Vic.: Bibliographic Services, 1978). Darling's volume indexes a total of thirty-seven anthologies and five periodicals from the years 1970 to 1976 (*Meanjin, Overland, Quadrant, Southerly*, and *Westerly*) and should be used in conjunction with Torre's work. For a comprehensive history of the short story in Australia, see Bruce Bennett's *Australian Short Fiction: A History* (St. Lucia: University of Queensland Press, 2002). More information is available on this work in chapter 2.

CONCLUSION

Conducting research on Australian and New Zealand authors can be challenging, especially for students and scholars residing outside those two countries. The difficulty in locating information is due, in part, to the British and American focus of core literary databases and indexes. The emergence of *AustLit* has greatly increased the accessibility of materials on Australian literature; unfortunately, not everyone has access to this essential tool. Even more problematic is the investigation of New Zealand literature, which does not have a presence in *AustLit* and is only marginally included in the *MLA International Bibliography* and *ABELL*. Fortunately, other resources allow for the discovery of primary and secondary materials by and about Australian and New Zealand authors. The specialized bibliographies and indexes described in this chapter can be a good place to begin your search, or you may use them to supplement information acquired through other means. Keep in mind that new resources (in print and online) are being published every day. The research strategies and methods outlined throughout the course of this book will improve your ability to locate and evaluate new scholarship efficiently and effectively.

NOTES

1. "Australian Public Affairs Full Text," Informit, http://www.informit.com.au/plustext_APAFT.html.

2. "About *AustLit*," *AustLit*, http://www.austlit.edu.au/about.

3. Faye Christenberry, "Bibliography of Australian Literature and Criticism Published in North America—2007," *Antipodes* 22.2 (2008): 178.

4. Adam Shoemaker, "A Checklist of Black Australian Literature," *Australian Literary Studies* 11.2 (1983): 255–63.

5. Wesley Horton, "Australian Aboriginal Writers: Partially Annotated Bibliography of Australian Aboriginal Writers 1924–1987," *Kunapipi* 10:1–2 (1988): 275–304.

Chapter Five

Scholarly Journals

The academic journal plays an essential role in promoting and disseminating literary scholarship. Scholars use journals as a means of making their research available to other experts in the field and adding insight into a work of literature or literary theme that has not been considered previously. These publications serve as a historical record of how academics have viewed the work of an author or a genre of literature over time. When researching Australian and New Zealand literature, it is important to become familiar with the major journals that feature criticism pertaining to these areas. Because Australia and New Zealand are considered part of the British Commonwealth, you should become acquainted with titles that focus on Commonwealth literature as well. If your research topic requires a broader examination of scholarship on Australia and New Zealand, it may be necessary to consult journals outside the scope of literature, such as those that publish reviewed articles on the history and culture of the two countries and their people. The goal of this chapter is to familiarize researchers with the most important titles devoted to academic scholarship on the literature, culture, and history of Australia and New Zealand. It will not cover "little magazines" or other periodicals that publish only creative works. For more information on these resources for Australian and New Zealand literature see chapter 7.

Journals featured in this chapter are grouped into four main categories: Australian literary studies, New Zealand literary studies, Commonwealth literary studies (these must publish content pertaining to Australia and New Zealand on a regular basis), and Australian and New Zealand cultural and historical studies. The entries in this chapter for each of the journals listed outline the scope of the publication; the information is mostly taken from the editorial statement located within each issue or on the journal's Web page. Sample articles appearing in recent issues are listed, to provide insight into topics representative of the journal's focus. When considering if a particular title is relevant for your research, check to see if the content is peer-reviewed, what topics are encouraged or sought for publication by the editor(s), the number of articles published in each issue, and the average length of essays accepted for publication. Some titles also include book reviews by scholars in the field. Scanning these reviews on a regular basis allows you to stay up to date on new or emerging areas of scholarship. This information will be noted for the journals described in this chapter. To locate similar facts about other scholarly publications not covered here, consult the *MLA Directory of Periodicals*. The *Directory* is available online through the *MLA International Bibliography*.

In addition to the *Directory of Periodicals*, other strategies to locating scholarly journals on Australian and New Zealand literary studies include searching your local library catalog or OCLC's *WorldCat*. The following subject terms are recommended for either resource, but note that additional terms do exist and may be discovered by consulting the LCSH:

Australian literature—Periodicals
Australian literature—History and criticism—Periodicals
New Zealand literature—Periodicals
New Zealand poetry—Periodicals

The National Library of Australia sponsors a tool specifically designed to locate online journals and other periodicals. *Australian Journals Online: The National Library's Database of Australian Electronic Journals* (www .nla.gov.au/ajol/) provides publication details and direct links to more than two thousand titles that focus on topics related to Australia, as well as those that feature scholarship by Australian authors. Journals listed in the database may be searched by keyword or browsed by a specific title or subject. More detailed information on *Australian Journals Online* is available in chapter 7.

The goal of this chapter is to provide an overview of the core journals dedicated to Australian and New Zealand literary scholarship. Keep in mind that additional periodicals beyond those covered in this chapter exist, and while they may not focus on Australia and New Zealand, they have published special issues on these areas in the past. Examples of these journals are the Spring/Summer 1993 issue of *Nimrod*, the Summer 2000 issue of *Granta* on "Australia: The New World," the *Victorian Periodicals Review* from Winter 2004 on "Australian, New Zealand, and South African Periodicals," and more recently, the Winter 2006 issue of *Manoa* entitled "Where the Rivers Meet: New Writing from Australia." By far, the most thorough means of identifying literary scholarship in periodical resources is to use the appropriate indexing tools, such as the *MLA International Bibliography* or *AustLit*.

Most of the journals described in this chapter are indexed in the *MLA International Bibliography*, *ABELL*, and *AustLit*. Be aware that there is often a time lapse between when a journal issue is published and when the content is loaded into the online versions of the *MLA International Bibliography* and *ABELL*. To see the most current articles available, scan the tables of contents of recent issues located in your library's periodical collection. If your library does not subscribe to a journal that looks important to your research needs, you still have alternatives, as most journals publish tables of contents online, allowing you to request specific articles through your library's interlibrary loan service. Unfortunately, few of the journals discussed in this chapter are included in two of the leading full-text journal packages in the humanities, *Project MUSE* and *JSTOR*. Some titles are accessible full-text through other databases and online resources. This chapter attempts to mention these resources for each journal, but note that coverage varies and database providers are constantly dropping and adding publications in their products.

AUSTRALIAN LITERARY STUDIES

Antipodes: A North American Journal of Australian Literature. The American Association of Australian Literary Studies, 1987–. Semiannual. ISSN: 0893-5580. www.australianliterature.org/Antipodes_Home.htm.

Australasian Drama Studies (ADS). University of Queensland, 1982–. Semiannual. ISSN: 0810-4123. www.latrobe.edu.au/drama/ads/index.html.

Australian Literary Studies (ALS). University of Queensland, 1963–. Semiannual. ISSN: 0004-9697. www.als.id.au/.

Hecate: An Interdisciplinary Journal of Women's Liberation. Hecate Press, 1975–. Semiannual. ISSN: 0311-4198. www.emsah.uq.edu.au/awsr/Home/home.htm.

Island. Sandy Bay, Tasmania: Island Magazine, 1990–. Quarterly. ISSN: 1035-3127. www.islandmag.com/.

Journal of the Association for the Study of Australian Literature (JASAL). Association for the Study of Australian Literature, 2002–. Annual. ISSN: 1447-8986. www.nla.gov.au/openpublish/index.php/jasal.

Meanjin. University of Melbourne, 1977–. Quarterly. ISSN: 0815-953X. www.meanjin.unimelb.edu.au/.

Overland. O. L. Society Ltd., 1954–. Quarterly. ISSN: 0030-7416.

Southerly: The Magazine of the Australian English Association. The Association, 1939–. 3/year. ISSN: 0038-3732. www.arts.usyd.edu.au/publications/southerly/.

Westerly. Nedlands: University of Western Australia, 1956–. Annual. ISSN: 0043-342X. www.westerlycentre.uwa.edu.au/magazine.

These titles constitute the core scholarly periodical sources available for criticism on Australian literature. Some of these journals, such as *Australian Literary Studies*, are devoted strictly to literary criticism and academic reviews of important books in the field. Others publish both critical interpretations of literature and primary works by Australian authors. *Antipodes* and *Meanjin* are excellent examples of journals that feature both primary and secondary works. Scanning these publications facilitates the discovery of current topics of interest to scholars in the field of Australian literary studies, as well as newly emerging Australian authors who may be analyzed by future scholars.

Antipodes: A North American Journal of Australian Literature was founded in 1987 by Robert Ross, who also instituted the first and only association in the United States devoted to Australian literature, the American Association of Australian Literary Studies. *Antipodes* publishes scholarly articles, book reviews, and author interviews, in addition to an impressive array of creative works by established and emerging Australian writers. Approximately seven essays on all aspects of Australian literature and culture are included in each issue. The length of articles is typically 3,000 to 4,000 words. Book reviews are limited to 750 words, arranged according to genre, and may be found in the back of each issue. Recent entries feature an analysis of religion in the poetry of Kevin Hart, an interview with Tara June Winch, and new fiction from Thomas Shapcott. The annual "Bibliography of Australian Literature and Criticism Published in North America" appears in the December issue. *Antipodes* is indexed from the very first issue forward by the *MLA International Bibliography*, *ABELL*, and *AustLit*. It is also indexed in the *Australian Public Affairs Information Service* (*APAIS*) from 1993 to the present. Full text of *Antipodes* is accessible through ProQuest's *Research Library Complete*, Chadwyck Healey's *Literature Online*, and Gale's *Literature Resource Center*. Tables of contents of issues from volume 1 to the present are listed on the journal's website.

Established in 1982, *Australasian Drama Studies* (*ADS*) is a fully peer-reviewed journal that publishes articles, interviews, book reviews, and production casebooks on the theater of Australia and other Pacific nations by international scholars. Community theater texts and published play texts appear on a regular basis, along with reviews of scholarly books. In all, approximately six essays of 4,000 to 6,000 words and eight to ten reviews are present in each issue. Book reviews are limited to 2,000 words in length. Recent articles discuss puppetry in the Australian colonies and in New Zealand, as well as the contributions of the Australian screenwriting pioneer Frank Harvey. Content is indexed in *AustLit*, *APAIS*, the *MLA International Bibliography* from 1982 to the present, and *ABELL* from 1984 to the present. Because it focuses on drama, *ADS* is also indexed in theater-specific resources, such as the *International Bibliography of Theatre and Dance* (see entry in appendix). Articles in *ADS* are available full-text in *APAFT: The Australian Public Affairs Full Text Service Database.* For more information on this resource see the entry in chapter 4. Tables of contents of *ADS* from 2001 to 2005 are available on the journal's website.

The oldest and most prestigious journal for the study of Australian literature is ***Australian Literary Studies (ALS).*** *ALS* was founded in 1963 by Laurie Hergenhan, now emeritus professor of Australian literature at the University of Queensland. *ALS* is published twice a year by the University of Queensland Press and includes scholarly articles on the Australian literary tradition and interdisciplinary issues that affect it, including sociocultural studies, postcolonialism, and nationalism. The journal offers critical assessments of writers, book reviews, and interviews with established and upcoming authors. The "Annual Bibliography of Studies in Australian Literature" is available in the May issue each year. For more detailed information on the bibliography see the separate entry in chapter 4 under "Serial Bibliographies." Typically, each issue of *ALS* presents eight to twelve articles of approximately 5,000 words each. Book reviews are limited to 2,000 words. Recent articles discuss the poetry of Judith Wright, Henry Lawson, and Gail Jones's work of fiction, *Black Mirror.* The *MLA International Bibliography, ABELL, AustLit,* and *APAIS* index *ALS* content from the first issue published in 1963 forward. Full-text articles are accessible through EBSCO's *Academic Search Complete* and Gale's *Literature Resource Center.* Unfortunately, *ALS* does not have much of a Web presence, so browsing through tables of contents without the aid of a subscription is not possible at this time.

Hecate: An Interdisciplinary Journal of Women's Liberation is published by Hecate Press in association with the Centre for Women, Gender, Culture, and Social Change Research, located within the School of English, Media Studies, and Art History at the University of Queensland. *Hecate* is a refereed journal that features material relating to women, especially articles that use feminist, Marxist, or other methodologies to interpret literature, history, and other cultural issues. In addition to secondary resources, a wide variety of creative works are included, such as prints, graphics, poems, short stories, and essays. Book reviews are not included in *Hecate,* as they are the focus of a separate publication, *Hecate's Australian Women's Book Review* (for more information on this source see the entry in chapter 6). Issues center on selected themes, such as women's history in academic journals and representations of motherhood in literature. Because *Hecate* is based in Australia, content often pertains to topics of interest to an Australian audience. Recent articles are "Women, Colonialism, History: Publishing on Women's History in Race and Colonial History Journals," by Jane Lydon[1] and "Bodies of De/Composition: Leprosy and Tattooing in Beatrice Grimshaw's Fiction and Travel Writing," by Clare McCotter.[2] *Hecate* is available full-text through ProQuest's *Research Library Complete* from 1983 to the present and in Gale's *Literature Resource Center* from 1992 to the present. The journal is indexed selectively in *ABELL* from 1977 to 1992, and even more selectively in the *MLA International Bibliography*. *Hecate* is indexed more comprehensively in *AustLit* and *APAIS*.

Island publishes short stories, poetry, extracts from forthcoming novels, and essays on topics of social, environmental, and cultural significance. The journal includes work from emerging as well as established writers, photography, illustrations, and other visual work, especially works pertaining to the environment. Recent issues feature a conversation on autobiographical writing by Tasmanian authors Robert Dessaix and Danielle Wood, and poetry by Kate Llewellyn and Bruce Dawe. Because *Island* is funded by Arts Tasmania, the Australia Council, and the University of Tasmania, the editors have focused their efforts on reaching a national readership and maintaining a strong Tasmanian identity. Perhaps as a consequence of having less interest in international issues and themes, *Island* is not widely accessible outside Australia and New Zealand. Content is only selectively indexed in the *MLA International Bibliography* and *ABELL* but is more comprehensively represented in *AustLit* and *APAIS*. Tables of contents from 2004 to the present are available through the journal's website.

The ***Journal of the Association for the Study of Australian Literature*** (***JASAL***) is a relatively new title in Australian literary scholarship, publishing its first issue in 2002. However, because it is sponsored by one of the leading organizations devoted to Australian literature, the Association for the Study of Australian Literature (ASAL), scholars should be aware of its existence. ASAL and its affiliated journal seek to promote the study of Australian literature and increase awareness of Australian writing throughout the world. *JASAL*'s editorial policy states that it accepts articles that examine Australian literature in all its forms and encourages comparative studies with other literatures. The journal is published at least once each year and usually another "special issue" follows, based on proceedings from the annual ASAL conference. Eight to twelve articles of ten to sixteen pages each are included in a typical issue, along with several book reviews of up to 4,000 words. Note that book reviews are not available in the special issue. Recent articles in *JASAL* include an examination of the relationship between writing, history, memory, and death in Brian Castro's *The Garden Book*, and trauma in Lily Brett's *Too Many Men*. Full text of all issues of *JASAL* from 2002 to the present is freely available, and new content is added as it is finalized for publication. *JASAL* is only indexed by *AustLit* and *APAIS*, so North American researchers are encouraged to go directly to the archive (available on the National Library of Australia's website though its open-access journal service, *Open Publish*) to see which articles have been published. Searching the archive is possible through browsing by issue, author, or title. You can also perform a keyword search and limit to the following fields: author, title, abstract, index terms, and full text.

Considered to be Australia's leading literary magazine, **Meanjin** was founded in Brisbane by Clem Christesen in 1940. The name of the journal is pronounced "Mee-an-jin" and is an Aboriginal word for the land on which central Brisbane resides. The journal relocated to Melbourne in 1945 at the invitation of the University of Melbourne. *Meanjin* is a quarterly publication that features analytical articles on Australian literature and arts, Australian culture, history, politics, and other contemporary issues. In addition to scholarly essays, issues contain fiction, poetry, and reviews of recent books. While the main focus is on Australia, *Meanjin* also covers topics of global concern. Each issue of *Meanjin* includes approximately fifteen articles of 4,000 to 5,000 words and five book reviews limited to 1,500 words. Recent content concentrates on indigenous Australia, presenting new poetry by Yvette Holt, an essay on recent Miles Franklin Award winner Alexis Wright, and an article on the relationship of Aboriginal poetry to the Aboriginal political voice. *Meanjin* is indexed in the *MLA International Bibliography*, *ABELL*, *AustLit*, and *APAIS*. Full text is available through Gale's *Literature Resource Center* from 2001 to the present.

The editors of **Overland** consider it the most radical of Australia's literary magazines. Publishing critical essays, fiction, poetry, reviews, artwork, and opinion pieces, the journal is committed to discussion of important literary, cultural, historical, and political issues in contemporary Australia. *Overland* has a tradition of publishing articles from alternative or minority viewpoints, providing a voice to those traditionally excluded from the mainstream media and publishing venues. The magazine attempts to "document lesser-known stories and histories, dissect media hysteria and dishonesty, debunk the populist hype of politicians, give a voice to those whose stories are otherwise marginalised, misrepresented or ignored, and point public debate in alternative directions."[3] A typical issue includes fifteen articles of 3,500 words each. Recent essays discuss the state of independent publishing in Australia, electronic books, and Australia's Native Title Act. *Overland* is also an excellent source for locating reviews of current books, such as Alexis Wright's *Carpentaria* and Richard Flanagan's *Unknown Terrorist*. Approximately fifteen reviews of 1,200 words each are available per issue. *Overland* is indexed in *APAIS* from 1963 to present, the *MLA International Bibliography* from 1960 to present, and *ABELL* from 1959 to present. More recently, *Overland* content is indexed in EBSCO's

Academic Search Complete (beginning in 2006), and in Gale's *Literature Resource Center* from 1997 to present.

Southerly: The Magazine of the Australian English Association is a refereed journal for the discussion of Australian literature, sponsored by the English Association and the Department of English at the University of Sydney. *Southerly* began publication in 1939 and is considered Australia's oldest literary magazine. A portion of each issue is devoted to a particular theme, ranging from Australian-Chinese relations to works by immigrant authors. Four to six scholarly essays of up to 5,000 words are included in each issue. Recent articles explore allusion in Robert Dessaix's novel *Night Letters* and the treatment of Chinese immigrants in Australian history. In addition to scholarly criticism, *Southerly* publishes short stories, fiction, and poetry by established and emerging Australian authors. Recent issues feature poetry by Kevin Hart and new fiction by Frank Moorhouse. Approximately four book reviews evaluating both primary and secondary works in Australian literature complete the content of a typical issue. *Southerly* is indexed in the *MLA International Bibliography*, *ABELL*, *AustLit*, and *APAIS*. Full text of the journal is available through Gale's *Literature Resource Center* from 1998 to the present.

Westerly is affiliated with the Westerly Centre at the University of Western Australia. The goal of the Westerly Centre and the journal is to stimulate and publish research in Australian literature and culture. For those interested in creative works by contemporary Australian authors, *Westerly* features an excellent array of new poetry and short fiction. Typically, five scholarly articles complement the creative writing that highlights each issue. In addition, three review essays outlining recent publications in poetry, fiction, and nonfiction serve to update readers on important new writing. Previous essays in *Westerly* discuss the work of contemporary novelists Kim Scott, Robert Drewe, and David Malouf. The tables of contents of issues back to volume 45 (2000) are available for browsing on the Westerly Centre's website. *Westerly* is indexed in the *MLA International Bibliography*, *ABELL*, *AustLit*, and *APAIS*. Unfortunately, full text is not available online through any vendor, but the editors are currently working to convert the entire back file of the journal to electronic text. This project is due to be completed soon.

NEW ZEALAND LITERARY STUDIES

Journal of New Zealand Literature (*JNZL*). Wellington: Department of English, Victoria University, 1983–. Annual. ISSN: 0112-1227. www.waikato.ac.nz/wfass/jnzl/index.shtml.

Ka Mate Ka Ora: A New Zealand Journal of Poetry and Poetics. Auckland: New Zealand Electronic Poetry Centre, 2005–. Semiannual. ISSN: 1177-2182. www .nzepc.auckland.ac.nz/kmko/index.asp.
Landfall: New Zealand Arts & Letters. Dunedin: University of Otago Press, 1947–. Semiannual. ISSN: 0023-7930. www.otago.ac.nz/press/landfall/index.html.
Poetry New Zealand (Poetry NZ). Auckland: Brick Row Pub. 1990–. Semiannual. ISSN: 0114-5770. www.poetrynz.net/.

Journal of New Zealand Literature (JNZL) is the only international, fully peer-reviewed journal devoted to New Zealand literary studies. Sponsored by the Department of Humanities at the University of Waikato, *JNZL* carries scholarly and critical essays on all aspects of New Zealand literature and cultural studies. Articles are typically 4,000 words each. Books of critical interest in the field of New Zealand literary studies are reviewed in *JNZL* and are limited to 1,500 words. Recent essays focus on Katherine Mansfield, Keri Hulme, Janet Frame, and Māori author Patricia Grace. Full text of *JNZL* from volume 22 (2004) to the present is available online through ProQuest's *Research Library Complete*. A full run of back issues from volume 1 (1983) to volume 24 (2006) is currently available in *JSTOR*. The journal is indexed in the *MLA International Bibliography* from 1993 to present, in Gale's *Literature Resource Center* from 1996 to present, and in *ABELL* from 1983 to the present. Selected full-text content is accessible through Chadwyck-Healey's *Literature Online*.

Ka Mate Ka Ora: A New Zealand Journal of Poetry and Poetics is sponsored by the New Zealand Electronic Poetry Centre, which is based at the University of Auckland. The journal publishes substantial essays (6,000–10,000 words each), review articles, historical reappraisals of poetry, close readings, and mixed-genre criticism of poetry and poetics. The goal of *Ka Mate Ka Ora* is to provide a site for discourse and debate about New Zealand poetry. The editors welcome contributions from poets, academics, essayists, and students from within New Zealand and overseas. "New Zealand" is interpreted broadly to include both expatriate and immigrant writers. However, the poetry discussed is not necessarily about New Zealand. Currently, there are eight issues of *Ka Mate Ka Ora* available. The most recent issue is dedicated to one of New Zealand's most established poets, James K. Baxter. Other issues feature an interview by Bill Manhire with Māori poet Hone Tuwhare and the transcript of a talk given by Ian Wedde for the launch of *Collected Poems* (Auckland: Holloway Press, 2007) by Charles Spear at the Gus Fisher Gallery in October of 2007.

Landfall: New Zealand Arts & Letters is the oldest existing journal to focus on New Zealand literature. Content features literary essays, poetry, short fiction, extracts from fictional and nonfictional works in progress, and commentary on New Zealand arts and culture. *Landfall* also publishes reviews of books on topics of interest to New Zealand. Writers from New Zealand and the Pacific

Islands are given first priority, but editors also encourage authors visiting new Zealand or whose work has a connection with the region to submit contributions to *Landfall*. Occasional works by Australian or other non–New Zealand writers are allowed. Most of the content featured in *Landfall* is creative writing. Two to five critical essays are available in each issue. Typical article lengths are four to twelve pages, and book reviews range from 1,000 to 2,000 words. Recent essays include a comparative study of writing and teaching in China, Australia, and New Zealand by Ouyang Yu and an essay on regionalism in New Zealand literature by Paula Morris. Primary works in *Landfall* are by emerging authors, such as Katherine Liddy, and well-established authors, such as former New Zealand poet laureate Bill Manhire. *Landfall* is indexed in Gale's *Literature Resource Center* from 1998 to the present, the *MLA International Bibliography* from 1960 to the present, and *ABELL* from 1950 to the present.

Poetry New Zealand (*Poetry NZ*) began in 1951 with the publication of Louis Johnson's *New Zealand Poetry Yearbook: An Annual Collection* (Wellington: A. H. & A. W. Reed, 1951–1964). The goal of the journal is to support poetry and poets, primarily from New Zealand, but also from any region of the world. *Poetry NZ* is interested in new writers who are striving to get their work recognized. Each issue features fifteen to twenty pages of poetry from a developing or established poet in order to draw attention to that poet's work. The rest of the issue is a selection of poetry from New Zealand and abroad, as well as book reviews and scholarly criticism. Recent articles include critical essays on New Zealand poets Alistair Campbell and Denys Trussell. Most of the material in *Poetry NZ* is primary literature, likely the reason it is not indexed in the *MLA International Bibliography*. However, it is selectively indexed in *ABELL*, and tables of contents are available on the journal's website for issues 22 to the present.

COMMONWEALTH LITERARY STUDIES

Journal of Commonwealth Literature (*JCL*). Sage, 1965–. Quarterly. ISSN: 0021-9894. jcl.sagepub.com/.

Journal of Commonwealth and Postcolonial Studies (*JCPS*). Department of English and Philosophy, Georgia Southern University, 1993–. Semiannual. ISSN: 1073-1687. class.georgiasouthern.edu/litphi/jcps/jcps.htm.

Journal of Postcolonial Writing (*JPW*). Routledge, 2005–. Semiannual. ISSN: 1744-9855. www.tandf.co.uk/journals/titles/17449855.asp. Former title: *World Literature Written in English* (*WLWE*). University of Texas at Arlington, 1971–2004. Semiannual. ISSN: 0093-1705.

Kunapipi. University of Wollongong, English Studies Program, 1979–. Semiannual. ISSN: 0106-5734. www.uow.edu.au/arts/kunapipi/.

SPAN: *Journal of the South Pacific Association for Commonwealth Literature and Language Studies.* University of Queensland, 1975–. Semiannual. ISSN: 0313-1459. spaclals.org/?page_id=23.
World Literature Today (*WLT*). University of Oklahoma, 1927–. Bimonthly. ISSN: 1535-9492. www.ou.edu/worldlit/.

Journal of Commonwealth Literature (***JCL***) has been published for approximately forty years and is internationally recognized as one of the leading critical and bibliographic sources in the field of Commonwealth studies. The primary focus of the journal is to bring together the latest critical essays on Commonwealth and postcolonial literature, including those on Australia and New Zealand, postcolonial theory, and colonial discourse. Approximately seven essays are included in each journal. Recent articles feature an examination of David Malouf's *An Imaginary Life*, a comparative essay on Richard Flanagan's *Death of a River Guide,* and Annie Proulx's *The Shipping News.* The fourth issue of *JCL* is dedicated to a comprehensive bibliography of recent publications that is essential for researchers in Australian and New Zealand literature. More in-depth information about this core bibliography can be found in chapter 4. Scholarly book reviews are also published in *JCL*, as are interviews with authors. *JCL* is indexed in *AustLit* and *ABELL* from 1965 to present, and the *MLA International Bibliography* from 1967 to present. For those with access to ProQuest's *Research Library Complete* or Gale's *Literature Resource Center*, *JCL* content is indexed from 1989 to the present. Full text of *JCL* is available electronically through *Sage Journals Online*.[4]

Sponsored by Georgia Southern University's Department of English and Philosophy, the ***Journal of Commonwealth and Postcolonial Studies*** (***JCPS***) is devoted to the promotion and/or study of the literature, performing arts, history, and politics of nations historically part of the British Commonwealth. The journal also covers the literature of countries colonized by other European powers in Africa, the Americas, Asia, and the Caribbean. Scholarly essays, interviews, and creative writings are all regular features of *JCPS*. Typically, each issue has five to six scholarly essays, each of 4,000 to 5,000 words in length. Book reviews are 1,200 to 1,500 words. Tables of contents beginning with volume 1 are available on the journal's website. Issues tend to focus on a designated topic or theme, such as "Postcolonial Gay and Lesbian Literature," or more recently, "Postcolonial Studies and Ecocriticism." *JCPS* is indexed in *AustLit*, the *MLA International Bibliography*, and *ABELL*. *AustLit* has the most up-to-date content of the three sources.

Journal of Postcolonial Writing (***JPW***) is devoted to the study of literature written in English. Its goal is to explore postcolonial writing of the modern era and publish articles that address issues pertinent to postcolonial studies. Topics accepted include analysis of the work of individual writers and an examination of classical texts of literature from a range of postcolonial and global perspectives. Interviews and profiles of postcolonial writers and theorists are available, as well as reviews of contemporary writing and critical analysis of postcolonial texts. Six to eight essays are featured in each issue, ranging in length from eight to fourteen pages apiece. Recent issues have been devoted to Indian literature and African literature. *JPW* is indexed in the *MLA International Bibliography*, *ABELL*, and *AustLit*. Full-text content online is not currently available.

Kunapipi is a biannual arts magazine of critical and creative writing that focuses on new literatures written in English. Its goal is to introduce work by new writers and promote access to critical evaluations of both emerging and established authors. *Kunapipi* publishes poetry, short stories, photography, and graphic art, along with criticism on literature, art, film, and dance. Interviews with contemporary writers, artists, and scholars are regularly featured. *Kunapipi* is the official journal of the European Association of Commonwealth Languages and Literatures, a subgroup of the Association of Commonwealth Literature and Language Studies. Content often features the literature of Australia and New Zealand. One of the many strengths of *Kunapipi* is that it makes an effort to promote works by and about minority authors. Often, issues are devoted to a particular theme, as reflected by a recent volume on "Birds." Here, readers will find poems by Australian author Chris Wallace-Crabbe and an essay on the importance of birds in postcolonial Australian literature and art by Adrian Franklin. Articles are typically between 3,000 and 5,000 words in length, and book reviews are limited to 3,000 words. *Kunapipi* is indexed in *ABELL*, *AustLit*, and the *MLA International Bibliography* from 1979 to the present. Unfortunately, the journal is not available full-text online in any resource.

SPAN: Journal of the South Pacific Association for Commonwealth Literature and Language Studies is issued biannually by SPACLALS, a subgroup of the Association of Commonwealth Literature and Language Studies. The editorship and place of publication for *SPAN* rotates between association members, which can make it difficult to track down issues. Content focuses on postcolonial, neocolonial, and diaspora literature in English from the British Commonwealth nations. More specifically, *SPAN* publishes critical articles and book reviews on postcolonial literatures of the South Pacific, which includes Australia and New Zealand. Issues contain eight to ten scholarly articles, one or two book reviews, and a wide selection of poetry and fiction from Australian writers such as Mudrooroo, John Kinsella, and Doris Pilkington. Recent scholarly essays have discussed the work of Samoan author Albert Wendt and Russell Soaba of Papua New Guinea. Selected full text of volumes 32 through 37

(1992–1993) is available for free from the *Culture and Communication Reading Room* at Murdoch University (wwwmcc.murdoch.edu.au/ReadingRoom/litserv/ SPAN/SPAN.html). According to information posted on the SPACLALS website, members of the association are compiling a detailed, multientry index of all issues of the journal. When completed, the information will be available free of charge (spaclals.org/). *SPAN* is selectively indexed by the *MLA International Bibliography*, *ABELL*, and *AustLit*.

Founded in 1927, **World Literature Today (WLT)** is the University of Oklahoma's bimonthly magazine of international literature and culture. Issues feature interviews with authors, poetry, and fiction from around the world, essays on writers and regional trends, author profiles, and coverage of cultural and political issues if they pertain to literary interests. *WLT* is not specifically dedicated to Commonwealth literature. However, because the goal of the journal is to publish articles on contemporary literary and cultural topics from all over the world (including non-English literatures), content on Australian and New Zealand authors is available on an intermittent basis. Twelve to fifteen articles (limited to 2,500 words) are published in each issue. Recently, Māori author Patricia Grace was featured as the twentieth laureate of the Neustadt International Prize for Literature. Approximately twenty-five book reviews (limited to 500 words) accompany the essays and primary works in *WLT*. An online index from 2002 to the present is available through the periodical's website. As a long-standing, prize-winning publication of information on international literature in all languages, *WLT* is indexed in many resources—*AustLit*, the *MLA International Bibliography*, *ABELL* from 1977 to present, and Gale's *Literature Resource Center* from 1989 to present. Full-text content of *WLT* is accessible through *Literature Resource Center* and ProQuest's *Research Library Complete* from 1994 to present.

AUSTRALIAN AND NEW ZEALAND
CULTURAL AND HISTORICAL STUDIES

Australian Aboriginal Studies (AAS). Australian Institute of Aboriginal Studies, 1983–. Semiannual. ISSN: 0729-4352. www.aiatsis.gov.au/asj/asj.html.
Australian Historical Studies (AHS). Routledge, 1988–. 3/yr. ISSN: 1031-461X. www .tandf.co.uk/journals/titles/1031461X.asp.
Australian Humanities Review (AHR). La Trobe University, 1996–. Irregular. ISSN: 1325-8338. www.australianhumanitiesreview.org.
Australian Studies Journal. British Australian Studies Association, 1988–. Semiannual. ISSN: 0954-0954. www.kcl.ac.uk/schools/humanities/depts/menzies/basa/ journal.html.

British Review of New Zealand Studies (*BRONZS*). New Zealand Studies Committee, University of Edinburgh, 1988–2006. Annual. ISSN: 0951-6204. Continued by *CNZS Bulletin of New Zealand Studies*. Birkbeck College, Centre for New Zealand Studies, 2008–2009. Annual. ISSN: 1758-8626. www.kakapobooks.co.uk/cnzs .htm.

Journal of the Polynesian Society (*JPS*). Department of Māori Studies, University of Auckland, 1892–. Quarterly. ISSN: 0032-4000. www.jps.auckland.ac.nz/index .php.

New Zealand Journal of History (*NZJH*). University of Auckland, Department of History, 1967–. Semiannual. ISSN: 0028-8322. www.arts.auckland.ac.nz/uoa/home/ about/departments-and-schools/history-1/newzealandjournalofhistory.

Australian Aboriginal Studies (**AAS**) is an interdisciplinary journal promoting scholarly research in Australian indigenous studies. The focus of *AAS* is on the humanities and social sciences disciplines. Issues are published twice a year and contain scholarly research articles, book reviews, news and information, obituaries, and correspondence. Reviews of autobiographies and literary works by Aboriginal authors are regularly featured. The "News and Information" section can be useful to researchers interested in Aboriginal literature, as it lists forthcoming publications and reprints of important titles, as well as acquisitions reports from libraries across Australia that collect materials on indigenous people. For researchers in Australian Aboriginal studies, this is the primary journal for keeping up to date with new scholarship, current information, and emerging experts in the field. *AAS* is indexed in *AustLit* and *APAIS*, with full text from 1998 to the present in Gale's *Expanded Academic Index*.

Australian Historical Studies (**AHS**) is a refereed journal concerned with Australian, New Zealand, and Pacific regional history. With a record of publishing scholarship from leading academics in the field, *AHS* is regarded as one of Australia's oldest and most respected journals. Since 1940, the journal has featured essays on all aspects of the Australian past, including heritage and conservation, archaeology, oral history, family history, and histories of place. In addition to scholarly articles, each issue contains a review essay as well as an extensive selection of book reviews. Full text of the journal is available in EBSCO's *Academic Search Complete* from 1995 to the present, with the latest year restricted to citations only. Content from the very beginning of *AHS* is indexed in *Historical Abstracts* (see entry in the appendix), in *APAIS* from 1988 to present, and in Gale's *Expanded Academic Index* from 1998 to present.

Australian Humanities Review (**AHR**) is a peer-reviewed interdisciplinary electronic journal. According to the editorial policy, *AHR* "provides a forum for open intellectual debate across humanities disciplines, about all aspects of social, cultural and political life, primarily (but not exclusively) with reference to Australia. It aims to present new and challenging debates in the humanities to both an academic and a non-academic readership, both within and outside of Australia" (www.australianhumanitiesreview.org/help .html#policy). The journal welcomes articles from scholars working in all disciplines of the humanities, including literary and film studies, cultural and media studies, gender studies, history, politics, philosophy, sociology, and anthropology. Creative writing is not included. *AHR* is one of the first e-only journals devoted to the humanities in Australia and has been extremely successful since the first issue appeared in 1996. A full archive is available on the journal's website. Unfortunately, *AHR* is not indexed in many resources. Only older issues are cited in *ABELL* (no new content since 2000), but all content is accessible for those with access to *AustLit*. If you do not have a subscription to *AustLit*, the best way to discover scholarly literature in *AHR* is to proceed to the journal's website and search there. The archive has been designed with multiple access points, allowing users to browse by issue, author, or by broad subject categories. All content may be searched by keyword as well.

Sponsored by the British Australian Studies Association, the *Australian Studies Journal* has as its goal the promotion of quality research on all aspects of Australia, including culture, geography, literature, history, law, political science, economics, and the media. First appearing in 1988, this fully refereed journal seeks to foster innovative critical approaches to topics pertaining to Australia and encourages authors to establish connections between traditionally distinct areas of research. *Australian Studies Journal* is published twice a year, with publications alternating between a themed issue and a general issue. Themed issues are typically based on the interests of the editors, or may be generated by the association's biennial conference. *Australian Studies Journal* features a comprehensive book review section, as well as an editorial preface that provides information on Australia-related events and initiatives that may be of interest to readers. Beginning in late 2009 *Australian Studies Journal* is available free online via the website of the National Library of Australia's *Open Publish* journal system (www .nla.gov.au/openpublish/index.php/australian-studies). Recent articles focus on book publishing in Western Australia, food and identity in Patrick White's novel *The Vivisector*, and the female Gothic in Elizabeth Jolley's novel *The Well*.

The *British Review of New Zealand Studies* (*BRONZS*) was the official journal of the New Zealand Studies Association (United Kingdom) from 1988 to 2006. The journal ceased with volume 15, but the subject matter is still useful to those interested in New Zealand literature, history, and culture.

Tables of contents for all issues of *BRONZS* are available on the association's website (www.nzsa.co.uk/bronzs.htm), and full text is accessible through EBSCO's *Academic Search Complete*. The New Zealand Studies Association replaced *BRONZS* with a new title, the *CNZS Bulletin of New Zealand Studies*. The first issue of the *Bulletin* was published November 2008. Sadly, the Center for New Zealand Studies ceased to exist in 2009, and the journal is no longer in print. However, like its predecessor, the first issue is still valuable, including essays on New Zealand film, Māori literature, and forty-one pages of previously unpublished poetry from important authors such as Jan Kemp, Fiona Kidman, C. K. Stead, and Ian Wedde.

Journal of the Polynesian Society (*JPS*) is sponsored by the Polynesian Society of the University of Auckland. The goal of the society and its affiliated journal is to promote the study of Māori and other Pacific Island people—their culture, society, history, and language. *JPS* is a quarterly publication that began with the founding of the society in 1892. Early issues of the journal contain indigenous texts and documentations of local traditions contributed by missionaries and other visitors to the islands. Among the variety of scholars who contribute articles to *JPS* are social and cultural anthropologists, archaeologists, historians, linguists, and physical anthropologists working in Micronesia, Melanesia, and Polynesia. More recent content documents research by sociologists, political scientists, and economists. Each issue contains one to three lengthy research articles, one shorter article, and several book reviews. Articles within the scope of the *MLA International Bibliography* are indexed. All content is cited in Gale's *Expanded Academic Index* from 1998 to the present, and full text is available in EBSCO's *Research Library Complete* from 2007 to the present. The most comprehensive indexing of *JPS* is through *Historical Abstracts*. Full text from volume 1 (1892) through volume 44 (1935) is available free through the University of Auckland (www.jps.auckland.ac.nz/browse.php).

The *New Zealand Journal of History* (*NZJH*) is published twice a year by the University of Auckland. Each issue contains approximately six scholarly articles and a lengthy section of current book reviews. The October issue of *NZJH* features a section called "Research," which lists completed theses and dissertations on history at the University of Auckland, as well as those in progress at other New Zealand universities. An author index to articles and reviews published in volumes 1 through 35 is available in PDF format on the journal's website. Tables of contents with abstracts are provided for more recent issues. *NZJH* is indexed from the beginning issue (1967) to the present in *Historical Abstracts*.

CONCLUSION

This chapter presents a list of core journals that focus on Australian, New Zealand, and Commonwealth literary studies. Selected titles that cover topics or disciplines outside of literature are described to a lesser degree. Because these journals present academic research on cultural and historical issues that can provide context for the creative works of a particular author or literary movement, an awareness of their existence may prove useful to your investigation. While all titles are dedicated to publishing and promoting scholarship on Australia and New Zealand, keep in mind that criticism on Australian and New Zealand literature will be available in other periodicals. The best way to ensure the discovery of the most relevant information on your topic is to use the appropriate indexing tools, such as the *MLA International Bibliography* or *AustLit*. If your research involves disciplines outside of literature, you should make use of other resources, such as *Historical Abstracts*. If you are not sure which database is relevant to a specific subject area, consult the items listed in the appendix, or ask your librarian for assistance. Availability of the journals covered in this chapter will vary by library, so be sure to check your local library catalog or consult with a librarian if you are not certain of the accessibility of a specific title.

NOTES

1. *Hecate*, no. 33 (2007): 164–68.
2. *Hecate*, no. 33 (2007): 81–106.
3. "About *Overland Magazine*," *Overland* home page, ehlt.flinders.edu.au/humanities/exchange/stu_work/switch_05/links/overland%20home%20page.htm (accessed 23 May 2010).
4. Sage Publications, *Sage Journals Online*, online.sagepub.com/ (accessed 23 May 2010).

Chapter Six

Literary Reviews

When searching for reviews of early Australian and New Zealand books, it is important to consider the origins of the literature itself. For example, when did Australian and New Zealand literature begin? Who would have reviewed these works and in what types of resources would the reviews appear? The earliest instances of "Australian literature" are travel narratives that were written by Europeans exploring or visiting the colonies in the late seventeenth century and early eighteenth century. The first travel journal published about the exploration of Australia was by British buccaneer William Dampier. Dampier's *Voyage to New Holland: The English Voyage of Discovery to the South Seas in 1699* (London: James Knapton, 1703) and Watkin Tench's *Narrative of the Expedition to Botany Bay* (London: J. Debrett, 1789) represent the inception of Australian literature. Similarly, Tasman's account of his exploration to Van Diemen's Land in 1642 is among the first writings to appear about New Zealand, but was not published until 1898 (*Abel Janszoon Tasman's Journal of His Discovery of Van Diemens Land and New Zealand in 1642*, Amsterdam: F. Muller, 1898).[1] After travel narratives, most of the early writings from Australia and New Zealand were produced by the colonists, recording their experiences in the new world. These were mostly historical or biographical writings that were published as letters, diaries, and journals, and appeared in newspapers rather than in book form. The first novel both written and published in the Australian colonies did not occur until 1830, when Henry Savery, a British convict who wrote sketches of Hobart life for the local paper, finished his three-volume work *Quintus Servinton: A Tale Founded upon Incidents of Real Occurrence* (Hobart Town: Henry Melville, 1830–1831). While Charles Tompson's *Wild Notes, from the Lyre of a Native Minstrel* (Sydney: Robert Howe, Government Printer at the Albion Press, 1826) is the first book of poetry published in Australia by an Australian-born author, contemporary poet Charles Harpur is widely considered the first poet to write in a uniquely Australian voice. Because book publishing was such an expensive venture and the potential audience too small to justify the expense, Charles Harpur and other colonial Australians published their works mostly in independent journals and newspapers of that time. Examples of these early papers are the *Australian* (1824–1848), the *Sydney Monitor* (1826–1841), and the *Colonial Times* (1825–1857). Two of the first journals that played a vital role in laying the foundation for Australian literature include the *Australian Magazine* (1821–1822) and the *Colonial Literary Journal* (1844).[2] These and other important periodicals will be discussed in more detail in chapter 7. For an excellent chronology of Australian literature from the beginning to the mid-twentieth century, see Hooton and Heseltine's *Annals of Australian Literature*, which is described in chapter 2. More information on the history of the Australian book publishing industry may be found in a three-volume series produced by the University of Queensland Press called *A History of the Book in Australia*. Volume 2,[3] which covers the years 1891 to 1945, and volume 3,[4] which explores publishing during the years 1946 to 2005, are both currently available. Unfortunately, the first volume, which encompasses the beginning of the book industry through 1890, is not yet published. For those interested in the history of book publishing in New Zealand, see Penny Griffith's *Book & Print in New Zealand: A Guide to Print Culture in Aotearoa* (Wellington: Victoria University Press, 1997).

The goal of this chapter is to provide guidance and information on locating reviews of Australian and New Zealand literature from its inception to the present. Resources are divided into the following four sections: twentieth-century and twenty-first-century reviews, eighteenth-century and nineteenth-century reviews, periodicals that feature book reviews, and author-specific reviews. You will not need to use all the materials discussed in a given section, but the tools you select may depend in part on availability. For example, *AustLit* is the single best source to consult for identifying reviews of Australian literature spanning all centuries. However, because *AustLit* is a subscription database, other tools must be considered for those without access. For researchers in North America, it is important to note that even though the United States is one of the largest markets for books exported from Australia, nonfiction and educational works make up the majority of these titles.[5] Unfortunately, many literary works are not readily available for purchase within the United States and Canada, although there have been improvements in recent years, thanks to distributors like International Specialized Book Services and Independent Publishers Group. Due to the fact that access to the literature is limited, relatively few works are reviewed in North American periodical resources. Often, reviews will only be available in Australian and New Zealand sources, and in some cases a review may not exist at all.

TWENTIETH- AND TWENTY-FIRST-CENTURY REVIEWS

ABRC: Australian Book Review Citations. O'Connor, A.C.T., 1990–. Annual. ISSN: 1038-393X.

Academic Search Complete. Ipswich, Mass.: EBSCO Publishing. www.ebscohost .com/thisTopic.php?marketID=1&topicID=633.

Annual Bibliography of English Language and Literature (ABELL). Cambridge: Bowes & Bowes, 1924–. Annual. Available online at www.proquest.com/en-US/ catalogs/databases/detail/abell.shtml.

AustLit: The Australian Literature Resource. Canberra, A.C.T.: University of New South Wales at Australian Defense Force Academy. www.austlit.edu.au/about.

Australian & New Zealand Theatre Record. Kensington, N.S.W.: Australian Theatre Studies Centre of the University of New South Wales. Monthly. (1988–1996). ISSN: 1032-0091. Former title: *Australian Theatre Record* (1987–1988).

Australian Public Affairs Full Text (APAFT). Melbourne: RMIT Publishing. Available online from 1995– at www.informit.com.au/plustext_APAFT.html.

Australian Public Affairs Information Service (APAIS). Canberra, A.C.T.: Government Printer, 1945–2000. ISSN: 0005-0075. Available online from 1978– at www .informit.com.au/indexes_APAIS.html.

Book Review Index (BRI). Detroit, Mich.: Gale, 1965–. 3/yr with annual cumulations. ISSN: 0524-0581. Available online at www.gale.cengage.com/BRIOnline/.

Combined Retrospective Index to Book Reviews in Humanities Journals, 1802–1974. Woodbridge, CT: Carrollton Press/Research Publications, 1982–1984.

Expanded Academic ASAP. Detroit, Mich.: Gale/Cengage Learning. www.gale .cengage.com/PeriodicalSolutions/academicAsap.htm.

Factiva. New York: Dow Jones & Reuters. factiva.com/.

Index New Zealand (INNZ). Wellington: National Library of New Zealand, 1987–. www.natlib.govt.nz/catalogues/innz.

Index to Book Reviews in the Humanities. Williamston, Mich.: Phillip Thomson, 1960–1990.

Index to New Zealand Periodicals. Wellington: National Library of New Zealand. Annual. (1966–1986). ISSN: 0073-5957. Former title: *Index to New Zealand Periodicals and Current National Bibliography of New Zealand Books and Pamphlets Published in . . .* Wellington: New Zealand Library Association. Annual (1950–1965). Former title: *Index to New Zealand Periodicals.* Dunedin: Otago Branch New Zealand Library Association, 1941–1950. (1940–1949).

LexisNexis Academic. Dayton, OH: Reed-Elsevier, Inc. www.lexisnexis.com.

New York Times Book Review Index 1896–1970. 5 vols. New York: Arno Press, 1973.

New Zealand Literature File (NZLF). Auckland: University of Auckland Library. www.library.auckland.ac.nz/subjects/nzp/nzlit2/authors.htm.

ProQuest Research Library. ProQuest Information and Learning. www.il.proquest .com/products_pq/descriptions/pq_research_library.shtml.

The Times Literary Supplement Index 1902–1939. 2 vols. Reading, England: Newspaper Archive Developments Ltd., 1978.

ABRC: Australian Book Review Citations is an index to books, serials, audio-visuals, and other items reviewed in approximately ninety major newspapers, academic journals, and general-interest magazines. The goal of this source is to continue the indexing of reviews previously offered through the *Index to Australian Book Reviews* (1965–1981)[6] and the *Australian Book Review Index* (1979–1984).[7] Even though there is no definitive indication that *ABRC* has ceased, no new volume has been published since the first, which contains reviews up to 1991. Materials included must have been published in Australia, published overseas by Australian authors, or feature significant Australian content. Emphasis is placed on disciplines within the social sciences and the humanities. Note that *ABRC* does not cover reviews that are published in major Australian literary journals, as these are expected to be in *AustLit*. This does not mean that there are no reviews pertinent to Australian literature in *ABRC*. However, it would be advisable to consult *AustLit* for literary topics and use *ABRC* for all other reviews of books pertaining to the humanities. Each volume has a title index, an author index, and a reviewer index.

EBSCO's ***Academic Search Complete*** is a multidisciplinary database that provides access to more than 7,100 full-text periodicals and indexing and abstracts for an additional 11,200 titles. Of these, more than six thousand are peer-reviewed journals. Some of the more important publications available in full text are *Australian Literary Studies* and *World Literature Today.* In addition to these journals, *Meanjin, Overland,* and the *Journal of Commonwealth Literature* are all indexed in *Academic Search Complete*. Even though EBSCO does not cover the number of Australian or New Zealand literary journals available in Gale's competing product, *Expanded Academic ASAP*, it does present quality indexing that makes searching for book reviews cleaner. For instance, in the advanced search screen you can limit results by the document type "book review." Because EBSCO takes the time to index the title of the book being reviewed, you can search within the field "reviews and products" and directly locate reviews of that specific title. The search will still work if you neglect to specify the title of the book in this field. However, you can expect to see false hits in this situation, as it performs a basic keyword search on the terms used.

The Modern Humanities Research Association's ***Annual Bibliography of English Language and Literature (ABELL)*** indexes reviews of books pertaining to literary criticism and theory. *ABELL*, discussed in more length in chapter 4, is an international bibliography of scholarship pertaining to English language and literatures. It does not supply citations to reviews of fiction, poetry, or other creative writing. When using the electronic version of *ABELL* to locate a book review, you have the option of limiting your search to a particular publication type, including "Reviews." If you know the International Standard Book Number (ISBN) of the book, you may search by it. Otherwise, searching for the title is the easiest means of querying the database. The online version of *ABELL* covers the years 1920 to the present and offers the advantage of linking to the full text of a review, if your library subscribes to the journal in electronic format. When using the print version of *ABELL*, look for book review citations under the name of the principal author entry. For example, reviews of Andreas Gaile's edited collection *Fabulating Beauty: Perspectives on the Fiction of Peter Carey* (Amsterdam: Rodopi, 2005), would be listed under "Peter Carey," located in the "English Literature: Twentieth Century: Authors" section. You could also find the review by looking for Gaile in the "Scholars" index.

AustLit: The Australian Literature Resource is the most comprehensive source for locating reviews on Australian literature, both in terms of primary and secondary works. As an index to scholarly literature, *AustLit* is discussed in more detail in chapter 4. Given the scope of the database and the fact that it includes material dating from the European settlement in Australia (1780) to the present, it is also an exceptional tool for identifying book reviews. *AustLit* indexes all the major Australian newspapers and journals that feature reviews (e.g., *Australian Book Review*, *Quadrant*, and *Hecate's Australian Women's Book Review*), as well as international journals that regularly review works of literature and literary scholarship. In total, *AustLit* contains citation information to the content of more than one thousand periodicals and major Australian newspapers. Dates of coverage will vary by source. To determine this information for a specific title, see the *AustLit* website under "Periodicals and Newspapers" (www.AustLit.edu.au/about/periodicals). There are several options for searching *AustLit*, but the most accurate strategy for locating book reviews is to perform a quick search on the title of the work in question. Figure 6.1 presents the information retrieved for the title *A History of the Book in Australia, 1891–1945: A National Culture in a Colonized Market*. Note the hyperlink to "Works About" on the bottom left-hand portion of the screen. Citations to reviews appear at the bottom of the record and are listed from earliest to most recently published, as illustrated by figure 6.2.

The guided search provides a means of quickly retrieving a review by a specific author, if you wish to do so. Simply limit your search to the form "Review" and type the name of the reviewer in the author field. Occasionally *AustLit* will miss reviews from North American journals and newspapers. To locate reviews from these sources, it is advisable to use a different tool, such as *LexisNexis Academic* or *Factiva* for newspapers, and *Expanded Academic ASAP* or *ProQuest Research Library* for magazines and journals. All these resources will be described in more detail later in this chapter.

Australian & New Zealand Theatre Record supplies full-text reviews of performances published in major newspapers across Australia. Reviews are arranged chronologically but may also be identified through an index to individual performances by title, director, and location. For those interested in theater reviews, this is a very important tool to consult. Unfortunately, *Australian & New Zealand Theatre Record* was published only from 1988 to

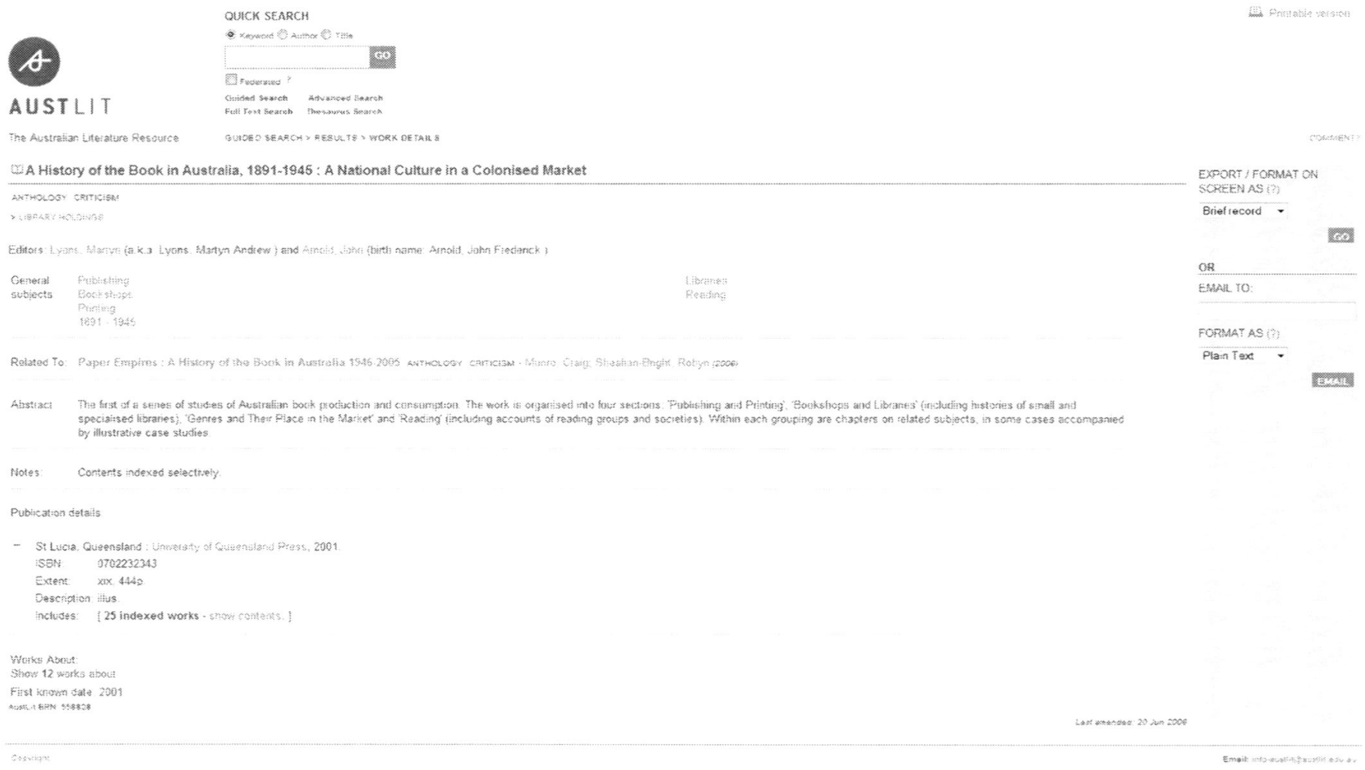

Figure 6.1. Modified *AustLit* record for *A History of the Book in Australia, 1891–1945: A National Culture in a Colonized Market.* Source: *AustLit.*

Works About:

1. ☐ [Untitled] REVIEW - Morrison, Ian *(2002)*
   Appears in: Bibliographical Society of Australia and New Zealand Bulletin vol.26 no.2 👥 2002 (pp.125-128)

2. ☐ [Untitled] REVIEW - Damousi, Joy *(2002)*
   Appears in: Lilith no.11 2002 (pp.131-134)

3. ☐ Book Industry Nurtured in the Bosom of Empire REVIEW - Maniaty, Tony *(2002)*
   Appears in: The Weekend Australian 26-27 January 2002, Books Extra (pp.6,7)

4. ☐ Bound Up in the British Way REVIEW - Borghino, Jose *(2002)*
   Appears in: The Sydney Morning Herald 2-3 February 2002, Spectrum (pp.10, 11)

5. ☐ Bookworld REVIEW - Carter, David *(2002)*
   Appears in: Australian Book Review no.238 February 2002 (pp.12-13)

6. ☐ A History of the Book in Australia, 1891-1945 REVIEW - Capp, Fiona *(2002)*
   Appears in: The Age 16 February 2002, Saturday Extra (p.9)

7. ☐ The Book in Australia REVIEW *(2002)*
   Appears in: Margin no.57 July - August 2002 (pp.27-30)

8. ☐ Australia, By the Book REVIEW - Anderson, Reg *(2003)*
   Appears in: The Courier-Mail 11 January 2003, BAM (p.7)

9. ☐ [Untitled] REVIEW - Cryle, Denis *(2003)*
   Appears in: The Australian Journal of Politics and History vol.49 no.1 2003 (pp.129-130)

10. ☐ [Untitled] REVIEW - Harvey, Ross *(2003)*
    Appears in: Australian Literary Studies vol.21 no.1 May 👥 2003 (pp.127-129)

11. ☐ [Untitled] REVIEW - Wegner, Jurgen *(2003)*
    Appears in: Biblionews and Australian Notes & Queries vol.28 no.1 2003 (pp.30-34)

12. ☐ A History of the Book in Australia REVIEW - Mead, Philip *(2009)*
    Appears in: JASAL no.9 👥 👥 2009

SHOW MARKED   SHOW ALL

First known date: 2001
AustLit BRN: 558828

Figure 6.2. Modified *AustLit* record for works about *A History of the Book in Australia, 1891–1945: A National Culture in a Colonized Market.* Source: *AustLit.*

1996. For more recent reviews of drama or theater performances, check one or more of the all-purpose databases (*APAIS, Expanded Academic Index*, and *LexisNexis Academic*) described in this chapter.

Australian Public Affairs Information Service (*APAIS*) is an interdisciplinary database offering access to published material on Australian political, economic, legal, social, and cultural affairs. Materials included are periodicals, newspapers, scholarly journals, conference papers, and books. *Australian Public Affairs Full Text* (*APAFT*) is the full-text counterpart to *APAIS*. Because *APAIS* indexes approximately 550 journals, and *APAFT* provides full text of more than 400 journals, these databases are highly recommended for locating book reviews on topics pertaining to Australia. Both are available via subscription and will be accessible through most Australian and New Zealand libraries. These resources are less likely to be available in the United States and Canada. Journals indexed that regularly feature reviews of literary works include *Antipodes, Australian Aboriginal Studies, Australian Academic and Research Libraries, Australasian Drama Studies, Australian Literary Studies, Hecate, Meanjin, New Literatures Review,*

Overland, *Quadrant*, and *Westerly*. More information on *APAIS* and *APAFT* may be found in chapter 4.

For many years **Book Review Index (BRI)** was the most comprehensive index available for book reviews published in a wide variety of periodical resources. Approximately five hundred periodicals and newspapers are currently indexed by *BRI*. Be aware that retrospective coverage varies by each title. Periodicals indexed range from the *Harvard Business Review* to the *Center for Children's Books: Bulletin*. General-interest magazines such as *Ms.*, *Time*, the *New Yorker*, and *Atlantic* are also included. A full list of periodicals indexed can be found in each print issue or online through Gale (www.gale.cengage.com/BRIOnline/). Some of the journals indexed in *BRI* that regularly review Australian books are *Arena Magazine* (1992–), *Australian Library Journal* (1997–), *Journal of Australian Studies* (1997–), *Magpies* (1991–), *Meanjin* (1988–), and *Quadrant* (1994–). The most important review source in Australia, the *Australian Book Review*, is indexed from 1991 to 2003 only. To locate a review in *BRI*, you will need to know the year the item was published, then check under the author's name in the appropriate annual or quarterly volume. Keep in mind that most book reviews are published within twelve to eighteen months of the publication date. Over the past several years, databases like Gale's *Expanded Academic ASAP*, *ProQuest Research Library*, and EBSCO's *Academic Search Complete* have strengthened their coverage of book reviews, making it less vital to consult *BRI*. However, it is still possible to identify reviews in *BRI* that are not available in any of the aforementioned resources.

Combined Retrospective Index to Book Reviews in Humanities Journals, 1802–1974 is a set of ten volumes that provides author and title access to approximately five hundred thousand reviews appearing in more than 150 humanities journals. As indicated by the title, dates of the sources consulted are from both the nineteenth century and the twentieth century. Thus, this tool may be used to identify reviews of early works on Australia and New Zealand, as illustrated by one example that appeared in the *Spectator* in 1888 on Walter Hazell and Howard Hodgkin's *The Australasian Colonies: Emigration and Colonization* (London: Edward Stanford, 1887). However, the *Combined Retrospective Index* appears to be stronger for items published in the twentieth century. You can locate reviews either by the author (listed alphabetically and covering the first nine volumes of the set), or by the title of the work (final volume in the set). As with all review sources, the number of reviews available will depend on the popularity of the author in question. A good example of this is a comparison of results for a lesser known but important writer from the early twentieth century, E. J. Banfield, versus that of Nobel Prize winner Patrick White. There are four reviews for Banfield, versus almost half a page for White. The *National Library Service Cumulative Book Review Index, 1905–1974* (Princeton, N.J.: National Library Service, 1975) may be used in conjunction with the *Combined Retrospective Index* but is of limited use when researching Australian and New Zealand authors. This is mostly because it is a cumulative index to only four sources: *Book Review Digest* from 1905 to 1974, *Library Journal* from 1907 to 1974, *Saturday Review* from 1924 to 1974, and *Choice* from 1964 to 1974. In terms of literature, these publications are more focused on American and British authors, so expect reviews of works from Pacific authors to be spotty. However, it is possible to be successful with some authors, as supported by the discovery of one review for E. J. Banfield's *Confessions of a Beachcomber* (London: T. F. Unwin, 1908). Note that the *Combined Retrospective Index to Book Reviews in Scholarly Journals, 1886–1974* (Woodbridge, Conn: Carrollton Press / Research Publications, 1979–1982) is a companion set to *Combined Retrospective Index to Book Reviews in Humanities Journals, 1802–1974* that supplies author and title access to more than one million book reviews appearing in 459 scholarly journals in history, political science, and sociology. Use this tool to locate reviews of books outside the areas of literature and literary scholarship.

An advantage to using Gale's **Expanded Academic ASAP** is that it provides cover-to-cover content for a number of important literary journals, including book reviews. As is the case with all periodical aggregators, publication dates for titles included will vary. You can perform a publication search to determine the exact date range a particular title will be available in the database. Many of the standard book review resources are featured, such as the *Times Literary Supplement* and *Library Journal*, but there are also several journals that focus on Australian literature and reviews of Australian creative works, such as *Antipodes*, *Australian Literary Studies*, *Overland*, *Meanjin*, and *Southerly*. *Expanded Academic ASAP* also lists reviews from two important New Zealand literary journals, *Landfall* and the *Journal of New Zealand Literature*. Due to inconsistent subject indexing, best results occur when you search for the author and title of a particular work. *Expanded Academic ASAP* does not offer the option to limit a search to a particular document type, so the most accurate means of locating reviews is to go to the advanced search screen, select "document title" as your default index, then look for the name of the literary work combined with the term "review." Be sure that you do not use the phrase "book review," as it and the term "review" are used inconsistently within the database. A faster way to find reviews is to perform a keyword search using the term "review" and the title of the work. You can expect to pick up a few false hits this way, but they are easily spotted in the list of results. *Expanded Academic ASAP* sorts results by three categories: academic journals, magazines, and newspapers. This sorting feature is handy in cases when you only wish to retrieve information from peer-reviewed sources. Even though *Expanded Academic ASAP* offers a category for newspapers, be aware that it indexes very few titles—one of note is the *New York Times Book Review*. For additional ways to locate reviews within newspapers, see *LexisNexis Academic* and *Factiva*.

Because **Factiva** is a product of Dow Jones Reuters Business Interactive, its primary purpose is to provide access to global news and business information. Sources derive from 118 countries and are published in twenty-two languages. However, because *Factiva* contains full-text coverage of major American, Australian, and New Zealand newspapers, it can be an option for locating book reviews. If you prefer that your reviews emanate from scholarly resources, newspapers should not be your first option. For works by lesser-known authors, it is possible that newspapers may be your only option. Some of the major Australian newspapers covered in *Factiva* include the *Australian*, the *Sydney Morning Herald*, the *Age* (Melbourne), the *Courier-Mail* (Brisbane), the *Advertiser* (Adelaide), the *West Australian* (Perth), the *Northern Territory News*, the *Hobart Mercury*, and the *Canberra Times*. A few of the New Zealand papers available are the *Nelson Mail*, the *New Zealand Herald*, the *Otago Daily Times*, the *Press* (Christchurch), and the *Waikato Times*. Because *Factiva* contains so much full text, it is recommended that you take time to limit your search as much as possible, otherwise a basic keyword search can produce many false hits. Limit your search by "subject," "political/general news," "arts/entertainment," then by "books." Be aware that the default date range may be limited to the last year. If your book was published prior to the previous year, remember to change the default. *Factiva* can be a tricky resource to use, so if you experience any problems, check with your local reference librarian for assistance.

***Index New Zealand* (*INNZ*)** contains abstracts of articles from approximately one thousand publications from 1987 to the present. Articles from older publications are being added retrospectively. The titles indexed in *INNZ* are popular magazines, academic journals, and major newspapers such as the *Otago Daily Times* and the *New Zealand Herald*. In addition to covering a broad range of publications, *INNZ* is an excellent tool to consult because it is updated daily and features substantial reviews of New Zealand and Pacific books. There are two ways to search *INNZ*—a simple search and an advanced search. For the purpose of locating book reviews, the advanced search offers the advantage of searching by the subject heading "book reviews." This ability to limit your search can be especially useful when researching one of the more prolific authors, such as C. K. Stead. Keep in mind that *INNZ* is an index, so if you want to see the full text, check your local library holdings for the source that published the review.

Originally, *Index to Book Reviews in the Humanities* was a comprehensive index to book reviews in all areas of the humanities. From 1971 onward, it became an index to reviews in selected humanities periodicals and chose to exclude books devoted to children's literature. Journals indexed are international in scope, so using this source as a means of locating reviews on Australian and New Zealand authors is promising. Note that the index uses code numbers in place of journal names, so be careful to double-check the front of each volume to identify the source in which your review will be located. A quick glance in volume 13 (1972) shows four reviews of Thomas Keneally's novel *The Chant of Jimmie Blacksmith* (Ringwood, Vic.: Penguin Books, 1972). The journals with reviews of Keneally's book are interesting to note: two are British publications—a London weekly titled the *Listener,* and the *Times Literary Supplement*— and a third source is *Orbis*, a quarterly published by the Foreign Policy Research Institute at the University of Pennsylvania. The variety of review sources indicates an attempt to be comprehensive in scope of coverage, something that can be beneficial when looking for lesser-known works.

The *Index to New Zealand Periodicals* has changed names several times over the years and finally ceased being issued in print in 1986. Instead, the National Library of New Zealand chose to put their efforts into the *Index New Zealand*, a database that provides access to journal articles, theses, reports, books, and conference papers published in or about New Zealand and the South Pacific. For older book reviews, the *Index to New Zealand Periodicals* is a good source to consult. It covers more than 180 serials, mostly from New Zealand, but it also includes content from international journals when the subject matter pertains to New Zealand. To access reviews, check the subject heading "Book Reviews," where citations will be listed alphabetically by author. You can also locate book reviews by author name. The titles of periodicals containing reviews are abbreviated, so be sure to use the "Guide to Periodicals Indexed" to determine the full title of the magazine or journal. At that point you can search your local library catalog to access the resource that published the review.

LexisNexis Academic (*LexisNexis*) is an excellent resource for locating reviews in major international papers, as well as national and regional newspapers within the United States and Canada. Content in *LexisNexis* is full text, so the information is retrieved immediately. There are two basic strategies to use when locating reviews in *LexisNexis*. For the quickest results, select the "power search" option, enter the title of the book, and add the term "review." The default search looks in all "Major World Publications," which allows the most options possible. However, if you prefer to focus your search on Australian newspapers or an alternative collection of resources, simply check the drop-down arrow under "Sources." Be sure to note the date range option at the bottom, and keep in mind the copyright date of your book. Results will be organized within several categories on the left-hand portion of the screen. Select the "newspapers" option to see a list of all the papers with articles or reviews on your book. By selecting a specific title, all the articles will appear on the right-hand side of the screen. A more precise way to search *LexisNexis* for reviews is to check the "News" tab on the top-left side of the screen. This allows you to search within specific fields such as the headlines and lead paragraphs of articles. Your result set should be smaller, with fewer false hits. Frequently, reviews of Australian and New Zealand authors will only be available through local newspapers, so selecting "Major World Publications" will be a good choice, as it will offer full text of many papers from the region.

The **New York Times Book Review Index 1896–1970** is a five-volume set that offers convenient access to reviews of books published in one of the oldest and most renowned newspapers in the United States—the *New York Times*. Each volume is an index to reviews through different access points, including author, title, byline (reviewers of works), subject, and category (anthologies, children's fiction, poetry, etc.). The category feature can be useful if you wish to focus your search on reviews by a particular genre. If your library subscribes to ProQuest's *Historical Newspapers*, you will have access to the full text of the *New York Times* from 1851 to 2006 online, including the book reviews. You can also search the online database for the document type "review." This can be helpful in identifying book reviews by some of the more well-established early Australian authors, such as Henry Lawson and Rolf Boldrewood. Do not expect to find reviews in the *New York Times* for most of the early authors, unless they are well known.

The **New Zealand Literature File** (*NZLF*) presents a selective list of New Zealand and Pacific authors with references to biographical and critical materials about their works. Citations to book reviews are also included. The *NZLF* was compiled initially by staff in the New Zealand and Pacific Collection of the University of Auckland's General Library to assist students enrolled in courses on New Zealand literature. The site is organized alphabetically by author. A typical entry contains a list of books by the author, followed by citations to scholarly criticism and reviews of the author's works. You can also find lists of primary materials by each author that were published in periodical resources. The information in *NZLF* is not comprehensive, but it is current. This is an excellent place to begin looking for reviews on a New Zealand author. Keep in mind that review sources are mostly from New Zealand periodicals, which can present more of a challenge for researchers in the United States and Canada. Interlibrary loan may be necessary to get the full text of items cited in the *New Zealand Literature File*.

Similar to other all-purpose periodical databases, ***ProQuest Research Library*** includes reviews published in selective literary journals, magazines, and newspapers. As with EBSCO's *Academic Search Complete* and Gale's *Expanded Academic ASAP*, dates of coverage will vary for individual titles. You can search for a specific publication to determine when coverage begins and whether it is available full text. An advantage to using *ProQuest Research Library* over *Expanded Academic ASAP* is the fact that you can limit a search by document type in the advanced search screen. Not only do you have the option of searching for a "book review," but there is also the ability to search for an "audio review," "film review," and "theater review." Results are sorted by magazines, scholarly journals, trade publications, and newspapers. *ProQuest Research Library* does not include as many scholarly journal reviews as *Expanded Academic ASAP*, but it is competitive with its full-text coverage of all-purpose literary review sources, like the *Times Literary Supplement, New York Review of Books,* and the *New Yorker*. Also, *ProQuest Research Library* offers more titles featuring movie reviews, so if you are interested in finding criticism on films based on Australian or New Zealand fiction, such as Peter Carey's *Oscar and Lucinda*, try *ProQuest* first.

The Times Literary Supplement Index 1902–1939 is a two-volume set that indexes 350,000 reviews appearing in the *Times Literary Supplement* (*TLS*) from the early twentieth century. Volume 1 covers A through K and volume 2, L through Z. Information contained in the two volumes is divided into three alphabetically arranged categories: personal names, titles, and subject. Using the first volume, you can find Boldrewood's *Bush Honeymoon*[8] by both author and title. To locate the review itself, you will need to consult the appropriate issue of the *TLS*. Additional subject categories that may be useful to those researching Australia and New Zealand include "Australia: literature," "Australia: travel," "New Zealand: literature," and "New Zealand: travel." Also, when applicable, the following headings can lead to reviews of edited collections, anthologies, and critical essays on specific authors or literary genres: "Authors: Australian," "Drama: Australian," "Poetry: Australian," and "Poetry: New Zealand." There is an additional three-volume set that indexes reviews from 1940 to 1980, so be sure to consult it if the work you are researching was published during this time period. If your library subscribes, Gale's *Times Literary Supplement Centenary Archive* is a full-text online version of *TLS* content from 1902 to 1990 (www.gale.cengage.com/pdf/facts/tls.pdf).

EIGHTEENTH- AND NINETEENTH-CENTURY REVIEWS

The tools discussed in the previous section will not be useful if you are looking for reviews of books published prior to the late twentieth century. The reason for this is that most standard online databases begin their coverage of periodicals with the 1970s or 1980s. This section will identify resources that provide either citations to book reviews or full-text reviews from periodicals published prior to the twentieth century. When looking for reviews of early Australian and New Zealand literature, remember that, because of the limited number of periodicals published in the region during the eighteenth and early nineteenth centuries, you will be using mostly American or British publications. To make the situation even more difficult, coverage of topics pertaining to Australia and New Zealand will be limited in these resources. *AustLit* contains citations to book reviews from all time periods, but coverage of older works is selective, and New Zealand authors are not covered at all. There are excellent indexes available for finding reviews of creative works in eighteenth-century periodicals, but those indexes will not be applicable to the literature pertaining to Australia and New Zealand, as works written about the region are nonfictional accounts of travel to and from the newly established British colonies. Thus, one of the standard tools for locating reviews from this period, Ward's *Literary Reviews in British Periodicals*, will be of little use to your research. If you wish to learn more about the tools that index creative works from the eighteenth century, see Keeran and Bowers's research guide to the British Romantic era.[9]

American Periodicals Series Online, 1740–1900 (APS). Ann Arbor, Mich.: ProQuest Information and Learning Company, 2000–. Available at www.proquest.com/en-US/catalogs/databases/detail/aps.shtml.

C19: Nineteenth Century Index. Ann Arbor, Mich.: ProQuest Information and Learning Company, 2005–. Available at c19index.chadwyck.com/home.do.

Nangle, Benjamin Christie. *The Monthly Review, Second Series, 1790–1815: Indexes of Contributors and Articles*. Oxford: Clarendon Press, 1955.

American Periodicals Series Online, 1740–1900 (APS) contains digitized images of the pages of American magazines and journals that originated between 1741 and 1900. The dates continue through the early twentieth century for many of the one thousand five hundred titles available in *APS*. In the advanced search feature you can limit to the document type "review," then look for a specific author or work. For instance, a search for Douglas Sladen's *A Century of Australian Song*[10] produces one full-length feature review from the *Literary World: A Monthly Review of Current Literature*. This particular review appears in 1890, a full two years after the publication of the anthology, so be careful if limiting your search to a particular date range. *APS* offers an excellent opportunity to locate book reviews of travel narratives and other reports from Australia and New Zealand, as it contains publications that are not strictly literary in nature. For instance, reviews of Charles Stuart's *Two Expeditions into* *the Interior of Southern Australia* (London: Smith, Elder and Co., 1833) may be found in the *American Quarterly Observer* and the *Bulletin of the American Geographical Society of New York*. Publications in *APS* that frequently include reviews of literary works by early Australian authors such as Katharine Susannah Prichard and Norman Lindsay are the *Bookman: A Review of Books and Life* and the *North American Review*.

C19: Nineteenth Century Index is an online index to British and American publications from the nineteenth century. *C19* is the electronic equivalent of the major indexing tools for the nineteenth century, including *Poole's Index to Periodical Literature* (1802–1906), *The Wellesley Index to Victorian Periodicals* (1824–1900), and *Palmer's Index to the Times* (1790–1905). There are many ways to search the database, but a basic search is very effective if you have a specific author and work in mind. For example, a search on Matthew Flinders's *A Voyage to Terra Australis* (London: G. and W. Nicol, 1814) results in articles from the key British periodicals the *Monthly Review* and *Annals of Philosophy*, both published in 1815. Searches may be limited to specific types of resources including periodicals, books, newspapers, and official (government) publications. If you chose to keep the search as open as possible, results are sorted by these resource types, allowing for quick identification of reviews published in periodicals and newspapers. If your library subscribes to ProQuest's *British Periodicals* database, which offers full text of magazines and journals from the seventeenth century through the Victorian age, you will be able to link directly from a citation in *C19* to the full-text article.

Some of the most important sources for reviews of books published in the eighteenth century include the *Gentleman's Magazine*, the *Monthly Review*, the *Critical Review*, and the *London Magazine*. As mentioned earlier, it can be difficult to locate reviews of nonliterary works in these publications. Fortunately, there exists **The Monthly Review, Second Series, 1790–1815: Indexes of Contributors and Articles**, which provides indexing for the journal during the height of British exploration to the South Seas. There is also an index to the first series (1749–1789), but for the purposes of locating reviews of early books written about Australia and New Zealand, content within the second series is more appropriate. The book is divided into two major sections, with the first comprising an index to authors/contributors to the *Monthly Review*. The second section is an index to the articles themselves and is arranged alphabetically by author. If a work was published anonymously, it will be listed alphabetically by title. Following each entry is a reference to the volume and page of the appropriate issue of the *Monthly Review*, along with the author or contributor of the review: "White, John. Journal of a Voyage to New South Wales. IV. 314. W[ales]." The index also lists biographical information about each contributor, and in this case it notes that William Wales had been on Cook's last two voyages as a scientific observer and was responsible for reviewing most of the publications concerning exploration of the South Seas.[11]

PERIODICALS THAT FEATURE BOOK REVIEWS

The following periodicals are extremely important to be aware of, as their primary focus is publishing reviews of Australian and New Zealand books. All four titles feature reviews of fiction, poetry, and literary scholarship, as well as other disciplines that may be of interest to researchers of Australian and New Zealand studies. These resources are particularly useful for identifying reviews of creative works by women or minority authors, who have been neglected by the more mainstream publications or databases discussed in this chapter.

Australian Book Review (ABR). Richmond South, Vic.: National Book Council (Australia), 1961–. Monthly. ISSN: 0155-2864 home.vicnet.net.au/~abr/.
Australian Multicultural Book Review. Upper Ferntree Gully, Vic.: Papyrus Publishing, 1993–2004. 3/yr. ISSN: 1039-7043.
Hecate's Australian Women's Book Review. Brisbane: Hecate Press, 1997–2000. ISSN: 1446-702X. 2001–. Available online only at emsah.uq.edu.au/awsr/recent/index.html. Former title: *Australian Women's Book Review*. St. Kilda East, Vic.: AWBR, 1989–1997. ISSN: 1033-9434.
New Zealand Books: A Quarterly Review. Wellington: Peppercorn Press, 1991–. Quarterly. ISSN: 1170-9103.

Australian Book Review (ABR) is Australia's oldest literary review source. *ABR* first appeared in 1961 and publishes book reviews, essays, commentaries, and creative writing. This monthly magazine is committed to "highlighting the full range of critical and creative writing from around Australia. . . . Its primary aims are several: to foster high critical standards; to provide an outlet for fine new writing; and to contribute to the preservation of literary values and a full appreciation of Australia's literary heritage" (www.australianbookreview.com .au/about-abr). A typical issue of *ABR* includes lengthy commentaries on books in all disciplines. For those interested in the humanities, it features reviews of current biographies, letters, essays, poetry, films, cultural studies, indigenous studies, fiction, and literary studies. It also covers nonliterary topics that focus on Australia, such as economics, politics, and international studies. An index to issues from 1990 to the present is available online (www.australianbookreview.com.au/past-issues/index). The website allows you to browse the contents of each year for a particular review. You can also search *Book Review Index*, *APAIS*, and *AustLit*, as these resources index the content of *ABR*.

Unfortunately, *Australian Multicultural Book Review* ceased publication in 2004. However, it is still an important resource for those interested in the work of authors from minority cultures within Australia. According to *Australian Multicultural Book Review*'s editorial policy, its goal is to offer reviews on a wide range of multicultural writing, including fiction, poetry, biographical essays, and historical texts. Issues also feature critical articles, interviews with authors, and a creative writing section that highlights new work by multicultural authors. *Australian Multicultural Book Review* does not appear to be indexed by *APAIS*, but reviews of literary works are included in *AustLit*. One note of warning for researchers outside Australia: this publication will be more difficult to obtain, as OCLC *WorldCat* indicates no holdings other than libraries within Australia.

Hecate's Australian Women's Book Review is the review magazine of the feminist journal *Hecate*, which in 1997 took over the publication formerly known as *Australian Women's Book Review*. Only books written by women are featured in *Hecate's*. The goal of the magazine is to provide women with information on small-press publications and books that might otherwise not be included in mainstream review sources. The contents of selected issues from volume 12 (2000) to the present are available online free of charge (emsah.uq.edu.au/awsr/recent/index.html). Unfortunately, there is no easy way to search the contents online other than browsing by individual issues. Thus, you may wish to search *AustLit* to identify a particular review, then check the online site for the full-text article. *Hecate's* is not indexed in any other major database or index, so for those without access to *AustLit*, browsing the contents online is the sole option for locating reviews.

New Zealand Books: A Quarterly Review is the only periodical available that focuses on reviews of books published in New Zealand. The journal is indexed from 2005 to the present through EBSCO's *Humanities International Index*.[12] *New Zealand Books: A Quarterly Review* began publication in 1991 and features reviews of books covering all aspects of New Zealand history, culture, politics, and literature. Unfortunately, few libraries outside New Zealand and Australia carry current subscriptions to the journal, so access for researchers outside the region will be limited.

AUTHOR-SPECIFIC REVIEWS

Bibliographies and critical guides to specific authors will often furnish citations to reviews of older and current works, all in one convenient list. While bibliographies of primary and secondary sources exist for many

Australian authors, very few have been published as monographs. The following resources represent a small sample of the available author-specific monograph-length bibliographies. Note that several of these titles are from important series discussed in chapter 4, "Print and Electronic Bibliographies, Indexes, and Annual Reviews." They are presented in this chapter because book reviews are a featured portion of their content. A better option for finding a bibliography that includes book reviews is to search an index to periodical literature, as more bibliographies are available as articles in scholarly journal literature. This is easily done by searching tools like the *MLA International Bibliography* or *AustLit*. In addition to author-specific bibliographies, you can often find lists of reviews in subject-focused bibliographies. Schürmann-Zeggel's *Black Australian Literature*, also discussed in chapter 4, devotes an entire chapter to reviews of works by Aboriginal and Torres Strait Islanders. More tips on locating author-specific bibliographies may be found in chapter 4.

Finch, Janette H. *Bibliography of Patrick White*. Bibliographies of Australian Writers. Adelaide: Libraries Board of South Australia, 1966.

Griffiths, Gareth, ed. *John Romeril*. Australian Playwrights. Amsterdam; Atlanta: Rodopi, 1993.

Hooton, Joy W. *A. D. Hope*. Australian Bibliographies. Melbourne: Oxford University Press, 1979.

Niall, Brenda. *Martin Boyd*. Australian Bibliographies. Melbourne: Oxford University Press, 1977.

Tasker, Meg. *Francis Adams (1862–1893): A Bibliography*. Victorian Fiction Research Guide 24. St. Lucia: Department of English, University of Queensland, 1996.

Tiffin, Chris. *Rosa Praed (Mrs. Campbell Praed) 1851–1935: A Bibliography*. Victorian Research Guides 15. St. Lucia: Department of English, University of Queensland, 1989.

Walker, Shirley. *Judith Wright*. Australian Bibliographies. Melbourne: Oxford University Press, 1981.

Zuber-Skerritt, Ortrun, ed. *David Williamson*. Australian Playwrights. Amsterdam: Rodopi, 1988.

The Libraries Board of South Australia published a number of author-specific bibliographies in the 1960s and early 1970s. The *Bibliographies of Australian Writers* series covers some of the more established authors such as A. D. Hope, Randolph Stow, Judith Wright, Hal Porter, and Patrick White. It also features some lesser-known authors, like R. D. Fitzgerald, Catherine Helen Spence, and Ian Mudie. Titles in this series are extremely valuable for identifying book reviews, as exemplified by Janette Finch's **Bibliography of Patrick White**. The bibliography contains a separate section called "Specific Reviews," which arranges items chronologically by White's work. All review sources are Australian and include both newspapers and journals. A convenient feature of the Libraries Board series is that brief reviews are separated from full reviews, so researchers can easily focus on the more substantial commentaries. Reprinted reviews also have their own category. For those who have access to the *Index of Australian Book Reviews*, please note that these bibliographies were published in coordination with the *Index*. Thus, reviews listed in the series are not available in the *Index of Australian Book Reviews* to avoid unnecessary duplication.

Rodopi's *Australian Playwrights* series is designed to "contribute to the promotion, analysis and better understanding of Australian drama in Australia and overseas" (i). The inclusion of reviews is inconsistent, however. Gareth Griffiths's work on **John Romeril**, one of the most prolific contributors to twentieth-century Australian theater, is a bibliography of primary materials and secondary materials pertaining to the author. The section on secondary materials features both critical interpretations of Romeril's plays, as well as reviews of his works. Ortrun Zuber-Skerritt's volume on **David Williamson**, one of Australia's most popular and successful playwrights, is an invaluable guide to locating interviews with the author, as well as critical interpretations of his works. Unfortunately, it only lists reviews of those plays of Williamson's that were released as films and does not list citations for performance reviews.

As mentioned previously in chapter 4, one of the best author-specific bibliographical series available is Oxford's *Australian Bibliographies*. These volumes were designed to be as comprehensive in scope as possible and thus contain citations to book reviews of the authors featured. Joy Hooton's bibliography on **A. D. Hope**, one of the most important poets in Australian literature, includes all works by him (whether published or unpublished) and references to him and his work in books, theses, manuscript materials, magazines, newspapers, and radio broadcasts for the years 1924 to mid-1975. Beginning on page 221 is a lengthy list of reviews, arranged chronologically by work. Reviews are from both Australian and British publications. Similar to the book on Hope, Shirley Walker's bibliography on **Judith Wright** attempts to cover all works by Wright, as well as references to her in books, theses, manuscript materials, magazines, newspapers, and radio broadcasts between 1925 and 1979. Beginning on page 175, there is a section specifically devoted to reviews, arranged chronologically by individual work. Commentaries are mostly from Australian publications, but some are from international sources. The final volume in this series, Brenda Niall's bibliography on **Martin Boyd**, attempts to record all secondary materials published about Boyd found in books, theses, periodicals, and newspapers from 1920 to 1976. However, the author notes that some reviews published in provincial newspapers and minor journals have likely been missed. Within each section, items are arranged in chronological order, and reviews begin on page 65. Reviews cited derive from internationally published sources.

Published by the University of Queensland Press, *Victorian Fiction Research Guides* are designed to cover minor or lesser-known writers active between the years 1860 and 1910. The coverage of reviews varies depending on the topic, so be sure to check the table of contents to determine if they are included. Meg Tasker's ***Francis Adams (1862–1893): A Bibliography*** provides lists of fiction and poetry published in collections, as well as short stories, poetry, and essays that appeared in newspapers and magazines. It also mentions information on locating manuscript materials, secondary resources on Adams, and reviews of his fiction, poetry, nonfiction, and plays. Most of the reviews are from Australian newspapers and magazines, but British publications are also represented. Chris Tiffin's ***Rosa Praed (Mrs. Campbell Praed) 1851–1935: A Bibliography*** features references to primary materials, secondary sources, reviews, and interviews with the author. Reviews cited are from a mix of British and Australian newspapers and magazines and are arranged chronologically by title of the work.

CONCLUSION

Thanks to interdisciplinary periodical databases such as *ProQuest Research Library* and Gale's *Expanded Academic ASAP*, the discovery of contemporary book reviews is less complicated today than it was when print indexes were the only option. Even better is the fact that many reviews are accessible full-text online through these databases, including those of interest to scholars of Australian and New Zealand literature. Still, keep in mind that you may need to consult a number of different resources to locate reviews of a particular book. The tools listed in this chapter should provide a good starting place for your search, but they are not the only options available. Be sure to check with your librarian if you encounter any difficulties or have any questions about which resources are most appropriate for your research.

NOTES

1. E. H. McCormick, *New Zealand Literature: A Survey* (London: Oxford University Press, 1959), 2–3.

2. Delys Bird, "The 'Settling' of English," in *Oxford Literary History of Australian Literature*, ed. Bruce Bennett and Jennifer Strauss (Melbourne: Oxford University Press, 1998), 29.

3. Martyn Lyons and John Arnold, *A History of the Book in Australia, 1891–1945: A National Culture in a Colonised Market* (St. Lucia: University of Queensland Press, 2001).

4. Craig Munroe and Robyn Sheahan-Bright, *Paper Empires: A History of the Book in Australia 1946–2005* (St. Lucia: University of Queensland Press, 2006).

5. "Book Publishing and Retailing," in *Yearbook Australia 2006*, http://www.abs.gov.au/websitedbs/D3310114.nsf/home/home?opendocument.

6. *Index to Australian Book Reviews* (Adelaide: Libraries Board of South Australia, 1965–).

7. *Australian Book Review Index* (Melbourne: Footscray Institute of Technology Library, 1979–1984).

8. Rolf Boldrewood, *Bush Honeymoon* (London: Fisher Unwin, 1904).

9. Peggy Keeran and Jennifer Bowers, *Literary Research and the British Romantic Era: Strategies and Sources* (Lanham, Md.: Scarecrow Press, 2005), 119–22.

10. Douglas Sladen, *A Century of Australian Song* (London, W. Scott, 1888).

11. Benjamin Christie Nangle, *The Monthly Review, Second Series, 1790–1815: Indexes of Contributors and Articles* (Oxford: Clarendon, 1955), 70.

12. *Humanities International Index* (Ipswich, Mass.: EBSCO Publishing, 2000–).

Chapter Seven

Magazines and Newspapers

Periodicals such as popular magazines, scholarly journals, and newspapers are important resources for the study of Australian and New Zealand literature. As previously discussed in chapter 5, journals represent a critical avenue for scholars to communicate ideas and distribute information about authors and their creative works. Some journals publish not only secondary literature, but the primary works themselves. In addition to consulting pertinent academic journals, you may also find it necessary to investigate other types of periodical resources, especially when studying an author from the nineteenth century or early twentieth century. Consulting newspapers and popular magazines from the period in which an author lived establishes context for better understanding his or her work. Because these resources are designed to convey information about current events and issues of local concern, reading articles from a Sydney or Melbourne newspaper from the late nineteenth century can shed light on day-to-day realities that may have affected the writing of a particular author. Also uniquely important to the study of early Australian and New Zealand literature is the fact that authors had little choice but to use newspapers and magazines for publishing their creative works. Due to the small and diffuse populations of Australia and New Zealand during their colonial period, book publishing was not a viable option. Even the early newspapers and magazines had a difficult time surviving, and for the most part only those located in more populated areas were successful.

The goal of this chapter is to highlight resources that will identify and locate magazines and newspapers from Australia and New Zealand that were available (and may still be available, in some cases) during the nineteenth and twentieth centuries. Primary emphasis will be on periodicals

143

that published literary works, book reviews, critical essays about literary works, and interviews with authors. The first section discusses resources that list or describe magazines and newspapers from Australia and New Zealand. Many of these are "union lists," tools compiled by libraries for the purpose of identifying holdings of specific resources and sharing that information with other libraries and potential researchers. Union lists used to be critical for determining what periodicals were available at a given library. However, with the emergence of the online catalog, union lists are no longer necessary, and few are being published today. Online catalogs have the advantage of being updated quickly and easily, so that new issues of a newspaper or magazine are reflected on the record upon receipt, and any title changes or frequency alterations are noted immediately. That said, the advantage of the printed union catalog is that it collects information on a specific type of resource (serials, in this case) and makes it available in one convenient source. Thus, you can scan through a list of newspapers and discover where copies were located, as well as see publication details about each title. Since union lists have mostly been abandoned as a means of accumulating current information, they are no longer useful for identifying new periodicals. When using these resources to determine library holdings, it is advisable to consult the online catalog to verify accuracy. Also, be sure to note the dates of coverage of each tool. Finally, keep in mind that union lists simply document the existence of a particular periodical—they do not index content.

Determining if and when an author published in a specific newspaper can be a significant challenge, as indexes to newspapers and early magazines are limited. Thankfully, for those interested in early Australian literature, scholars have created bibliographies and other tools specifically designed to document early literary contributions to periodicals. Unfortunately, less information is available for New Zealand literature, but as more and more early newspapers are being digitized and made available online, searching full text for the existence of a particular poem or creative work is becoming a reality. Be prepared to find gaps, however, as some periodicals simply do not have an index to their content.

The second section of this chapter focuses on nineteenth-century periodicals and resources that identify as well as discuss their significance to Australian and New Zealand literary history. Similarly, the third section will concentrate on twentieth-century periodicals. Because libraries are making significant advances in digitizing early newspapers and periodicals, the final section of this chapter provides information on digital archive projects that feature Australian and New Zealand periodicals.

IDENTIFYING MAGAZINES AND NEWSPAPERS: GENERAL RESOURCES

Australian Journals Online (AJOL). Canberra, A.C.T.: National Library of Australia. www.nla.gov.au/ajol/.

Guide to Australian Newspapers. www.newspapers.com.au/ (accessed 8 September 2010).

Newspapers in Australian Libraries: A Union List. Part 2: Australian Newspapers. 4th ed. Canberra, A.C.T.: National Library of Australia, 1984.

Union Catalogue of New Zealand Newspapers Preserved in Public Libraries, Newspaper Offices, and Local Authority Offices. Wellington: New Zealand Parliamentary Library. 2nd ed. 1961.

Union List of New Zealand Newspapers before 1940 Preserved in Libraries, Newspaper Offices, Local Authority Offices, and Museums in New Zealand. Wellington: National Library of New Zealand, 1985.

Union List of Serials in New Zealand Libraries. Wellington: National Library of New Zealand. 3rd ed. 1969.

Australian Journals Online (AJOL) is the National Library of Australia's database of Australian electronic journals, newspapers, magazines, and newsletters. The database lists publication details and direct links to more than two thousand titles that feature local and overseas works with Australian content or authorship. It also lists websites that advertise or promote Australian journals. Dates covered vary from title to title, but most of the resources are from the mid-to-late twentieth century. Titles appearing in *AJOL* may be available in *PANDORA*, the National Library's archive of selected Australian online publications. For more information about *PANDORA*, see chapter 8 on microform and digital collections pertaining to the study of Australian and New Zealand literature. Journals in *AJOL* can be browsed by title or broad subject categories derived from the *APAIS Thesaurus*, which is available online (www.nla.gov.au/apais/thesaurus/about.html). A subject browse search on *literature* retrieves sixty hits. The full record of each journal (title, URL, subject headings, a brief description, publisher, and other details) may be viewed by linking from the brief record list. The advanced search feature allows users to search within the title, subject, and entire record content for key terms. Limits to four types of resources (journals, newspapers, promotional sites, and abstract sites) may be performed in the advanced search. The *AJOL* database lists all known online Australian journals, including those that are no longer active. To avoid retrieving inactive sites, be sure to use the *search* function rather than the *browse* function, as defunct journals will be retrieved in a browse search. Use *AJOL* to discover small literary magazines, such as

Thylazine: Australian Journal of Arts, Ethics & Literature and *Jacket Magazine*, that are dedicated to poetry, fiction, and other creative writing. Please refer to chapter 5 on scholarly journals to see additional titles that feature both scholarly criticism and creative writing.

Guide to Australian Newspapers is a commercial site that maintains a list of active newspapers, the majority of which have an online presence. Users can browse newspaper titles by state or territory and search by town or city of publication. Direct links to each newspaper are provided for quick access, but keep in mind that most papers only post current material online. To determine what dates are available for a particular source, you must check the website and verify coverage there. For instance, the *Canberra City News* displays content from December 17, 2009, to present. For historical information you will need to consult an index (if available) to identify specific articles on a topic, then locate a library with holdings to the paper of interest. This will be the case for all but a small portion of titles that have been digitized by projects such as the Australian Newspapers Digitisation Project, also sponsored by the National Library of Australia. More information on this important project will be available later in this same chapter.

Newspapers in Australian Libraries: A Union List is a two-volume set designed to list every newspaper held in seventy-eight libraries across Australia. Because part 1 is devoted to overseas newspapers, it will not be discussed here. Part 2, however, features only those titles published within Australia and Papua New Guinea. The 4,006 papers included in the union list are arranged alphabetically by name of state or territory, then by town of publication, and finally, by title. Notes for frequency of publication, publication history, library holdings (both print and microfilm), and holdings within newspaper offices are available for each title. For those who may be unaware of the geographic origination of a particular paper, a separate title index is available to point them to the main entry. Because the holdings information focuses on Australian libraries, it will be of limited use to researchers in other countries. However, using OCLC's *WorldCat* to identify a local library with holdings of a particular paper or requesting specific articles through interlibrary loan may be the best options for those who reside in the United States or Canada.

The **Union Catalogue of New Zealand Newspapers Preserved in Public Libraries, Newspaper Offices, and Local Authority Offices** is a finding list of all newspapers held in thirty-two public libraries in New Zealand, ten libraries in Australia, the British Museum in London, and major New Zealand newspaper offices. The idea behind the catalog is to document as many papers as possible that were once published or are still being published in

New Zealand. Thus, dates covered will vary from title to title, ranging from the 1840s to the 1960s. Papers are listed under the town in which they were published. If a paper changed names over time, earlier titles are provided. Frequency of publication is given in the case of weekly or monthly papers. The *Union Catalogue* is designed to be a finding aid, but it also attempts to include as much bibliographical information as possible about each paper recorded. Having all variations of a title can be important to those interested in historical research, as newspapers tend to change names over time. An example to note is the *Christchurch Star*, which changed names three times between 1868 and 1935. Because the main section of the *Union Catalogue* is arranged geographically, a separate, alphabetically arranged title index will assist researchers in identifying information on a specific paper of interest.

The original purpose of the ***Union List of New Zealand Newspapers before 1940 Preserved in Libraries, Newspaper Offices, Local Authority Offices, and Museums in New Zealand*** was to ascertain holdings and condition information for New Zealand newspapers in order to locate quality copies for a preservation microfilming project. The data gathered in this volume serves an additional function in that it empowers researchers with a unique tool for identifying early New Zealand newspapers and holdings by date. A select number of newspapers were excluded from the project, such as those focusing on sports, prohibition, religion, and titles created for the armed forces. Entries are arranged geographically according to place of publication, then alphabetically by title. Dates of first and last issues are listed, along with the place of publication, if it differs from the title under which it is entered. Also, frequency of publication, sources where the contents are indexed, and library holdings are available. Of particular interest is the notation of indexes to newspapers, if they exist. There is a separate title index in the back of the volume, so that information within the main section of the book can be accessed by publication name. For researchers within New Zealand, Kathryn Peacocke's *Newspaper Indexes in New Zealand: A Guide* (Hamilton: University of Waikato Library, 1994) may be consulted to locate libraries that have produced in-house indexes to content for many of the newspapers in the *Union List*. This information will be of less use to those outside New Zealand, as many of the indexes are card files that must be used in person.

The ***Union List of Serials in New Zealand Libraries*** contains approximately forty thousand serial titles owned by nearly two hundred libraries in New Zealand. The contents of this six-volume set include periodicals and other serial publications issued by societies, institutions, government agencies, and other important organizations. Items are not restricted to being published in New Zealand or about New Zealand. Coverage will vary by title, but because the

goal is to document all serial publications available in the designated libraries, dates range from the 1840s to the late 1960s. Excluded are newspapers, as
they are covered by the *Union Catalogue of New Zealand Newspapers*. Each
publication is entered under the current or latest-known form of its name. Notes
added under each entry record the bibliographical history of that particular publication. References to earlier names are also available. Because this is a union
list, the holdings for each library are listed, which may be of use to researchers
within New Zealand. For those in the United States and Canada, you may wish
to check OCLC's *WorldCat* for libraries with holdings in your area. If your
research pertains to early Māori periodicals, it would be useful to consult the
chapter devoted to serials in Parkinson and Griffith's work, *Books in Māori,
1815–1900: An Annotated Bibliography.*[1] This annotated list of newspapers,
magazines, almanacs, and official publications established prior to 1901 contains detailed descriptions of content and publication histories for each title.

FINDING NINETEENTH-CENTURY
MAGAZINES AND NEWSPAPERS

The small population of Australia during the nineteenth century resulted in
a limited market for local writers and for specialized newspapers and magazines. The history of newspaper and magazine publication in Australia before
1880 is an unfortunate one—many were created, but only a handful were able
to find enough subscribers to survive for more than a few years. However,
nineteenth-century newspapers and magazines were essential to the development of Australian literature because they were the primary communication
outlet for local writers. Book production was not feasible at that time, given
the limited market and high printing costs.[2] The situation was similar in colonial New Zealand. And like in Australia, most early New Zealand periodicals
had a short life span, as inhabitants were spread thin and local publications
had to compete with popular European titles.[3] For more information on the
history of the press in New Zealand, see Griffith, Harvey, and Maslen's *Book
& Print in New Zealand: A Guide to Print Culture in Aotearoa* (Wellington:
Victoria University Press, 1997). An excellent introduction to the origins of
the newspaper press in Australia, including circulation statistics, advertising
trends, and other pertinent issues, is Henry Mayer's *The Press in Australia*
(Melbourne: Lansdowne Press, 1964). A similar work that focuses on the
history of the magazine industry in Australia is Frank Greenop's *History of
Magazine Publishing in Australia* (Sydney: K. G. Murray, 1947). For those
interested in the history of magazines that featured literary content in the
nineteenth century, reading Elizabeth Webby's chapter in *The Book in Aus-*

tralia: Essays Towards a Cultural History[4] is highly recommended. There are also works devoted to the history of the press in specific regions of Australia, such as George Henry Pitt's *The Press in South Australia: 1836 to 1850* (Adelaide: Wakefield Press, 1946), and R. B. Walker's *Yesterday's News: A History of the Newspaper Press in New South Wales from 1920 to 1945* (Sydney: Sydney University Press, 1980). The next section of this chapter outlines sources that identify important periodicals from nineteenth-century Australia and New Zealand. Some of these tools are simple checklists, while others offer historical context for a particular magazine or newspaper. For researchers with access to *AustLit*, please note that some of the early Australian periodicals (such as the *Bulletin* and the *Bunyip*) have been indexed in the database. A complete list of magazines in *AustLit* is available online (www .austlit.edu.au/about/periodicals).

Andrews, Barry G., and William H. Wilde. *Australian Literature to 1900: A Guide to Information Resources*. American Literature, English Literature, and World Literatures in English: An Information Guide Series 22. Detroit, Mich.: Gale, 1980.

Johnson-Woods, Toni. *Index to Serials in Australian Periodicals and Newspapers: Nineteenth Century*. Canberra, A.C.T.: Mulini Press, 2001.

Lindesay, Vane. *The Way We Were: Australian Popular Magazines 1856–1969*. Melbourne: Oxford University Press, 1983.

Park, Iris M. *New Zealand Periodicals of Literary Interest*. Wellington: National Library Service, 1962.

Pong, Alfred. *Checklist of Nineteenth Century Australian Periodicals*. Bundoora, Vic.: La Trobe University Press, 1985.

Stuart, Lurline. *Australian Periodicals with Literary Content, 1821–1925: An Annotated Bibliography*. Melbourne: Australian Scholarly Pub., 2003.

Webby, Elizabeth. *Early Australian Poetry: An Annotated Bibliography of Original Poems Published in Australian Newspapers, Magazines & Almanacks before 1850*. Sydney: Hale & Iremonger, 1982.

Section 5 of *Australian Literature to 1900: A Guide to Information Resources* consists of an annotated list of secondary resources pertaining to the history of nineteenth-century Australian journals, magazines, and newspapers. The later half of the section is devoted to individual newspapers and periodicals from the nineteenth century. This list is extremely useful, as the annotations contain important facts about each periodical, including editors, prominent staff members, and notes on major Australian authors who contributed to each source. As expected, the most significant entry in this category is the *Bulletin* (Sydney). In addition to detailed publication information, a large section devoted to Australian authors who wrote about the role of the *Bulletin* in promoting literary nationalism is available. Andrews and Wilde also cover lesser-known periodicals from Sydney and Melbourne, as well as core titles from Hobart, Brisbane, and Perth. Finally, it is important to note that entries in *Australian Literature to 1900: A Guide to Information Resources* will mention known indexes to content for various regional presses in Australia, if they exist.

Toni Johnson-Woods's ***Index to Serials in Australian Periodicals and Newspapers: Nineteenth Century*** is a unique and valuable tool for locating serialized fiction in nineteenth-century Australian periodicals. Only novel-length serials (more than forty thousand words) are featured, and because the focus is on colonial literature, materials must have appeared in publications prior to 1899. Periodicals in the *Index to Serials in Australian Periodicals and Newspapers* fall into two main categories: weekly newspapers, such as the *Sydney Mail*, and popular magazines, such as the *Australian Journal* and *Melbourne Punch*. Three separate indexes allow researchers to identify serialized fiction by author, by title, and by the periodical in which it appeared. The periodical index serves an additional function, as brief publication histories are available for each title. The author index is divided into two separate categories—"imported" and "colonial"—allowing users to pinpoint writers living in Australia during its earliest period. For an index to poetry published in early Australian newspapers and magazines, see the following entry on Elizabeth Webby's *Early Australian Poetry: An Annotated Bibliography of Original Poems Published in Australian Newspapers, Magazines & Almanacks before 1850*. Additional resources for locating fiction and poetry published in anthologies and other resources may be consulted in chapter 4, "Print and Electronic Bibliographies, Indexes, and Annual Reviews."

It was not until 1855 that Australia produced its first popular magazine, the *Melbourne Punch*, which had a life span reaching to the early twentieth century (1925). Vane Lindesay's ***The Way We Were: Australian Popular Magazines 1856–1969*** is a history of the popular magazines that played a significant role in forming the earliest national image of Australia. Many of these magazines were founded by distinguished writers of the day, such as Henry Kendall, Marcus Clarke, and Rolf Boldrewood. The periodicals featured in Lindesay's work were selected because they published creative works and reviews of literary works on a regular basis. Further, because the focus is on early Australian authors and their associations with contemporary magazines, a thorough index allows researchers to identify specific publications to which an author contributed. An example of such an affiliation is Banjo Patterson's connection with the *Bulletin* and *Aussie*. Illustrations are plentiful in *The Way We Were*, so readers can see actual pages—advertisements, cover photos, cartoons, and editorials—from publications like *Humbug* and the *Australian Journal*. One chapter is devoted to children's magazines that existed between 1920 and 1955. It may be useful to note that Frank Greenop's *History of Mag-*

azine Publishing in Australia features a chapter on the *Melbourne Punch*, as well as other popular weekly and monthly magazines of the nineteenth and early twentieth centuries.

Iris Park's *New Zealand Periodicals of Literary Interest* is a guide to resources that contain original writing from New Zealand published between 1850 and 1960. Park also attempts to document the development of the literary magazine in New Zealand. Periodicals are listed chronologically, with annotations designed to reflect the purpose of each publication (whether it seeks to present literary content versus entertainment), the type of literary works typically featured, as well as basic facts about the publication itself (frequency of publication, editor, dates of publication, changes in name, etc.). A separate appendix includes a list of marginal items, or those publications examined by the author but rejected, based on content being mostly outside the scope of literature. An alphabetical list of all periodicals described may be found in the back of the volume. Finally, an index to authors mentioned in annotations completes this essential work on New Zealand literary periodicals. Researchers may use this index to identify specific titles to which a particular author contributed writing. An example is the magazine *Mate*, which featured poetry and stories by core authors Frank Sargeson, Janet Frame, and James K. Baxter. Unfortunately, there are limited resources available that index early New Zealand periodicals. For two additional resources that index early New Zealand newspapers, see the entries for *Niupepa: Māori Newspapers* and *Papers Past* in the final section of this chapter, devoted to digital archives of periodicals.

Alfred Pong's *Checklist of Nineteenth Century Australian Periodicals* is an attempt to compile a single-source bibliography of all major Australian periodicals that were published before 1945, the year when the *Australian Public Affairs Information Service* (*APAIS*) began indexing newspapers, scholarly journals, popular magazines, and other resources pertinent to the study of Australian humanities and social sciences. For more detailed information on *APAIS*, see the entry in chapter 4 under "National Bibliographies and Indexes." Pong concentrates his efforts on all weekly or less frequently published periodicals from the nineteenth century. Annual publications, daily newspapers, and government gazettes have been excluded, as these titles are covered mostly by the National Library's *Newspapers in Australian Libraries: A Union List*. The *Checklist of Nineteenth Century Australian Periodicals* consists of short entries arranged alphabetically by title. For each title, volumes and dates published and place and frequency of publication are listed. Name changes are available, when applicable. Annotations accompany selected entries, when the author felt it necessary to comment on a particular title. Unfortunately, there is no subject index to the *Checklist*, so researchers will not be able to identify periodicals that focus on literature or other humanities-related content, unless using a known title. However, since there are only forty-nine pages of content, scanning entries for relevant titles is a viable option.

Of the resources available on early Australian periodicals, Lurline Stuart's ***Australian Periodicals with Literary Content, 1821–1925: An Annotated Bibliography*** is perhaps the most critical to consult. Because Stuart chronicles literary periodicals from the nineteenth century to the first quarter of the twentieth century, this is a gold mine of information for those interested in researching early Australian authors. Note that this work is a revised and updated version of an earlier edition (*Nineteenth Century Australian Periodicals: An Annotated Bibliography*. Sydney: Hale & Iremonger, 1979). All periodicals listed in Stuart's bibliography contain creative writing, such as essays, fiction, and poetry. Those with only minor literary content or no literary content have been excluded. Newspapers have also been excluded. Entries are listed alphabetically by title and include dates of publication, publisher/editor information, a brief description of content, and library holdings within Australia. Because early contributors often used pseudonyms or left their work unsigned, Stuart has attempted to note the names of known contributors after the summary of content, along with the names of writers who signed their literary contributions. Additional features that supplement the bibliography are a chronology of magazines by date, which allows readers to see a list of publications by year from the earliest (*Australian Magazine*, 1821) to the latest in 1925, and an index of printers, publishers, editors, and major contributors, so that specific writers and the magazines in which they were published may be readily identified.

The single best index to early Australian poetry exists today due to the dedicated work of Elizabeth Webby. Webby's contribution to Australian poetry scholarship began in 1978 with an article published in the first volume of *Push from the Bush: A Bulletin of Social History Devoted to the Year of Grace 1838* (Canberra, A.C.T.: 1838 Volume Collective of the Australian Bicentennial History, 1978–1988) and culminated with her book ***Early Australian Poetry: An Annotated Bibliography of Original Poems Published in Australian Newspapers, Magazines & Almanacks before 1850***. Webby notes in her introduction that in the early nineteenth century, poetry was both a more popular and a more public form of literary expression than it is today. Further, poetry was a regular feature of most early Australian newspapers. According to Webby, to study the literature of Australia prior to 1850 is to study poetry, and to read the work of lesser-known writers reveals the cultural and intellectual life of the period. Because so few of the authors of early poetry can be identified, items in the bibliography are arranged chronologically, rather than alphabetically by author. Content includes the title of the poem (or first line if it is untitled), author, date, and place of composition (if available), date of publication, and page reference. Brief comments on the content of each poem have been added by Webby, except when the title makes this irrelevant. *Early Australian Poetry: An Annotated Bibliography of Original Poems Published in Australian Newspapers, Magazines & Almanacks before 1850* is arranged by the region where newspapers, magazines, and almanacs were published, then further categorized by city. Regions include New South Wales, Tasmania, Western Australia, South Australia, and Victoria. An index of newspapers, magazines, almanacs, and identifiable poets completes this essential volume on early Australian poetry.

FINDING TWENTIETH-CENTURY MAGAZINES AND NEWSPAPERS

Australian Indigenous Index (INFOKOORI). Sydney: State Library of New South Wales. library.sl.nsw.gov.au:1084/search.

Bennett, Bruce, ed. *Cross Currents: Magazines and Newspapers in Australian Literature.* Melbourne: Longman Cheshire, 1981.

Day, A. Grove. *Modern Australian Prose, 1901–1975: A Guide to Information Sources.* American Literature, English Literature, and World Literatures in English: An Information Guide Series 29. Detroit, Mich.: Gale, 1980.

Denholm, Michael. *Small Press Publishing in Australia: The Late 1970s to the Mid to Late 1980s,* vol. 2. Footscray, Vic.: Footprint, 1991.

Tregenza, John. *Australian Little Magazines, 1923–1954: Their Role in Forming and Reflecting Literary Trends.* Adelaide: Libraries Board of South Australia, 1964.

The *Australian Indigenous Index* (**INFOKOORI**) is produced by the State Library of New South Wales and is an index primarily to the *Koori Mail*, a national newspaper published in the region that focuses on the indigenous people of Australia. Coverage begins in May 1991 and continues to the present date. The database also indexes biographical information from a variety of magazines published for Aboriginal populations, including *Our Aim* (1907–1961), *Dawn* (1952–1969), *New Dawn* (1970–1975), and one of the most significant periodicals of its kind, *Identity* (1971–1982). Historical information about Aboriginal people and communities from additional New South Wales newspapers is being added on a regular basis. Researchers can identify content in the *Australian Indigenous Index* through a basic keyword search on the title, subject, and author fields. Thus, an author search on "Noonuccal, Oodgeroo" will retrieve sixteen items by this important Aboriginal writer. Changing the search to the subject field produces more than sixty articles written about her. The advanced search allows more focused queries, as users can limit their search by type of publication (book review, interview, etc.), newspaper source, and to articles that contain certain features, such as illustrations or maps. Limiting to a particular date range is also an option in the advanced search. Keep in mind that this tool is an index only, so while you may discover poetry or short fiction published by an Aboriginal author, you will need to locate a copy of the text through other means. This may be achieved by searching your local library catalog for newspaper holdings, or requesting a copy of the item through interlibrary loan.

Bruce Bennett's *Cross Currents: Magazines and Newspapers in Australian Literature* is an excellent introduction to Australian newspapers and magazines from the very beginning of Australian literary history to the present day. An additional factor that makes this work essential is its emphasis on early and contemporary serials that published primary works and reviews of Australian literature. *Cross Currents* is a valuable resource for gaining insight into the challenges faced by the early Australian press. Most of the content focuses on specific publications from the twentieth century, providing historical information and context for prominent literary titles like the *Angry Penguins* and *Australian Literary Studies*. Other chapters in *Cross Currents* are devoted to "little magazines" of the 1970s and book reviewing trends in Australian newspapers during the mid-twentieth century. For additional resources on the history of the little magazine in Australia, see the entry on Michael Denholm's chapter.

Similar to his section on nineteenth-century periodicals, A. Grove Day's bibliography in *Modern Australian Prose, 1901–1975: A Guide to Information Sources* lists publication information on Australian literary magazines, as well as noteworthy secondary resources about them. The section on twentieth-century serials compiles and describes general periodicals of interest to those researching an author who lived and wrote during this period. Of particular note is the final portion of the bibliography entitled "Selected Literary Journals." The publications in this ten-page section are a mix of periodicals currently in print and out of print, all devoted to Australian literature and the book trade industry in Australia. Sample titles from Australia are the *Australian Book Review* (1961–) and the *Australian Bookman* (1905–1906). Publications from other parts of the world are noted if they feature articles and/or reviews about Australian literature. Ceased title *British Book News* (1941–1993) is an example, as it contained reviews of books produced in Australia. If secondary sources about a noteworthy periodical have been identified, they are listed in an annotation following the publication information. No library holdings are provided for the titles in the section on twentieth-century serials, so be sure to check your local library catalog or OCLC's *WorldCat* to determine where copies of a particular title might be held.

For researchers interested in learning more about the history of the little magazine in Australia during the twentieth century, it is advisable to consult several publications, two of which are written by Michael Denholm. The final chapter in *Small Press Publishing in Australia: The Late 1970s to the Mid to Late 1980s*, volume 2, lists and describes approximately 377 titles. Note that the periodicals in Denholm's work are not exclusively devoted to literature. Some will focus on fiction or poetry, but because Denholm's goal was to be comprehensive in scope, other titles specialize in subjects such as music, theater, and art. Researchers should note that since this volume begins with the late 1970s, content does not duplicate the material presented by John Tregenza or Michael Dugan (see the following). Entries are arranged alphabetically, and detailed publication histories are presented for each title. For entries featuring creative works, Denholm includes information on key authors who contributed literary content. For an illuminating, succinct history of the little magazine in Australia during the twentieth century, see Denholm's chapter in *The Book in Australia: Essays Towards a Cultural & Social History*.[5]

The first Australian little magazine published after World War I was *Vision: A Literary Quarterly* (May 1923–February 1924). In the three decades following the war, some fifty Australian little magazines appeared, few of them lasting more than four issues.[6] Tregenza's work, *Australian Little Magazines, 1923–1954: Their Role in Forming and Reflecting Literary Trends*, provides a history of these magazines, including one of the most famous in Australian literary history, the *Angry Penguins*. Of particular interest to researchers is the annotated bibliography of forty-eight core magazines that were published during this period. Only periodicals with substantial literary content are examined. The list is arranged chronologically and features names of editors and holdings information for sixteen major Australian libraries. Excluded titles are theater magazines, annual anthologies, and university and college magazines. Because Tregenza lists authors who contributed to each title, the index allows researchers to identify specific writers and the periodicals in which they published. Michael Dugan's "Little Magazines 1968–77: A Selective Checklist"[7] presents brief entries on thirty-seven additional titles that came into existence after the period covered by Tregenza. Thus, it may be useful to consult the list in Dugan's checklist, if your research takes you further into the twentieth century.

DIGITAL ARCHIVES OF AUSTRALIAN AND NEW ZEALAND PERIODICALS AND NEWSPAPERS

Australian Newspapers, 1803–1954. Canberra, A.C.T.: National Library of Australia. trove.nla.gov.au/newspaper.

Australian Periodical Publications 1840–1845. Australian Cooperative Digitisation Project. www.nla.gov.au/ferg/.
Niupepa: Māori Newspapers. Hamilton: University of Waikato. www.nzdl.org/niupepa/.
Papers Past. Wellington: National Library of New Zealand. paperspast.natlib.govt .nz/cgi-bin/paperspast.

The National Library of Australia recently released a free online service that enables full-text searching of selected early newspapers. Part of eight different collections available in *Trove*, **Australian Newspapers, 1803–1954** features papers published in each state and territory from the 1800s to the mid-1950s. The first Australian newspaper, the *Sydney Gazette and New South Wales Advertiser* (1803), is included in the service. By 2010 the National Library plans to have forty million searchable articles in the database. Because the library is devoted to making quality services available to users free of charge, searching options in *Australian Newspapers* are numerous. Researchers can browse the content of a particular title by date (year and month) or look for publications by state or territory. Content is assigned to four category types (such as advertising versus news), and users can see lists of the most frequently searched tags. "Tags" are basically subject headings, so quick links to all articles pertaining to "Japanese War Crimes" or "gold mining" are readily available. A powerful advanced search feature promotes the exploration of terms within the full text, headings, headings plus the first four lines, and captions of papers. These options are extremely important when searching such a large collection of full-text information. Limits available in the advanced search are by date, newspaper title and location, article length, article categories (advertising, family notices, news), and articles with illustrations. Results can be sorted by date—earliest first or latest first. The default sort is by relevance. Note that, on first glance, some of the images from older papers can be a bit blurry, but the software allows for zooming in on portions of the text, making it clearly legible. For more information on the wealth of information available in *Trove*, including suggestions for searching digitized maps, photographs, and other archival materials, see chapter 9.

Australian Periodical Publications 1840–1845 provides free access to digital copies of Australian serials first published between 1840 and 1845. This content is available thanks to the efforts of the Australian Cooperative Digitisation Project, a collaborative venture between the University of Sydney Library, the State Library of New South Wales, the National Library of Australia, and Monash University Library. Users can browse individual titles that are arranged alphabetically and chronologically, or search tables of contents for specific terms. So far, only one journal (*Colonial Literary Journal and Weekly Miscellany of Useful Information*) may be searched full text, but others will be available to search more extensively in the future. In addition to the more than seventy journals available in the archive, the project features scanned images of four fiction titles published during the same time period (www.nla.gov.au/acdp/fiction.html). These titles, William Harvey Christie's *A Love Story by A Bushman*, Charles Rowcroft's *Tales of the Colonies*, Thomas McCombie's *Adventures of a Colonist*, and Mary Vidal's *Tales of the Bush*, are available through *SETIS* (*Sydney Electronic Text and Image Service*) at the University of Sydney (setis.library.usyd.edu.au/oztexts/acdp.html) as transcribed text based on optical character recognition. High-resolution TIFF images of the pages are also available. For more information on the resources available through *SETIS*, see entries in chapters 8 and 10.

Niupepa: Māori Newspapers is an online collection of historic newspapers published primarily for a Māori audience between the years 1842 and 1932. The collection consists of more than seventeen thousand pages taken from thirty-four separate periodicals that were originally reproduced on microfiche by the Alexander Turnbull Library. Approximately 70 percent of the collection is written in Māori, with only 3 percent in English. Another 27 percent of the content is bilingual. Periodicals in the database fall into three main categories, including government sponsored, Māori initiated, and religious. Facsimile images of the original pages and bibliographic commentaries for each newspaper title are presented, as well as English abstracts for each issue. Content may be browsed by title or date. Keyword searching of the full-text content, English abstracts, and bibliographic details is available. More information about the history of the Niupepa Collection can be found in Jennifer Curnow, Ngapare Hopa, and Jane McRae's work, *Rere Atu Taku Manu! Discovering History, Language & Politics in the Māori Language Newspapers* (Auckland: Auckland University Press, 2002).

Papers Past comprises more than one million pages of digitized New Zealand newspapers and periodicals covering the years 1839 to 1932. Fifty-two publications from all regions of New Zealand are available to search for free. Discovering content in *Papers Past* may be achieved through searching and browsing. Searching is the most powerful way to locate information, as it allows users to enter a keyword or term and limit to a particular date range, newspaper, and a selection of three different content types—articles, advertisements, and illustration captions. Users may browse *Papers Past* by year, region, or by a specific newspaper title. Regions are divided into fourteen categories, enabling the identification of papers by area of the country. Results are best when searching for a known item, such as *Verses from Maoriland*, by Doris Wilcox (London: G. Allen, 1905). Searching the title of the novel as a phrase produces nine book reviews from a mix of early magazines and newspapers. Search terms are highlighted within the text, allowing users to easily locate the item of interest. This can save time, as several books may be reviewed in a single article.

CONCLUSION

Magazines and newspapers are important resources for the discovery of early creative works and for providing historical context for the writing of a particular author. They are also excellent sources for uncovering content valuable to literary scholarship, such as book reviews, interviews, and editorials by important Australian and New Zealand authors. The challenge to using these resources is being able to ascertain which periodicals existed during a particular time period, and even more difficult, identifying specific works in these publications that were written by or about a particular author. Fortunately, many tools are available that list and describe early periodicals. Literary scholars like Bruce Bennett, Elizabeth Webby, and Michael Denholm have published core works that describe newspapers and magazines of the nineteenth and early twentieth centuries. Further, these scholars have made great efforts to supply citation information on Australian authors' contributions to these publications. *AustLit* also plays an important role in indexing literary content from early papers and other periodicals in the database. Still, very few all-purpose indexes to newspapers exist today, making research difficult, especially without access to the sources themselves. Researchers outside Australia and New Zealand will find this particularly challenging. As more and more of the early papers and magazines are digitized by national libraries and cooperative projects between core organizations and educational institutions, locating information will become easier to manage. In the meanwhile, researchers must be prepared to consult multiple reference tools to discover information contained in magazines and newspapers. This chapter attempts to address ways in which contemporary and historical periodicals may be identified and located, as well as describe existing tools that index literary content.

NOTES

1. Phil Parkinson and Penny Griffith, *Books in Māori, 1815–1900: An Annotated Bibliography* (Auckland: Reed, 2004), 739–816.

2. Elizabeth Webby, "Before the Bulletin: Nineteenth Century Literary Journalism," in *Cross Currents: Magazines and Newspapers in Australian Newspapers*, ed. Bruce Bennett (Melbourne: Longman Cheshire, 1981), 3–4.

3. Clark Stiles, "Periodicals," in *Book & Print in New Zealand: A Guide to Print Culture in Aotearoa*, ed. Penny Griffith, Ross Harvey, and Keith Maslen (Wellington: Victoria University Press, 1997), 138–39.

4. Elizabeth Webby, "Journals in the Nineteenth Century," in *The Book in Australia: Essays Towards a Cultural & Social History*, ed. D. H. Borchardt and W. Kirsop (Melbourne: Australian Reference Publications, 1988), 43–65.

5. Michael Denholm, "The Little Magazine in the Twentieth Century," in *The Book in Australia: Essays Towards a Cultural & Social History*, ed. D. H. Borchardt and W. Kirsop (Melbourne: Australian Reference Publications, 1988), 88–95.

6. John Tregenza, *Australian Little Magazines, 1923–1954: Their Role in Forming and Reflecting Literary Trends* (Adelaide: Libraries Board of South Australia, 1964), 2.

7. Michael Dugan, "Little Magazines 1968–77: A Selective Checklist," *Australian Literary Studies* 8.2 (1977): 222–25.

Chapter Eight

Microform and Digital Collections

Microform and digital collections are primary-resource formats that are comparatively easy to locate and to use. While original texts, documents, and images can be difficult and costly to access, these handy proxies go far in equalizing the availability of otherwise out-of-reach items. With these alternatives, a researcher may look at the reproduction of a hard-to-find text without having to endure the potential expense of traveling to see the original. Today, many digital and microform products produce extremely authentic images that accurately represent the original. In spite of this authenticity in image creation, researchers often still need to travel to use the original items. Reproductions, however, arm the researcher with an advanced familiarity, allowing for a better-focused research trip and decreasing the chances of ill-fated, uninformed travels. See chapter 9 for further discussion of primary resources held in archival and manuscript collections.

Today, digital resources are increasingly commonplace and high quality, and both students and faculty logically come to expect that they will be able to locate a digital version of an item that they need for research. On the other hand, microforms, due to their unfriendly reputation, frequently send library users looking long and hard for a different format, and often for a different resource altogether. While many microform products are making the move to the digital milieu, this process is neither quick nor cheap.

In the early 1900s microforms presented what was an enduring answer to the chronic library dilemma of too little space in which to house resources. Microforms exist as reels, fiche, and cards, and one unit can hold hundreds of pages and save countless linear feet of shelf space. These reproductions also serve as preservation aids for fragile, rare, and valuable materials. The reformatted items can be reproduced and disseminated to other libraries, usually from a corporate vendor. For many researchers, the surrogates eliminate the need to use the original print items, thereby saving wear and tear on the original. Importantly, microforms have not been victim to technological obsolescence; they can be read with a light source such as a flashlight and a magnifying glass, although chances are that this approach will never be necessary. In spite of its value, the microform has not been popular with library users. It is not going away, however, and vendors are still actively developing microform collections. Many existing microform collections do not have a lucrative prospective consumer pool that would warrant the time and money needed for a vendor to digitize them, so do not expect all microforms to be available electronically any time soon. Happily, in recent years many microform reader machines have been equipped with scanners that allow researchers to easily reformat microform into electronic files. This advancement lets users create their own electronic documents to do with as they please—e-mail them, save them to USB drives, print them, etc.

If you are unfamiliar with microforms, remember that your librarians will be able to help you with the machines that enable you to read them. There are four main types of microforms. The most familiar and easy to use are microfilm and microfiche; less common and more arduous are ultra-fiche and the micro-opaque card. Microfilm will be on a reel resembling a small movie film reel; the film is threaded through the reader and projected on a viewing screen. Microfiche is a flat page of film that slides into a reader and is similarly projected. Ultra-fiche looks like shrunken microfiche. You will rarely see ultra-fiche, and it is even less often that you will see a machine that can actually read this format. Finally, there is the micro-opaque card, which is also sometimes referred to as micro-print. This is more common than the ultra-fiche, and it looks like a page of thick paper with many small page images printed on it. Readers for this format are relatively accessible and will sometimes have printers or scanners connected to them.

The digital revolution, however, can now be seen clearly in libraries, where many products that would have been microformatted years ago are instead being digitized. Some microform collections have also been digitized, and sold again, to libraries. There are two major types of digitization projects: ones run by vendors, who sell their product to libraries, and ones developed as grant- or institutionally funded projects created by faculty and librarians. Particularly in text-heavy academic areas such as literature and theater, countless digital humanities initiatives are now striving to deliver academically sound and often peer-reviewed resources to the scholarly community and beyond, free of charge.

With both microform and digital collections, discovery can be a problem for the researcher. These collections can be very large, and therefore it can be a daunting task to figure out what is actually in them. With digital collections you have the luxury of online keyword searching to help you discern their contents, and often a well-crafted Google search will lead you into a collection; projects that were developed by vendors or publishers will often include finding aids on the vendor website, a sales tool as well as a useful guide for researchers. Similarly, microform finding aids are often available on vendor websites; these are usually the same guides that accompany the microform set if a library purchases it. This relatively new service provided by vendors significantly enhances the ease with which a researcher can determine the existence of important resources. Library catalogs are also good places to look for microform and digital collections and items within those collections, but the catalogs are inconsistent in their coverage. Sometimes a library catalogs a collection as one item, and other times a library catalogs each individual item from a collection. The same is true for digital collections, if they are in a library catalog at all.

The goal of this chapter is to explore the tools that are useful for finding and using microform and digital collections of potential value for research projects in the literature of Australia and New Zealand, as well as to look at a few resources that warrant particular attention. Because many newspapers and periodicals are available digitally and in microforms, remember to take another look at chapter 7 for more information on these resources.

LOCATING MICROFORM AND DIGITAL RESOURCES

Dodson, Suzanne Cates, ed. *Microform Research Collections: A Guide.* 2nd ed. Westport, Conn.: Meckler Publishing, 1984.

Frazier, Patrick, ed. *A Guide to the Microform Collections in the Humanities and Social Sciences Division of the Library of Congress.* Washington, D.C.: Library of Congress Humanities and Social Sciences Division, 1996. Online at www.loc.gov/rr/microform/guide/ (accessed 7 January 2010).

Microform Collections. Chester, Vt.: Readex. Online at www.readex.com/readex/?content=98 (accessed 17 January 2010).

Microfilm Collection Guides. London: Adam Matthew Publications. Online at www.adam-matthew-publications.co.uk/collections_az/index.aspx (accessed 17 January 2010).

Scholarly Resources Online Guides. Detroit, Mich.: Primary Source Media, Gale-Cengage. Online at www.gale.cengage.com/psm/guides.htm (accessed 17 January 2010).

UMI Research Collections. Ann Arbor, Mich.: ProQuest. Online at www.proquest.com/en-US/catalogs/collections/rc-search.shtml (accessed 17 January 2010).

WorldCat. Dublin, Ohio: OCLC. www.oclc.org/firstsearch.

Several guides exist to help researchers navigate through microform collections. Remember that the guides are only one way to locate useful microform collections. While figuring out what is in a microform collection can be exasperating, if you find what you are seeking, the effort is worth it. Knowing that a collection exists will not help you much unless you can ascertain what is in it. The resources in this section will be a great help in this endeavor.

Over the past three decades, the Library of Congress has produced an expanding guide to microform sets it has created. Because these microform collections are held by many libraries and are also widely available through interlibrary loan, the guide has the potential to be immeasurably useful to researchers. Edited by Patrick Frazier, *A Guide to the Microform Collections in the Humanities and Social Sciences Division of the Library of Congress* has been mounted on the library's Web page, distinctly enhancing its ease of use. While the guide is not functionally searchable, you do have the option to navigate through it alphabetically by title, as well as by the two main alphabetical index sections, A through J and K through Z. In any of these sections, you can use your Web browser's *find* option to search for specific words. For example, if you searched the subject index for *Australia*, you would find an entry for *Australian Biographical Archive*. Then you could locate that full entry in the alphabetical title list, where there is further information about the collection. In this case, the resource tells you that the collection has a guide, the three-volume *Australasian Biographical Index*, and it is also indexed as part of the online subscription service *World Biographical Index*. Additionally, *Microform Research Collections: A Guide*, edited by Suzanne Cates Dodson, covers approximately four hundred collections, selectively. This resource covers important research collections that are available on microform. Cross-referenced and arranged alphabetically by title, individual entries include, when appropriate, reviews for the item, scope, and content summary. If you use this guide to locate microform collections, be advised that it is a good idea to check on whether the collection has been digitized. It is thoroughly indexed and should be consulted, in spite of its age.

Helpfully, many microform vendors have placed finding aids online, a gesture that at once advertises their collections and helps users discover them. Web searching can often uncover these collections. For example, a Google search for *Australia colonial life* will return a hit early in the list for Adam Matthew Publication's microform product titled *Australia: Colonial Life and Settlement*. This publisher makes available descriptions and content lists for all its microform products. The item list for the collection is searchable with the *find* command on your Web browser. From the Adam Matthew Web page, you have the option to look at collections alphabetically by title, or by broad subject area in the **Microfilm Collection Guides**. Keep in mind that there may be useful information about literary topics from New Zealand and Australia in collections from the nineteenth and twentieth centuries that do not appear at first to be appropriate. Use your *find* command to search the contents, and search broadly. Remember that *empire* or *imperialism* in the nineteenth century can be a good indication that Australia and New Zealand may be covered in the collection. Similarly, if you search these terms in collections and finding aids, you may also discover materials that are related to Australia or New Zealand as parts of the British Empire. The Gale-Cengage corporation also makes lists of microform content online in its **Scholarly Resources Online Guides**. While this publisher may not have as many pertinent resources, it is still worth a quick investigation. Readex's **Microform Collections** and ProQuest's **UMI Research Collections** catalogs also provide collection descriptions, but they do not offer the same depth of indexing. Of note, however, is the ProQuest *Australia and New Zealand Catalog*, more than forty pages of collection descriptions with substantive connections to these countries.

WorldCat is likely the tool that reaches farthest and offers the broadest coverage of microform resources, and it should be used in concert with other discovery tools. Keep in mind that *WorldCat* will find microform collections even if you are not necessarily looking for them. Figure 8.1 represents a *WorldCat* record for *Woman Suffrage in New Zealand* by Lady Stout. The record lets the researcher know that this is on a microfilm reel and is part of the *History of Women* series. The original publication information is given, and in the notes field is the information for the microfilm publication. Both are important for you to cite the source correctly.

The series field in figure 8.1 explains that *Woman Suffrage in New Zealand* is in the microfilm collection *History of Women*, on reel 954. For more information about the series, a title search for *History of Women* will retrieve the record represented in figure 8.2. This record will include important information, such as the editor of the collection (Miriam Young Holden) and the number of reels in the set (1,247).

There is no one best way to find a microform collection or an item within a collection, and you will often locate microforms without intending to do so. In the same vein, there is not one mega-index that you can go to for digital collections. Your library and librarians will be excellent resources for guidance and suggestions. Library Web pages frequently list open-access (free) electronic collections, in addition to those to which your library subscribes. Most library catalogs will list resources to some degree and at varying levels of detail.

Figure 8.1. Modified *WorldCat* record for *Woman Suffrage in New Zealand.* Source: *WorldCat.*

SELECTED COLLECTIONS

Australian Joint Copying Project, Microfilm of Material in the Public Record Office, London, and Manuscript Material in Other Repositories, Relating to Australia, New Zealand and the Pacific (AJCP). Canberra, A.C.T.: National Library of Australia, 1948–.

Council of Australian University Libraries. *Australasian Digital Theses Program (ADTP)*, at adt.caul.edu.au/ (accessed 16 January 2010).

Defining Gender Online. London: Adam Matthew Publications. Online at www .adam-matthew-publications.co.uk.

Eighteenth Century Collections Online (ECCO). Farmington Hills, Mich.: Thomson Gale. www.gale.com.

Empire Online. London: Adam Matthew Publications. Online at www.adam-matthew-publications.co.uk.

History of women.
Miriam Young **Holden**
1975-1979
English ◆ Book : ▦ Microform 1247 reels : ill. ; 35 mm.
New Haven, Conn. : Research Publications,

GET THIS ITEM

Availability: **FirstSearch indicates your institution owns the item.**
Libraries worldwide that own item: 54 ⬠INDIANA UNIV
◉ Search IUCAT for availability

Find Items About:

Title: **History of women.**

Author(s): Holden, Miriam Young.

Publication: New Haven, Conn. : Research Publications,

Year: 1975-1979

Description: 1247 reels : ill. ; 35 mm.

Language: English

Contents: Reels 1-934. [Printed books]--reels 935-962. [Pamphlets]--reels 963.
Photographs.--reels 964-995. Manuscripts.--reels P1-P253. Periodicals.

SUBJECT(S)

Descriptor: Women -- History.
Women -- United States -- History.

Note(s): Microfilm of selected materials on women before 1920 from the Arthur and
Elizabeth Schlesinger Library on the History of Women in America, Sophia Smith
Collection, Jane Addams Memorial Collection, the Galatea Collection, Miriam Y.
Holden Collection, Ida Rust Macpherson Collection and others.

Figure 8.2. Modified *WorldCat* record for *History of Women*. Source: *WorldCat*.

National Library of Australia. *Digital Collections*, at www.nla.gov.au/digicoll/ (accessed 16 January 2010).

National Library of Australia. *PANDORA: Australia's Web Archive*, at pandora.nla.gov.au/ (accessed 16 January 2010).

National Library of New Zealand / Te Puna Mātauranga o Aotearoa. *Digital Collections*, at www.natlib.govt.nz/collections/digital-collections (accessed 16 January 2010).

Project Gutenberg Australia, at gutenberg.net.au/ (accessed 16 January 2010).

SETIS (Sydney Electronic Text and Image Service), at setis.library.usyd.edu.au/index.html (accessed 18 January 2010).

University of Auckland. *New Zealand Electronic Poetry Centre*, at www.nzepc.auckland.ac.nz/ (accessed 18 January 2010).

University of Auckland Library. *Early New Zealand Books Project*, at www.enzb.auckland.ac.nz/ (accessed 16 January 2010).

University of Sydney Library et al. *Australian Cooperative Digitisation Project*, at www.nla.gov.au/acdp/ (accessed 16 January 2010).

University of Waikato. *New Zealand Digital Library Project*, at www.nzdl.org/cgi-bin/library.cgi (accessed 18 January 2010).

Victoria University Library. *New Zealand Electronic Text Centre*, at www.nzetc.org/ (accessed 18 January 2010).

Victorian Popular Culture. London: Adam Matthew Publications. Online at www .adam-matthew-publications.co.uk.

While knowing how to discover and locate items within a microform collection will serve you well, there is one very important collection that must be mentioned. The ***Australian Joint Copying Project, Microfilm of Material in the Public Record Office, London, and Manuscript Material in Other Repositories, Relating to Australia, New Zealand and the Pacific*** (***AJCP***) is an endeavor that began after World War II. This project created microform copies of documents associated with Australia, New Zealand, and the Pacific that were owned by British repositories and archives. Although these are not "literary" in the traditional sense, these types of primary resources are of interest to literary scholars who study the Oceanian region, in large part because the writing is still young. In recent years, cultural studies have become an important part of literary studies, and documents such as these are of principal importance. The documents held by the Public Records Office (now the National Archives) in London kept them occupied from 1948 to 1958 and resulted in more than seven thousand microfilm reels. They are arranged by the department or office from which they originated (Home Office, Colonial Office, War Office, and more). After the Public Records Office microfilming was complete, records from the British Library, the National Libraries of Ireland, Scotland, and Wales, and many other libraries, archives, and other record-laden offices were added. The project continued into 1997 with a variety of library and archives partners. The collection covers a broad historical range. It is divided into two large sections, the Public Records Office Series and the Miscellaneous Series collections from other institutions. A set of handbooks accompanies the collection so that researchers can navigate the overwhelmingly large resource.

There are few vendor-produced electronic collections that are of much use in the study of the literature of Australia and New Zealand. Other pertinent collections are the product of individual and institutional initiatives to create freely available resources online. The Gale-Cengage corporation's ***Eighteenth Century Collections Online*** (***ECCO***) offers access to thousands of digital images of 150,000 books, broadsides, and sermons published in the eighteenth century in England and its colonial territories. This is a strong source for publications that chronicle the colonization and exploration of lands touched by British imperialism. Because this collection is so broad, it is an excellent place to find works that, odds are, very few people have ever read. For example, a search for "New Zealand" will retrieve *The Travels of Hildebrand Bowman, esquire, Into Carnovirria, Taupiniera, Olfactaria, and Auditante, in New-Zealand; in the Island of Bonhommica . . .* , a lengthily titled novel that features perceptions of the recently discovered New Zealand.

ECCO's contents are based on the *English Short Title Catalogue*, which provides a canonically unbiased approach to a century of English-language publishing. *ECCO* is organized into themed sections: "History and Geography" (travel writing, biography, sports, and history); "Social Science" and "Fine Arts" (business, politics, music, the arts, and collectibles); "Medicine, Science, and Technology" (agriculture, technology, medicine, science, and cookbooks); "Literature and Language" (all genres); "Religion and Philosophy" (prayer books, Bibles, debates, and sermons); "Law" (cases, laws, and commentaries); and "General Reference," which acts as a catch-all category that takes in almanacs, directories, dictionaries, catalogs, and reference books for many professions and pastimes.

The texts in *ECCO* have been scanned from microfilm, and the text searching is based on the OCR software used on the images to enable a search engine to decipher the images and recognize the words as text. This process is not perfect, and the software will sometimes interpret words and letters incorrectly. To accommodate this possibility, the *ECCO* interface has a fuzzy-search option that widens a keyword search to near-hits as well as exact matches. For example, this option allows the search engine to consider alternative spellings and font differences (such as the long "s" that to our twenty-first-century eyes looks like an "f"). The publications are enhanced by added indexing information that incorporates, when available, such fields as author birth and death dates, title, edition, publication information, and physical description of the item.

Adam Matthew Publishing, once known predominately for its unique microfilm collections, has a few digital collections that are promising for your research if you are looking for underexplored primary resources and manuscripts. Particularly useful if you are doing work in the nineteenth century, these products include first-person impressions of the countries by travelers and explorers, letters from settlers to these countries to family at home, and initial reactions by people seeing these countries, native populations, and flora and fauna for the first time. Most appropriate is ***Empire Online***, an international collection of documents connected to empire studies. Documents in this resource come from the British Library, the Bodleian Library, the Victoria and Albert Museum, Church Mission Society Archive, the National Archives of Canada, the National Library of Australia, State Records from New South Wales, the National Library of Scotland, and the Minneapolis

Institute of Arts, among others. Document types feature journals, logs, correspondence, periodicals, diaries, government documents, missionary records, travel writing, children's literature, maps, memoirs, and more. Photographs, posters, and illustrations are also featured in this collection.

Two other collections developed by Adam Matthew are *Defining Gender Online* and *Victorian Popular Culture*, both of which similarly treat the nineteenth century. **Defining Gender Online**, covering the years 1450 to 1910, comprises pamphlets, college records and exams, commonplace books, diaries, periodicals, letters, ledgers, government papers, all genres of creative writing, and conduct literature. The collection is divided into five broad sections: "Conduct and Politeness," "Domesticity and the Family," "Consumption and Leisure," "Education and Sensibility," and "The Body." **Victorian Popular Culture** is uniquely positioned to be an indispensable resource for researching nineteenth-century popular culture. Organized into three broad areas, "Spiritualism, Sensation, and Magic"; "Circuses, Sideshows, and Freaks"; and the forthcoming "Music Hall, Theatre, and Popular Entertainment," this database presents a variety of hard-to-find primary resources that cover the growing academic interest in popular culture.

The Adam Matthew electronic resources all feature considerable contextualizing information that helpfully assists both students and scholars in searching, navigating, and making sense of these resources' contents. The collections are all augmented by introductions that preface the collection overall, as well as by scholarly essays that treat varying aspects of the broad topics listed previously. They also include, when available, chronologies, biographies, bibliographies, teaching resources, slide shows, canned popular searches, links to external resources, and alphabetical lists of names, places, and topics.

The **Australian Cooperative Digitisation Project** (also called *Ferguson 1840–45*), funded by the Australian Research Council, created *Australian Periodical Publications 1840–1845* and *Fiction 1840–1845* (see chapter 8 for more information on these projects). The project is a joint effort of the University of Sidney Library, the State Library of New South Wales, the National Library of Australia, and the Monash University Library, with support from other institutions and corporations. The fiction collection has only four titles, William Harvey Christie's *A Love Story, by A Bushman*; Thomas McCombie's *Adventures of a Colonist, or, Godfrey Arabin the Settler*; Charles Rowcroft's *Tales of the Colonies, or, The Adventures of an Emigrant*; and Mary Theresa Vidal's *Tales for the Bush*.

These titles are available from the **SETIS** (**Sydney Electronic Text and Image Service**) Web page. *SETIS* is a project based at the University of Sydney that offers open access and subscription access to full-text, historical, humanities primary resources in ten themed collections. *Australian Literary and*

Historical Texts is the largest and most inclusive of the components, featuring fiction, poetry, and plays, as well as literature of discovery, exploration, and settlement. With more than three hundred texts, this excellent collection is free online and features transcribed text as well as page images for most items. *Australian Classic Works* is a small collection of twenty-five texts that are free online and also available for purchase through the Sydney University Press print-on-demand program. The titles were selected via a survey of teachers at the university level across the country and can also be searched through the *Australian Literary and Historical Texts* interface. The selection was based on the perceived importance of a text to the cultural heritage of Australia and the need that these texts be easily accessible. The *Australian Federation Full Text Database* covers the *Debates of the Federal Conventions of the 1890s*, important foundational documents from the early years of the state. Other components are *Australian Poets: Brennan—Harford—Slessor*; *Classic Texts in Australian Taxation Law*; *Joseph Henry Maiden Botanical Texts*; *Professor John Anderson Lectures Notes and Other Writings*; *Journals of Inland Exploration*; and *First Fleet and Early Settlement*. For long-distance research, the *SETIS* databases provide unmatched texts and high-quality illustrations (particularly important for works of exploration and travel).

The National Library of Australia **Digital Collections** is a significant project to digitize selected parts of the collection in order to increase ease of access for Australians and beyond. Selecting items that are of cultural and historical significance to the country, the library is continuing to add thousands of items to the digital collections annually. There are several format groupings that comprise the NLA's *Digital Collections*. The *Books and Serials* collection currently contains close to two thousand books, serials, and ephemeral publications. This collection is searchable and also can be browsed by author, title, and date. Links from the *Digital Collections* page will take you into a catalog search that presents the list of items in the selected grouping. More than one thousand three hundred of the digitized books are Australian, and there are eight hundred that are categorized as "overseas."

Impressively, the online picture collection contains more than one hundred thousand images from the library's holdings. From the picture collections page a link will take you into the picture catalog. From there you can conduct a search or browse the online collection by creator, name, subject, series, or title. A search or browse will return a set of small images with descriptive terms accompanying each image. The descriptions include the dimensions and medium of the original work, as well as creator and date. Researchers are allowed to download images for research, but if they want to use the images for other reasons, such as in publications, they must request permission through a link on the image page.

There is also a beautiful map collection of more than eight thousand map images. This collection could be particularly useful for researchers who are writing about the early literature from Australia that is characterized by accounts of exploration and settlement. The link to "Digitised Maps" will take you to a browsable list that features a series of filters (author, subject, series, and so on) along the right side of the screen. By clicking on the map image, you will open a window with a larger map. From there you can zoom in to certain areas, examine the entire map, or print. Concise bibliographic information is at the top of the screen, and a link is provided that leads to a more robust catalog record with a detailed physical description and subject headings. Other collection topics of possible tangential interest include Australian printed music from the nineteenth and twentieth centuries and an oral history collection. The manuscripts collection will be discussed in greater detail in chapter 9. These collections are the result of great care and effort to replicate the originals effectively in digital media. The National Library of Australia *Digital Collections* have the potential to guide an exploring researcher into interesting projects or to surprise a scholar with unexpected finds.

A product started by the National Library of Australia is ***PANDORA: Australia's Web Archive*** (the name reflects the goal of the project: Preserving and Accessing Networked Documentary Resources of Australia). The project began because the developers saw the impending mass of new online publications that would need continued access and preservation. While the National Library started *PANDORA* in 1996, it is now a collaborative effort among ten libraries and cultural institutions. In addition to the National Library, the partners are the Australian Institute of Aboriginal and Torres Strait Islander Studies, the Australian War Memorial, the National Film and Sound Archive, the Northern Territory Library, the State Library of New South Wales, the State Library of Queensland, the State Library of South Australia, the State Library of Victoria, and the State Library of Western Australia.

PANDORA collects online resources that are by Australian authors, about Australia, or are otherwise meaningful or appropriate to Australia or Australians. The collections can be searched on the *PANDORA* Web page, or they can be browsed by broad subject areas including the arts, business, defense, law, health, the humanities, indigenous Australians, culture, science, sports, and travel, among others. It is also part of the *National Bibliographic Database* discussed in chapters 3 and 4.

Project Gutenberg Australia is an outgrowth of *Project Gutenberg*, which began in 1971 with a grant that funded $100 million of computer hours that had been given to Michael Stern Hart at the University of Illinois. He used the time to type in the Declaration of Independence, the American Bill of Rights, the U.S. Constitution, the Bible, Shakespeare plays, and then various classics. In 1993 there were one hundred titles in *Project Gutenberg*, and this number has grown to almost twenty thousand, all accomplished by volunteers. All *Project Gutenberg* texts are in ASCII (American Standard Code for Information Interchange) format, chosen because it is one of the most widely supported formats by text readers. The titles in *Project Gutenberg* all appear in this simple text, but it is easily converted by word processing programs to look like a more standard readable page.

The collections available through *Project Gutenberg Australia* are broad and deep. From the introductory page, you will be able to select the "Search Site" option to look for particular authors or titles. Helpfully, you also have several browsable themed collections of specifically Australian publications. The *Library of Australiana* includes both books written by Australians and about Australia. As seems to be the norm for an Australiana collection, this one proudly features creative writing as well as the culturally significant literature of travel, exploration, and settlement. *Australia's Greatest Books* contains classics based on Geoffrey Dutton's 1986 *The Australian Collection: Australia's Greatest Books*, discussed in chapter 2. This collection provides access to the titles from the list that are no longer under copyright and features many authors who were involved in early exploration of Australia. Representative titles include E. J. Banfield's *The Confessions of a Beachcomber*, David Carnegie's *Spinifex and Sand*, Edward John Eyre's *Journals of Expeditions of Discovery into Central Australia*, Ethel Pedley's *Dot and the Kangaroo*, and Watkin Tench's *A Complete Account of the Settlement at Port Jackson / A Narrative of the Expedition to Botany Bay*, among many others.

Project Gutenberg Australia has also digitized the 1949 *Dictionary of Australian Biography* by Percival Serle, covered in chapter 2. Here you can find more than one thousand biographies of influential Australians who died prior to 1942. There are several exploration sections, such as *Australian Explorers*, which is structured along a chronology with links to books. Other collection topics include land and sea explorers, exploration journals, and several links to time lines. The collection of explorers' journals offers a wealth of primary literature from the initial European visits to Australia. The *First Fleet* collection has links to journals kept by some of the officers with the first fleet that traveled to Australia from Great Britain, transporting convicts.

The ***Australasian Digital Theses Program (ADTP)*** provides access to thousands of doctoral dissertations from Australian universities. This cooperative effort is the result of a partnership spearheaded by the University of New South Wales with the University of Melbourne, the University of Queensland, the University of Sydney, the Australian National University, the Curtin University of Technology, and Griffith University. More than forty institutions now participate in the project. Because doctoral dissertations are often at the cutting edge of scholarship, and because they can be difficult to get, especially when they are not from the United States, the *ADTP* presents researchers with a large collection of scholarship that may be otherwise hard to locate. The collection can be explored with a simple keyword search or with a robust advanced search that features many options unique among database functions. You can also browse by author, title, or school/department. The default is to search for digital theses, but you can broaden the search to cover citations of theses that have not been digitized.

The *Early New Zealand Books Project* is a product of the University of Auckland Library using books from the University's Special Collections / Kohikohinga Motuhake. While the project's goal is to create a digital collection of books about New Zealand from the nineteenth century, publication dates run from 1807 to 1940. Plans for the future encompass adding more titles and adding a subject/author search function. Currently the titles are simply in a chronological list. Texts are searchable by keyword and are encoded based on the standards set forth by the Text Encoding Initiative (TEI). The project has digitized images, notably maps, and gives links to high-resolution images from the scanned pages. Like many of the Australian collections, this one also values the narrative reports of travelers, settlers, and explorers, particularly with the insight they present on early encounters with the Māori culture. An extensive index accommodates variant spellings, which is quite helpful with Māori words.

The University of Auckland also hosts the *New Zealand Electronic Poetry Centre*, a portal for poetry in New Zealand. The site includes information about authors, poetry created for the digital environment, essays and interviews with poets, poetry journals, and recordings of poems read aloud. The *New Zealand Electronic Poetry Centre* also covers poetry and digital poetry initiatives of the Pacific Islands.

The National Library of New Zealand / Te Puna Mātauranga o Aotearoa *Digital Collections* offers twelve collections of varying potential value for research into the literature of New Zealand. The *Sir Donald McLean Papers* have more than one hundred thousand pages from letters, telegrams, notebooks, and diaries from the middle decades of the nineteenth century, when McLean was an important figure in the government, particularly in relations with the Māori after the Treaty of Waitangi in 1840. You can search the entire collection or specific parts, or browse individual sets within the collection. The *Ranfurly Collection* has drawings, photographs, diaries, and reports of Lord Ranfurly, who was the governor of New Zealand from 1897 to 1904, and can be browsed or searched. The *Transactions of the Royal Society of New Zealand* has digitized the publication from 1868 to 1961. The content is predominantly scientific, but literary studies are increasingly exploring historical scientific texts with a literary or cultural studies approach. This collection would be invaluable if you were interested in the early scientific literature from New Zealand. Additional collections of potential tangential interest include *Discover*, with more than 2,500 photographs, paintings, and audiovisual files designed to support the arts component of the New Zealand school curriculum; and the *Kilbirnie-Lyall Bay Community Centre Oral History Project* has audio and video interviews of seven residents of the Wellington area as they recall the 1920s and the changes they have seen.

The National Library, with the National Digital Forum, has also developed *Matapihi*, a database that lets a user search across digital collections developed by several different organizations. Digital collection contributors include the Alexander Turnbull Library, National Library of New Zealand / Te Puna Mātauranga o Aotearoa; Archives New Zealand / Te Rua Mahara o te Kāwanatanga; Auckland Art Gallery / Toi o Tāmaki; Auckland City Libraries / Tāmaki Pātaka Kōrero; Auckland War Memorial Museum / Tamaki Paenga Hira; Christchurch Art Gallery / Te Puna o Waiwhetu; Christchurch City Libraries / Ngā Kete Wānanga o Ōtautahi; Museum of New Zealand / Te Papa Tongarewa; New Zealand Electronic Text Centre; New Zealand Film Archive / Ngā Kaitiaki O Ngā Taonga Whitiāhua; Otago Museum; Puke Ariki; *Te Ara / The Encyclopedia of New Zealand*, Ministry for Culture and Heritage; the University of Auckland Library; University of Canterbury / Te Whare Wānanga o Waitaha; and the University of Otago Library and Hocken Collections.

The Victoria University Library has created the **New Zealand Electronic Text Centre**, a digital collection that provides access to primary documents connected to the history of New Zealand and the Pacific Islands. The collection can be browsed or searched using the navigational tools on the right side of the page. You can browse through broad subject divisions: autobiography, biography, journals, and correspondence; Māori and Pacific Islands (contemporary or historical); language; literary history and criticism; literature; history; and science. The collection contains more than 1,500 literary works and more than 150 works of criticism or literary history. Users can also browse and search various individual projects, in addition to all projects together. Some of the more than thirty collections that may be particularly useful for literary research incorporate *Ancient History of the Māori*, which covers prayers, songs, and proverbs among other areas; *New Zealand Journal of Media Studies*; *New Zealand Texts Collection*, featuring both fiction and nonfiction; *Nineteenth-Century Novels Collection*, which aims is to develop a thorough representative collection of New Zealand novels from the nineteenth century and will include shorter works; *Print History Project*, 160 years of the Wellington print industry to the twenty-first century; *Sport*, a New Zealand literary journal; *New Zealand Railways Magazine*, 1926–1940, with fiction and nonfiction; *Turbine*, a twenty-first-century literary journal from the International Institute of Modern Letters at Victoria University; *Typo, A Monthly Newspaper and Literary Review,* 1887–1897; and the *William Golder Electronic Edition*, a poetry collection. The project also has a blog (nzetc.blogspot.com/) that has been updated at least twice a month in recent months. The blog makes available information about titles that have been added to the collection.

The ***New Zealand Digital Library Project*** out of the University of Waikato has as its goal the development of open-access technology that supports digital library initiatives. Several collections are listed on the Web interface, but many of them will not be overly useful for literary research. The most potential lies with the *Indigenous Peoples* collection, which has many documents about the Māori as well as Aborigines and Torres Strait Islanders, and Māori Niupepa Collection. Items in the overall collection include contemporary and historical documents, humanitarian organization information, bibliographies, and literary works through *Project Gutenberg*.

CONCLUSION

While this chapter tries to be thorough, it is the nature of electronic resources to be in a state of constant change. Those projects created by corporate vendors tend to remain stable, but content will frequently be added to some resources as well as removed. Open-access resources often exist in a difficult and uncertain situation, as funding can be transitory, and sustainability is always a concern. Open-access resources can sometimes change location, and even worse, they can be left unattended. More often now, however, you will see that large open-access resources have considerable institutional support for their ongoing existence. Remember that while the resources covered in this chapter are useful if you have a particular item for which you are searching, they are also excellent places to explore. Even the microforms are filled with potential books and other documents that you may not find otherwise. The online resources have browse functionality, and the microforms will have a guide or an online finding aid. Use them, and you may find wonderful resources that are just waiting to be discovered. With all these resources, be patient. There are many places to look, and many ways to search.

Chapter Nine

Manuscripts and Archives

A research project that incorporates manuscripts and archives can be an intellectually exhilarating and unpredictably rewarding experience. It can also be confusing, difficult, and frustrating. Your dedication to the undertaking and degree of preparation for this type of research endeavor will directly influence your ensuing degree of success. Using archives and manuscripts is becoming much easier than it once was because institutions are increasing the availability of archival and manuscript resources online. Many repositories are now digitizing parts of their collections at varying levels of quality or thoroughness. There may still be times, however, when you will be in a situation in which you need to travel to an archives or special collection to look at original documents. These institutions are markedly different from a conventional research library, and a little groundwork before you start studying at an archival or manuscript repository will go a long way toward easing the transition, positioning you for a successful experience.

Often, the collection that you want to use will unfortunately be located in far-flung regions. Even more difficult is the distinct possibility that you will find more than one collection you would like to use, and they are located nowhere near each other. As mentioned in chapter 8, traveling to other institutions can be a drain on both your finances as well as on your time, and this may be an endeavor that you are not willing to undertake. Luckily, today you can avail yourself of a few extremely helpful services that these special repositories are offering. Many institutions are digitizing their manuscripts and archival collections, so if you are fortunate enough to need something that has been converted already, then you will be able to complete a great deal of your research from home. Interlibrary loan services are also available from many of these collections, usually with considerable restrictions. Remember, however, that not all archives and manuscripts are distantly removed. Many universities in the United States support research-level libraries that have impressive collections of manuscripts and documents, as well as early editions of books and authors' papers. Even in the United States you will be able to find useful historical resources for the study of literature from Australia and New Zealand.

If you are considering the possibility of using an archival collection, you should be well prepared before arriving at the repository. Importantly, hours at many repositories are significantly more restrictive than at other libraries. It is a good idea to contact the collection administrators before you plan your trip. Frequently it will be necessary for you as a researcher to work with a librarian or archivist in order to effectively navigate a collection, and often these experts will be so familiar with their repository's holdings that they will lead you to similarly appropriate materials either in their own institution or in other external yet complementary collections. Depending on the institution, you will find certain rules in place that you have to follow in order to use the materials. It is standard practice that you will have to register as a researcher and then sign in on subsequent visits. Some institutions require that you have a letter of reference from your own library or that an individual at the institution you are visiting sponsors your visit. These institutions differ from other library collections in that you are usually not allowed to browse the shelves to locate what you need. Instead, you have to request items, and usually you will only be able to use one item at a time. You will not be allowed to take anything out of the building, and you are frequently restricted to a reading room where staff members monitor the visitors. Often, you will not be permitted to use a pen, and institutions will provide pencils. Some will let you bring in notepads, but many will supply paper for you to use. When you leave the reading room, your papers will likely be checked by staff to make certain that you are only taking out your own notes. This security is important because there are very clever people who go to great lengths to steal valuable material from archives and manuscript collections. Increasingly these institutions are allowing laptop computers into the reading rooms. Not all of these practices apply to all archives and manuscript repositories, but they do reflect the norm, so be prepared for them.

WHAT MAKES AN ARCHIVE?

Archival research is quite different from the research that you would undertake in a library, and an understanding of what you can find in an archives will be important as your research progresses. The theories behind archives and archival organization are complex, and this section cannot effectively cover all details. It will, however, briefly cover some important information. It is beneficial to understand the word: *archives* with the letter "s" is the form that is approved by the Society of American Archivists (www.archivists.org). Without the "s," the word usually operates as a verb, or is used as reference to a backup file for computer files.[1] The organization's definition, here considerably condensed, characterizes an archives as materials that have permanent significance and that were generated or received by an individual, family, or organization. These materials can include letters, contracts, ephemera, cricket bats, fishing poles, immigration papers, manuscripts . . . the list is virtually endless.

Archival organization is decidedly different from a standard library arrangement. Intellectual organization of archives groups materials from an individual collection together; for example, the papers, books, letters, manuscripts, and pictures that belonged to an author will all be listed together in a finding aid. Items connected to that author but belonging to a different collection in the same archives will often be noted on the finding aid. The physical arrangement of these items, however, will be based on the type of material. Papers and manuscripts will most likely be kept in one area of the archives, while photographs may be somewhere else where the environmental conditions are right for photographs. Home movies will be in yet another place, and so on. Because access and preservation are of the utmost importance in an archives, careful attention is paid to the physical care and location of the items, and the physical location should be clearly noted in the finding aids. Browsing the finding aids provided by the archives will be as close as you can get to browsing the archival stacks.

Until you reach the point of fairly advanced research, it is likely that you will not need to use archival resources. If, however, you are located near an archives that has appropriate holdings, then you have a perfect opportunity to venture into this type of research. As this chapter discusses, there are many archival repositories in the United States that hold papers of writers from Australia and New Zealand. Additionally, there are archival resources that include letters and documents from the early years of exploration and settlement in both countries. Archives are usually filled with resources that no one has ever investigated fully, and by undertaking this type of research you always have the chance that you could discover something new, something that no one else has detected in the past, or something that could call into question a long-held belief in the literary canon. For example, you could uncover a poetic diary kept in the margins of an account book from a trip to New Zealand, or an unknown play that was hidden among records for a colonial theater in Australia. This is the fun part—knowing that one small photo, illustration, or scrap of paper could push your project into another realm of discovery.

Not only is there the potential of finding new material, but also the potential that you will see something that maybe hundreds of others have seen but not understood. Your background and knowledge can bring a fresh interpretation or recognition to an accepted history.

ARCHIVAL RESEARCH: HOW TO PREPARE

Once the decision is made, you need to do some preliminary work before heading to an archives. Early on, it is a good idea to make sure that you are not visiting an archival collection to look at resources that are accessible elsewhere with fewer restrictions. Often, books included in archival collections will be available on the shelves of your library or through interlibrary loan services, and either one is easier and less expensive than archival use. Remember that for years microforms have been a worthy surrogate media for manuscripts and other papers, and now it is not uncommon to find archival resources on digital media (see chapter 8). Do not waste valuable archives research time on items you can find elsewhere, unless you have already looked at the reproduction and decided that you must see the original document. It is also important to be aware of exactly what you need to see from a collection. Use the finding aids created by the institution in order to prioritize what you need to see. Time may not allow for you to look at everything in a collection.

Now, most archival repositories have some type of presence on the Internet, and you should take advantage of the information provided to potential researchers. You will be able to find this information for many institutions on their Web pages, and you should be prepared for the policies and procedures of the institution before you arrive. Expect to be required to leave your bags (including computer cases and shells, purses, briefcases) and outerwear in lockers outside the reading room. If this is a problem for you, do not bring anything that you are unwilling to store. Do not try to beg an exception. Rules are in place to protect the collections, and visitors have to abide by the rules if they want to use the collections. Be aware that you may have to wait to receive the items you request. Once you make a request, then someone working for the archives has to retrieve the item, and depending on the staffing and number of active researchers, this can take some time.

It is a smart move to contact an archival institution before you arrive. As mentioned previously, the staff is usually very helpful and extremely familiar with the holdings. Contacting the institution before you arrive will give you the chance not only to talk with staff, but also to be connected with the person or people who are best suited to help with your research. Archives often have uncataloged collections, and conversations with staff may be the only way you would know about these collections. Similarly, they will be able to tell you about collections at other institutions that might be of use to you.

There are a few additional realities of archival research that are significantly different enough from traditional library research to warrant mentioning. It is easy for an enthusiastic researcher to become sidetracked with all the potentially interesting material that one may find in an archival collection, especially if it has a minimal finding aid. In this type of situation you could spend a great deal of time looking for something that logically should be in the collection but is not. Looking this closely, however, can lead either to distraction and wasted time and effort or to unexpected new directions for your research. While potential distraction can monopolize your time, so too can the effort you may have to put forth in using the items you request. Much of what is held in an archives will be old and fragile, so you will need to take care with the physical items so as not to damage them. Some items will already be damaged due to age and use and therefore can be difficult to decipher. Occasionally, repositories will have created surrogates either on microformat or paper, and you may be asked to accept those instead of originals. Rarely will you be able to scan or photocopy items yourself, but rather you will have to order reproductions. All of this is time-consuming, so be prepared; care and patience are necessary for working with archival materials. Also, be open to new directions that you may discover while using these sources.

ARCHIVES AND THEIR POLICIES

Not all archives will have the same policies and procedures, but similarities exist across most. Looking at two specific examples will convey a sense of what you might expect to encounter. Both the University of Texas's Harry Ransom Humanities Research Center (www.hrc.utexas.edu) and the Special Collections of the Paterno Library at Pennsylvania State University (www .libraries.psu.edu/psul/speccolls/rare_books.html) have strong manuscript collections connected to Australian writers, so they will be appropriate to look at here. Both are open to the public and welcome researchers from around the world.

The Harry Ransom Center has a narrative guide to the collections that is available both in print and online from their Web page, as well as a select sample of their collections digitized and available online. The finding aids represent collections added since 1990, and for those cataloged before 1990 you will need to contact staff at the library. On the "Using the Collections" page, the Harry Ransom Center explains that before using the collection, users must register, present identification, and watch a demonstration about the center and how to handle fragile and valuable materials. Users have to create a research account through which they can request materials. The Harry Ransom Center has placed its policies and forms online (copyright procedures, use of proxy readers, reading room rules, and exhibit loan requirements), along with information about fees associated with duplication and publication of materials from the collection. Importantly, hours of operation are posted online, and special collections usually have markedly fewer operational hours than traditional open stacks libraries. The Harry Ransom Center also closes during intersession times. Be sure to check with any special collection to avoid visiting during a week in which the library is closed.

Similarly, the Eberly Family Special Collections Library in the Paterno Library at Pennsylvania State University provides information about disability access, hours, and location, in addition to useful advice about parking, public transit, visitor housing, and places to eat near the collections. The registration process includes presenting identification and storing belongings in keyed lockers. Researchers have to show identification again as they stop at the reference desk for a research consultation and begin requesting items. The Web page suggests that traveling researchers contact the library staff before beginning the trip. There is a series of rules for handling the material, and it is pointed out that older and extremely fragile materials may be replaced with copies. The Pennsylvania State University Special Collections Library states in many places on its website that it is useful for potential researchers to consult with staff before undertaking the trip to the library, and staff e-mails are available on most pages throughout the site. Keep in mind that most librarians and curators at archives and special collections are truly happy to help researchers use their materials.

LOCATING RELEVANT ARCHIVES AND MANUSCRIPTS

Albinski, Nan Bowman. *Australian Literary Manuscripts in North American Libraries: A Guide*. Canberra, A.C.T.: Australian Scholarly Editions Centre, ADFA, and the National Library of Australia, 1997.

Ash, Lee. *Subject Collections: A Guide to Special Book Collections and Subject Emphases as Reported by University, College, Public, and Special Libraries and Museums in the United States and Canada*. New Providence, N.J.: Bowker, 1993.

National Historical Publications and Records Commission. *Directory of Archives and Manuscript Repositories in the United States*. Phoenix, Ariz.: Oryx Press, 1988.

As is true with microforms and digital resources, there is no one particular foolproof method for locating archival or manuscript collections. Since collections are often assembled piecemeal by individuals with particular interests, and complementary resources can be in distant collections, certain complexities are associated with locating and accessing the resources you may need. Conversely, there are also many collections of authors' papers that have been carefully maintained by either the author, or a manager, agent, or other person close to the writer. There are several tools a researcher can use to determine the existence and location of archival and manuscript collections, and it is likely that you will be best served using a broad combination of them. Conveniently, many of the useful guides and directories are easily accessible online through the national governments and several universities in Australia and New Zealand.

Nan Bowman Albinski's print guide, *Australian Literary Manuscripts in North American Libraries: A Guide*, is a thorough overview of Australian manuscripts available in the United States and Canada. She suggests that American repositories are underexplored for their connections to Australian literature. In particular, the papers that belong to agents and publishers should be of interest to researchers. Her book is arranged alphabetically in one list that includes authors, editors, journals, and associations that are either Australian or have strong ties to Australia. The resource uses Australian in a broad sense, referring to natural-born Australians as well as settlers and visitors who were significantly influenced by their Australian experiences. Similarly, the concept of "literary" reaches beyond the traditional to include history and some writings in the social sciences. Individual entries vary in length depending on the amount of material held and the number of different institutions that have archival collections for the particular author or subject. Entries comprise a short description of the types of items within a collection—sometimes only one letter, and other times comprehensive lists of manuscripts, photos, contracts, and so on. An extensive introduction provides details on the types of collections covered in this volume: single author, American publishers and agents, British publishers and agents, editors, literary friendships, and other collections. A useful list of abbreviations follows the introduction. Before the alphabetical list begins, an annotated page explains how to read the individual entries, and a researcher will be well advised to mark this page for future reference. In addition to American holdings, the entries make reference to the major Australian holdings. Entries are helpfully cross-referenced to each other. This volume is an extremely useful resource, in spite of its age. Although changes in archival collections are slow, they do happen; for example, Pennsylvania State University's collection is listed as being in the Pattee Library, but renovations and additions in 2000 resulted in the special collections being relocated to the new Paterno Library.

There are a few noteworthy guides to archives and manuscript repositories in the United States that include some resources pertaining to the literature, history, and culture of Australia and New Zealand. *Subject Collections: A Guide to Special Book Collections and Subject Emphases as Reported by University, College, Public, and Special Libraries and Museums in the United States and Canada* began publication in 1958 and is a longstanding and thorough compilation of subject-centric collections, with the seventh edition appearing in 1993. The descriptive entries in this compilation are completed by librarians who are familiar with the collections and institutional priorities. When an institution does not return the survey for an updated entry, the publishers simply use the old text and include a note letting the user know that this particular description is from the earlier edition.

The most recent edition, although technically fairly dated, provides information of 65,818 collections held at 5,882 different institutions. Entries are arranged alphabetically by subject and then geographically by U.S. state or Canadian province within the larger subject division, with helpful cross-references to guide your navigation of the more than two-thousand-page resource. Within the entry you will find a concise overview of each individual collection, details on formats, and addresses and other contact information such as phone and fax numbers and Web and e-mail addresses—which may well have changed since the book was published. Most useful entries will be found under the broad topics of Australia and New Zealand. Subheadings include general, description and travel, authors, literature, music, discovery and exploration, ethnology, government publications, history, politics and government, Aborigines, authors, folklore, languages and literature, and law.

The *Directory of Archives and Manuscript Repositories in the United States*, published by the National Historical Publications and Records Commission, is another older but still potentially useful resource to consult. This volume is arranged alphabetically by institution, and it includes more than four thousand repositories. As with the preceding *Subject Collections* volume, the contents of this volume are dependent upon the participating institutions' responses to the call for information. Entries comprise the name of the institution, mailing and street address, and phone number; because of the date of publication, there is no Internet information (Web addresses, e-mail contacts). Useful entries for New Zealand and Australian literature are not abundant, but some small collections might be valuable, such as an oral history from New Zealand and other Pacific Island nations regarding the Māori, and missionary and church records connected to travels in Australia.

Two important resources that you should make sure to check if you are researching specific authors are the *Dictionary of Literary Biography* series and the *Dictionary of Australian Biography* that were covered in chapter 2. Both these resources usually contain information about manuscript and personal papers collections in their bibliographies. Additionally, remember to be mindful of citations and references to archival collections as you proceed in your research. You will quite likely encounter mention of letters, papers, and more as you delve into the history of an author or a particular work.

WEBSITES FOR LOCATING ARCHIVES AND MANUSCRIPT COLLECTIONS

Abraham, Terry. *Repositories of Primary Sources*, at www.uidaho.edu/special-collections/Other.Repositories.html (accessed 25 May 2010).

Alexander Turnbull Library, National Library of New Zealand. *Tapuhi*, 2009, at www.tapuhi.natlib.govt.nz (accessed 2 February 2010).

Archive Finder. Ann Arbor, Mich.: ProQuest Information and Learning Co. www.archives.chadwyck.com/

ArchiveGrid. Dublin, Ohio: OCLC. www.archivegrid.org/web/index.jsp.

Archives New Zealand, n.d., at www.archives.govt.nz (accessed 2 February 2010).

Archives New Zealand. *The Community Archive*, 2009, at thecommunityarchive.org.nz.

ArchivesUSA. Ann Arbor, Mich.: ProQuest Information and Learning Co. www.archives.chadwyck.com (accessed 2 February 2010).

Australian Society of Archivists Inc. *Directory of Archives*, n.d., at www.archivists.org.au/directory-of-archives (accessed 2 February 2010).

Hocken Library, University of Otago. *Hakena*, n.d., at hakena.otago.ac.nz/nreq/Welcome.html (accessed 2 February 2010).

Library of Congress. *Index to Personal Names in the National Union Catalog of Manuscript Collections, 1959–1984*. Alexandria, Va.: Chadwyck-Healey, 1988.

———. *Index to Subjects and Corporate Names in the National Union Catalog of Manuscript Collections, 1959–1984*. Alexandria, Va.: Chadwyck-Healey, 1994.

———. *National Union Catalog of Manuscript Collections* (*NUCMC*). Washington, D.C.: Library of Congress, 1961.

———. *National Union Catalog of Manuscript Collections* (*NUCMC*) at www.loc.gov/coll/nucmc/oclcsearch.html (accessed 25 May 2010).

National Archives. *ARCHON*, n.d., at www.nationalarchives.gov.uk/archon/ (accessed 15 March 2010).

National Archives of Australia. *Australian Security Intelligence Organisation* (*ASIO*), n.d., at www.naa.gov.au/about-us/publications/fact-sheets/fs69.aspx (accessed 2 February 2010).

National Inventory of Documentary Sources in the UK and Ireland (*NIDS*), Teaneck, N.J.: Chadwyck-Healey, 1983–.

National Library of Australia. *Trove*, at trove.nla.gov.au (accessed 28 January 2010).

National Library of Australia. *Catalogue*, n.d., at catalogue.nla.gov.au (accessed 2 February 2010).

State Library of New South Wales. *PICMAN: An Index to Pictures and Manuscripts*, 2007, at acms.sl.nsw.gov.au/search/SimpleSearch.aspx (accessed 2 February 2010).

University of Queensland. *Fryer Library Finding Aids*, 2010, at www.library.uq.edu.au/fryer/manuscripts (accessed 2 February 2010).

University of Western Australia. *Guide to Australian Literary Manuscripts*, n.d., at findaid.library.uwa.edu.au (accessed 2 February 2010).
Victoria University of Wellington. *New Zealand Literary Archive,* n.d., at www .victoria.ac.nz/library/collections/jcbr/archives.aspx#literary (accessed 2 February 2010).

Currently, most archives and special collections have websites through which researchers can access information on use and contents of a collection. The thoroughness of the websites will run the gamut from extreme detail to little more than contact information, depending on the size, staffing, and funding of the institution. This section will discuss a few of the most useful guides that will help you discover Web resources provided by repositories.

Developed by the National Library of Australia, ***Trove*** comprises papers and records (letters, diaries, and other archival materials), photographs, maps, sheet music, recordings, newspapers, published books and theses, reports, data, conference proceedings, and more. Some of the contents include the full text, while elsewhere you are provided citations and location information. *Trove* searches forty-five million records from the National Library as well as the *Australian National Bibliographic Database* (see chapter 3), *Pictures Australia* (see chapter 8), *Music Australia* (see chapter 8), *Australian Research Online*, as well as *Project Muse, PubMed, Hathi Trust* (a collaborative digital repository that currently has over twenty-five U.S. universities and libraries participating), and other international Web resources. Of special note is that *Trove* encompasses the former *Register of Australian Archives and Manuscripts* (*RAAM*), which was until 2010 a separate online database from the National Library but conveniently has been absorbed into *Trove*. Full text is searched for *Australian Newspapers, PANDORA*, the *Internet Archive*, the tables of contents made available through the Library of Congress, and the National Library's manuscript finding aids.

A simple search for *Botany Bay* will retrieve a variety of books, journals, articles, photos, illustrations, newspaper articles, maps, recordings, archived websites, and archival resources. Each individual record can represent one or many items. A book that has several editions will be represented by one record, but once you access that record you will see all the various editions. The search for *Botany Bay*, for example, returns citations for twelve editions of John Lang's *Botany Bay, or, True Tales of Early Australia*. The records for the individual volumes indicate where each volume is held and if it is available online (often indicated rather uncertainly as "possibly available"). The same search also provides the citation and holdings information for 122 archival items, such as Richard Atkins's unpublished *Journal of a Voyage to Botany Bay and South America, 1791–1810*. Any search will look through all the divisions of material unless you select only one format to search. For archival material, select "Diaries, Letters, Archives" from the introductory page.

The University of Western Australia hosts the ***Guide to Australian Literary Manuscripts***, an outstanding resource that is directed pointedly at archival research for literature studies. It makes available electronic finding aids for more than eighty collections of literary archival holdings. This free resource can either be searched or browsed; the simplest approach to explore the finding aids is the alphabetical browse option that allows you to look at a lengthy list of authors. You will immediately see the alphabetical author list when you open the guide (by clicking on "open the guide"). The interface does appear dated, but the information it offers is inestimably important to archival literary research. If, for example, you are interested in the papers of Peter Carey, then you would logically click on his name. The next screen that appears tells you that the University of Queensland holds the Carey papers and provides a Web address, e-mail, and mailing address/location for the collection. The split-screen window has navigational elements on the left side and content on the right. You can move forward or backward one page at a time by using the arrows on the right side. You can also select a specific part of the finding aid by using the navigational headings on the left side of the screen. The first screen of the finding aid gives the name of the collection and the holding library or archives. Usually, a summary screen follows, with a brief abstract and information regarding the size of the collection. Information that follows can include the collection's scope, biographical notes, notes on the arrangement of the collection, access and use permissions, citation preferences, and finally a list of folders and items in the collection.

The database has a small search box at the bottom of the screen. From the initial screen with the alphabetical list, you can type in a term, or terms, and search the entire database. If you search for the word *script*, you would retrieve a list of 186 hits that appears in the right side of the split screen. Clicking on any item in the list will take you to where the word appears in a finding aid, while maintaining the navigation screen on the left (in which the other hits in the collection are noted). If you are looking at a specific collection's finding aid, you can search within that collection. Buttons at the bottom of the screen indicate that you can select certain parts of a collection finding aid to export or print, but copying and pasting seems to work much better. While this resource does not give you full-text access to archives and manuscripts, it is one of the most useful resources you will find for locating and ascertaining the content of literary manuscript collections. Included with the *Guide to Australian Literary Manuscripts* is an electronic version of *Western Australian Writing: An On-line Anthology*, which gives users access to the complete content of this anthology.

In addition to these large, overarching guides that are designed to bring together many archival and manuscript repositories across Australia, there are also several smaller, institution-specific collections of finding aids. These guides will continue to be important because you cannot rely on the completeness of the larger guide aggregators. Institutions update their finding aids regularly, but the larger sites may not always be up to date with the most recent additions from the participating institutions.

The National Library of Australia's *Catalogue* searches more than half of the library's finding aids in addition to the cataloged collections. After running a search in the catalog, you will see an option to narrow the search by format, such as manuscripts and online resources. The National Archives of Australia has a unique collection of *Australian Security Intelligence Organisation* (*ASIO*) files that were kept on authors and literary groups, in addition to others. *ASIO* began keeping these records in 1949, and several of these were released in 1983 under the Archives Act. While many of these files have not yet been released, the collection at the National Archives can be useful. Literary groups covered feature the Australian Book Society, the Left Book Club, the Realist Writers Group, and many others. More than twenty twentieth-century authors are represented in this collection. The University of Queensland's Fryer Library provides a list of finding aids to hundreds of manuscript collections through the *Fryer Library Finding Aids*. The collections can be browsed by the topics of Australian literature and Australian poetry. The State Library of New South Wales has developed *PICMAN: An Index to Pictures and Manuscripts*. It encompasses pictures and manuscripts that the library added to its holdings after 1992. Finally, the Australian Society of Archivists Inc. produces a *Directory of Archives* that is available on the society's website. An extension of the 1992 print edition, the Web version is updated by the society when it receives changes from the archival collections in the list. A lengthy inventory, the directory can be browsed alphabetically by the name of the repository. It can also be searched by keyword. Individual records for archives have, when available, contact information and location, opening hours, collection focus, major holdings, website address, and titles of guides to specific collections.

New Zealand also has a healthy combination of guides to archives and manuscript repositories and guides created by individual institutions to aid researchers in navigating their own collections. The most far-reaching of the guides is *The Community Archive*, earlier called the *National Register of Archives and Manuscripts*. The history of this project dates to 1954 with the publication of the *Union Catalogue of New Zealand and Pacific Manuscripts in New Zealand Libraries. The Community Archive* is the cooperative product of a partnership between the New Zealand Society of Archivists, the Archives and Records Association of New Zealand, the Library and Information Association of New Zealand Aotearoa (LIANZA), the National Library of New Zealand, and Archives New Zealand. Contributors can add and edit descriptive records to highlight their collections. Because *The Community Archive* is open to contributors adding their own collection, this resource can act as a discovery tool for collections that you may otherwise never find.

Users can browse *The Community Archive* by selecting one of the categorized collections: subject, place, people, contributor, and tag. If you selected to browse *subject*, you would be able to navigate through an alphabetical list of broad subjects, including literature. Within the literature category are subcategories for books and writing. The 124 items under the broad term of literature include papers of literary authors, as well as records, diaries, and correspondence of others. The main list gives a brief description of collections, and the complete records offer information on the individual, the range of the collection, links to the holding institution, and valuable links to other related collections. This database has a feature that you will be seeing more of in the future—the ability to browse by tags added by users. If you select to browse by tags, you will retrieve a constantly changing alphabetical list of descriptive terms added by users. Terms in smaller font are searched less frequently, while large and colored fonts represent more sought-after terms. This feature allows for user-identified interconnectivity among collections that may not have been realized by those who officially add and describe collections. Although user-added tags are not likely the only way you will want to explore this database, by using this option you may encounter resources that you would not come across otherwise. Users can also search the database by keyword, contributor, medium, year, and type.

Archives New Zealand houses the archives of the New Zealand government. Starting with establishment of a British government in 1840, the records represent a broad array of subjects connected to the culture, history, and government of New Zealand. The national office is located in Wellington, with regional offices in Auckland, Christchurch, and Dunedin. In addition to governmental records, the national office holds genealogical records, immigration records, and coroners' records, among others. While on the surface these offices may seem to hold only government records, there are indeed collections of interest to literary research. A search of the catalog *Archway* (www.archway.archives.govt.nz) will reveal many potentially important collections. A simple search of the word *literary* retrieves more than seven hundred records, including an investigation on literary patronage; and a search for "Mansfield" retrieves records for a memorial minute book and for many Katherine Mansfield memorials across the country, in addition to trustees' minutes for a Mansfield memorial fellowship. *Archway* includes 1.2 million records from government offices, but there is no available online full-text content.

The Alexander Turnbull Library collections at the National Library of New Zealand include a large assortment of manuscripts created independently of government offices. The *Tapuhi* database will search these unpublished resources held by the National Library. From the *Tapuhi* page, you can select to search the Manuscripts and Archives Collections; Drawings and Prints, Ephemera and

New Zealand Cartoon Archive Collections; Photographic Collections; Combined Pictorial Collections; or Combined Collections. Although its appearance and functionality are dated, *Tapuhi* is packed with records that lead researchers to useful resources. Once you choose the collection you want to search, then you will have to select the type of search: broad, title, record number, language, subject, date, name, place, descriptive notes, and Iwi/Hapu (for searching Māori tribes and subtribes). A broad search for fiction will retrieve records for Ngaio Marsh, Frank Sargeson, and Katherine Mansfield, in addition to many other writers, organizations, institutions, and offices. A search on fiction as a subject will take you to a classified list from which you can pick broader terms such as prose literature or narrower terms such as love stories and historical fiction. Records for individual items will provide the record title, collection, restrictions, physical description (often now electronic files), and, when available, links to the item. *Hakena*, the catalog for the Hocken Library collections at the University of Otago, searches exactly like *Tapuhi* and presents results in the same format. A smaller collection, the Hocken Library nevertheless has strong holdings in the literature of New Zealand. The **New Zealand Literary Archive** is located at the Victoria University of Wellington, and it collects the papers of authors connected to the university. Small, it nevertheless holds papers of Jenny Bornholdt, Alistair Te Ariki Campbell, Patricia Grace, and Witi Ihimaera. Most of the major universities have archival repositories, some of which are also in the *Community Archive*. Although this chapter has mentioned several university archives, it is by no means exhaustive. Because the *Community Archive* is not a complete inventory of all the possible archives in New Zealand, you may also want to explore the archives at individual universities.

The online resources covered so far lead you to archives in Australia and New Zealand, and the distance between a researcher in the United States and these repositories can often be insurmountable. There are, however, resources held in U.S. archives and manuscript repositories, and these are considerably easier to access. Similar to the *National Union Catalog* (see chapter 3), the **National Union Catalog of Manuscript Collections** (**NUCMC**) is a multi-volume and confusingly difficult set of books that for years were the best method to discern what manuscripts were held by libraries and archives in the United States. The print volumes were published from 1959 to 1993, with one thousand four hundred institutions and seventy-two thousand collections represented. The set has two indexes: **Index to Personal Names in the National Union Catalog of Manuscript Collections, 1959–1984** and **Index to Subjects and Corporate Names in the National Union Catalog of Manuscript Collections, 1959–1984**, with 1985 and 1986 having their own indexes.

Now, however, the *NUCMC* volumes are searchable via OCLC's *World-Cat* through an open-access service in cooperation with the Library of Congress. From the "Simple Search Form" of this free resource you can search for Sylvia Ashton-Warner, for example, and the results screen will present six resources from the *NUCMC*. The fifth record represents the Sylvia Ashton-Warner collection. The subscription *WorldCat* (see chapter 2) also has some of the *NUCMC* records and includes holdings information; it does not include the complete *NUCMC*, but it does have other archival materials not present in the *NUCMC*. If you have access to the subscription *WorldCat*, you will be best served to search both resources. These resources have similar but not identical contents, so a keyword search in *WorldCat* limited to archival material will return comparable, but not the same, results as the OCLC *NUCMC* search. Figure 9.1 represents the *WorldCat* record for the Sylvia Ashton-Warner collection via the Library of Congress gateway. This record provides the user with the same type of information that is in the subscription version of *WorldCat*. Along with a short note on the holdings, the record will usually

Author: Ashton-Warner, Sylvia.
Title: Sylvia Ashton-Warner collection, 1929-1972.
Description: 34.5 linear ft.
Notes: In part, copies.
              New Zealand author, poet, and teacher; b. 1908; d. 1984.
              Manuscripts, correspondence, printed material, notebooks, diaries, professional
              material, illustrations, financial material, audiotapes, photographs, and memorabilia.
              Includes material regarding the Aspen Community School
              Teaching Center.
              Finding aid in the repository.

Subjects: Blaustein, Julian -- Correspondence.
          Gottlieb, Robert, 1931- -- Correspondence.
          Huxley, Julian, 1887-1975 -- Correspondence.
          Marsh, Ngaio, 1895-1982 -- Correspondence.
          McCall, Monica -- Correspondence.
          Mitgang, Herbert -- Correspondence.
          Paton, Alan -- Correspondence.
          Read, Herbert Edward, Sir, 1893-1968 -- Correspondence.
          Read, Margaret Ludwig, Lady -- Correspondence.
          Zanuck, Darryl Francis, 1902-1979 -- Correspondence.
          New Zealand literature -- 20th century.
          New Zealand poetry -- 20th century.
          New Zealand literature -- Women authors.
          New Zealand poetry -- Women authors.
          Women authors, New Zealand -- Diaries.
          Location: Boston University, Howard Gotlieb Archival Research Center
                    (Boston, Mass.).
Control No.: ocm70978841

Figure 9.1. Modified *WorldCat* record for Sylvia Ashton-Warner collection, 1929–1972. Source: *NUCMC* via OCLC *WorldCat* / Library of Congress.

list extensive subject headings that characterize the contents of the collection. This particular record includes names of many people with whom Sylvia Ashton-Warner corresponded, as well as other broad headings that describe both her and her work.

A thorough Web guide to archives worldwide, *Repositories of Primary Sources* has been developed under the supervision of the University of Idaho Special Collections by Terry Abraham. Although the list for American and Canadian sites is considerably more extensive, the international sites for Pacific nations are still useful. From the front page, select "Asia and the Pacific" to retrieve a list of archives arranged alphabetically by country, and by repository name within each country. Australia and New Zealand are the best represented, but there are other Pacific islands that could be of interest as your research progresses. One caveat should be mentioned regarding this site: not all links are current. If you hit a link that takes you to an error page, simply shorten the URL until you get to the institutional or organizational page and navigate from there.

There are also a couple of subscription-based resources that will help researchers locate archival repositories. Frequently a library will subscribe to one of them, but not both. *Archive Finder* is an online product that combines *ArchivesUSA* and the *National Inventory of Documentary Sources in the UK and Ireland (NIDS)* index. *ArchivesUSA* includes listings for more than five thousand institutions and more than one hundred sixty thousand collections of archival and manuscript materials in the United States, and the *National Inventory* index is a guide to a microfiche collection of finding aids to collections in repositories in the United Kingdom and Ireland. It also includes the *NUCMC* from 1959 to 2006, contact and location information for repositories, and links to finding aids when available.

ArchiveGrid, an OCLC product, provides access to finding aids for close to one million collection descriptions from more than 2,500 libraries, archives, museums, and other cultural institutions. Coverage is international, and the national libraries of Australia and New Zealand are both contributing institutions. In addition to these institutions, there are potentially thousands of collections that could be useful for a scholar researching the literature of either country. With the proliferation of free online finding aids such as the ones discussed previously, this resource and *Archive Finder* are more a luxury than a necessity. The convenience of being able to search across thousands of repositories at once, however, can make your research much easier. To search *ArchiveGrid* you enter terms into one simple search screen. In order to craft an advanced search in this database, you may be best served to review the section in chapter 1 about constructing Boolean searches and to look at the database search tips page. *ArchiveGrid* uses some unique syntax and symbols for commands in the search. Read the search tips and refer to them frequently as you use the database. Once you find a collection of interest, clicking on the title will open a page for the holding institution. From there you can navigate through the finding aid as well as the information about using the collection at the institution.

Researchers should also be aware of the National Archives of the United Kingdom. Here you can find records pertaining to Australia and New Zealand and their national relationships to the United Kingdom. Collections such as *Transportation to Australia 1787–1868* have great potential for researchers interested in Antipodean history, culture, and literature. The National Archives also has a directory called ***ARCHON***. This directory is a searchable and browsable compilation of archival repositories that have holdings listed in the indexes of the *National Register of Archives*.

CONCLUSION

If you have the opportunity to incorporate archives and manuscripts into your research, you also have the potential to expand your work into areas that may be as yet unexplored or underexplored. Using personal papers and manuscripts presents a researcher with the possibility of new discoveries. The early steps of archival research have been simplified as a result of the increasing number of finding aids that can be found online. A secondary effect, however, is that there are so many promising places to explore that you can lose time just looking around. Remember that diversion has long been a part of the research experience, and that exploring possibilities online may lead you to new resources. Archival research is not appropriate to all levels of student or scholar, but if you have easy access to archival collections, it would be worth a look. The decision is yours as to how deep you want to delve into these types of resources.

NOTE

1. Richard Pearce-Moses, *A Glossary of Archival and Records Terminology*, www.archivists.org/glossary/term_details.asp?DefinitionKey=156.

Chapter Ten

Web Resources

Previous chapters have presented a variety of Internet resources of value to those studying Australian and New Zealand literature. While some of these materials are free of charge to the user, such as national union catalogs and selected digitized issues of older newspapers and magazines, other tools are accessible only through a subscription service, such as *AustLit* and the *MLA International Bibliography*. Even though copyright restrictions prevent many materials from becoming freely accessible on the Web, more and more content is being scanned and digitized for public consumption. While the Web cannot deliver all the information needed for your research, it can be an effective tool for locating certain materials. This chapter focuses on publicly available Internet sites such as scholarly gateways, electronic text archives, author websites, and a sampling of cultural and historical resources of interest to scholars of Australian and New Zealand literature. Remember that while quality content does exist on the Internet, there are many sites that are less reliable. To ensure that you are selecting only the best, most authoritative resources, look carefully at the websites in question and keep the following criteria in mind:

Authority. Can you identify the author or sponsor of the site? Check to see if the site is based at an academic or government institution. If it is hosted by an individual, can you locate information about the author, such as academic credentials, which will indicate that the person is qualified or has expertise in the field?

Currency. Can you easily determine the last time the site was updated, or if it is maintained on a regular basis? This can be extremely important if the content you are seeking is time-sensitive.

Scope/Audience. What is the subject matter and range of coverage? Also, it is important that you obtain a sense of the audience targeted by the website.

Is the content intended for high school students, college students, or another group altogether?

Objectivity. Does the material covered reflect any particular bias on the part of the author? If so, does that bias affect the overall use or value of the website?

Accuracy. How reliable is the information presented in the website? Can you verify the material in other resources? Does the author cite sources so you can verify them?

While these criteria are particularly important when researching information on the Web, they can also be used to evaluate other resources you may be considering for your project.

SCHOLARLY GATEWAYS

Anglistik Guide, at www.anglistikguide.de/ (accessed 14 February 2010).
Australian e-Humanities Gateway, at vega.library.usyd.edu.au/_ehum2/public/ (accessed 21 February 2010).
Intute, at www.intute.ac.uk/ (accessed 14 February 2010).
Te Puna Web Directory, at webdirectory.natlib.govt.nz/ (accessed 5 January 2010).
Zeroland, at www.zeroland.co.nz/literature.html (accessed 21 February 2010).

Scholarly gateways can be extremely useful tools for navigating the world of Internet information. Because they are designed to capture and organize the best sites available on a particular topic, using one can save considerable time and eliminate much of the guesswork involved in researching materials on the Web. Especially beneficial are guides created by scholars or individuals with an in-depth knowledge of a particular subject, as these will incorporate only the most appropriate content. Further, gateways that are maintained on a regular basis are the most effective to use, as they ensure the discovery of up-to-date information and eliminate frustrating encounters with dead links. As you become more experienced in using scholarly gateways, you will notice no two are exactly alike. The organization, searchability, and scope of subjects covered vary greatly from one tool to the next. The gateways described here are particularly useful when researching Australian and New Zealand literature, history, and culture. All are created and hosted by research institutions or, in the case of *Zeroland*, an individual with an educational background in literature. Other gateways to Web resources exist, but if you decide to use them, be sure to investigate the quality and reliability of the tools before dedicating a great deal of time to searching their content.

Anglistik Guide is a subject gateway to scholarly Internet resources on Anglo-American language and literature. The guide is part of the literature section in the *Virtual Library of Anglo-American Culture*, sponsored by the State and University Library of Göttingen, Germany. *Anglistik Guide* provides several ways to search for specific content, but also offers a simple browse option for those who prefer to discover information through that method. Browsing by subject or source type allows you to select from five major categories, including "New Literatures," where both Australian and New Zealand content is classified. Currently, there are ninety-one sites under "English Literature in Australia" and twenty-seven under "English Literature in New Zealand." Brief records with ratings are available for author websites, associations, electronic text sites, and scholarly journals. Browsing by source type allows you to focus on four categories of materials—information providers (libraries, archives, museums), factual/reference works (encyclopedias, dictionaries, and directories), bibliographic sources (virtual libraries, bibliographic databases, and catalogs), and information sources (journals, teaching materials, and virtual exhibits). Both the simple and advanced search features allow you to identify more specific tools. For instance, an advanced search using the term "Australia" combined with the source type "Organizations and Societies" produces four results. The value of consulting websites of organizations concerned with Australian and New Zealand studies is discussed further later in this chapter, under "Current Awareness Resources."

The *Australian e-Humanities Gateway* is a searchable database containing details of current projects in the e-humanities field across a broad spectrum of disciplines in Australian universities. The *Australian e-Humanities Network* project is the result of a partnership between the Australian Academy of the Humanities, the University of Sydney, and the University of Newcastle, developed in response to the advances in digital technology that are transforming the nature of humanities research worldwide. The aim of the project is to facilitate access to the latest digital resources and to encourage communication between researchers in the e-humanities field. Content may be searched through a basic and advanced keyword search, as well as by an alphabetical browse by title. Detailed descriptions are available for each site. An alternative to the *e-Humanities Gateway* is *Australia's Culture Portal* (www .cultureandrecreation.gov.au/), sponsored by the Australian government's Department of the Environment, Water, Heritage, and the Arts. This site features news articles and links to websites on all aspects of Australian culture, including literature. Unfortunately, due to budget restrictions, the government decided to discontinue the portal beginning in July 2010, but content is archived in PANDORA. For more information, see chapter 8.

Intute is a free online service created by a consortium of seven British universities that helps individuals find the best Internet resources available on a specific topic. Subject specialists within these universities and their partners review and evaluate thousands of websites to assist in the selection of the most authoritative sites for your research. Because all disciplines are covered by *Intute*, users have the option to browse content by category or search for a specific subject. Within the "Modern languages and area studies" category, you can further select by language or country. Categories of interest within the area "Australasia" include "Australian Aborigine studies," "Australian studies," "Māori studies," and "New Zealand studies." Resources listed under the "Australasian" category of languages and literature target the needs of those researching Australian literature. Subcategories are presented on the right-hand portion of the screen for further browsing, or you may search the content and limit by type of information (e-books, images, maps) or by time period. *Intute* indexes approximately forty-one sites, including those for authors, journals and magazines, digital archives, and associations and organizations devoted to Australian and New Zealand literary studies. Detailed descriptions of each website provide immense assistance in determining the usefulness of the information to your research needs.

The aim of **Te Puna Web Directory** is to offer a subject gateway to selected New Zealand and Pacific Island Internet information resources that help libraries, their users, and all New Zealanders meet their professional, educational, cultural, and personal information needs. The National Library of New Zealand's directory of Internet-accessible New Zealand information sources allows users to search or browse content. Broad subject categories of interest to those researching New Zealand authors are "Arts and Literature" and "Māori." Under "Arts and Literature" are sections pertaining to "Languages and Linguistics" and "Literature." Sections within the literature category offer links to individual websites for authors like Janet Frame and Katherine Mansfield, as well as lists of journals and magazines devoted to New Zealand poetry, drama, and fiction. Separate pages concentrate on similar resources for Māori arts and literature.

Zeroland is designed to provide a systematic and comprehensive overview of the best, most authoritative Web pages on arts and culture from around the world. Topics covered are indexed alphabetically by subject, genre, period, name, and country. Disciplines featured are the visual arts, performing arts, philosophy, literature, and film. Within the literature section users may focus on a particular genre or topic, but the most direct access to content on the literature of Australia and New Zealand is through the category based on country. The *Zeroland* gateway to information on Australian literature (www .zeroland.co.nz/australia_literature.html) and the gateway to New Zealand literature (www.zeroland.co.nz/new_zealand_literature.html) are excellent places to begin looking for freely accessible resources on the Web. Categories of information vary, but each tool includes associations and organizations devoted to the study of the literature, electronic text sites, and magazines and journals publishing both primary and secondary materials. Of particular note is the section on authors. Here you will find author-maintained Web pages, biographical descriptions housed on Wikipedia, and links to full-text poetry or prose online. Approximately one hundred websites are available for Australian literature. The information on New Zealand literature is even more robust, presenting additional categories for online literary criticism, literary events, and blogs devoted to the discipline. Well over one hundred links are listed on the main page for New Zealand literature, and there is an additional page on individual authors and another page committed to New Zealand literary journals and magazines. Because *Zeroland* is updated weekly, few broken links are evident, making this an extremely valuable and reliable tool for identifying current Web content.

ELECTRONIC TEXT ARCHIVES

Australian Literary Compendium, at www.australianliterarycompendium.com/ (accessed 26 May 2010).
Colonial Australian Popular Fiction, at www.apfa.esrc.unimelb.edu.au/home.html (accessed 13 January 2010).
New Zealand Electronic Poetry Centre, at www.nzepc.auckland.ac.nz/ (accessed 14 January 2010).
Open Scholar, www.nla.gov.au/openscholar.html (accessed 11 January 2010).
SETIS (Sydney Electronic Text and Image Service), at setis.library.usyd.edu.au/index .html (accessed 14 January 2010).

Due to Australian and New Zealand copyright laws, full-text literary content available free of charge on the Internet is limited. Materials that are more likely accessible are those no longer under copyright, such as nineteenth-century poetry and fiction, or selective works from contemporary authors who have given permission to post the information on the Web. For Australian literature, the National Library of Australia and the University of Sydney are leading the way in digitizing early texts and offering them at no cost to the public. Similarly, the University of Auckland and the National Library of New Zealand have accomplished much in digitizing important texts for the study of New Zealand literature, history, and culture. Many major university libraries are actively building institutional repositories of materials produced by faculty and researchers at those institutions. Books, papers, theses, and other works are digitized and offered to the public with few restrictions, in an attempt to support a model of open access to information. These institutional repositories, sometimes referred to as digital libraries, can be useful when researching Australian and New Zealand literature. Most are still in the early stages of development but will continue to grow over time. For a directory of repositories around the world, including those at Australian and New Zealand institutions, see the *Directory of Open Access Repositories* (*OpenDOAR*), sponsored by the University of Nottingham (www.opendoar.org/). In *Open-DOAR* you can search for repositories by country or by broad subject areas, including language and literature. Brief descriptions of content and links are featured for quick access to each site.

The ***Australian Literary Compendium*** seeks to introduce new readers, writers, and researchers to a diverse range of Australian authors and literature. The website offers teaching materials, links to information, author profiles, and a newly established, refereed e-journal called the *Journal of Australian Writers and Writing*. Each of these components will be updated on a regular basis, with the goal of establishing an ongoing conversation about contemporary and colonial Australian writing. The project also supports scholarship in traditional Australian literary studies and encourages new and creative approaches to teaching and analyzing Australian writing. In addition to the resources on the website, a series of in-depth radio programs on Australian writing will be produced for the Australian Broadcasting Corporation Radio National twice a year. These programs will be posted with accompanying transcripts, podcasts, and essays by Australia's leading scholars. The material may be downloaded free of charge by schools, universities, and individuals interested in broadening their understanding of Australian writing. The *Journal of Australian Writers and Writing* will post new content twice a year on Australian literature. Scholarly essays will be included, along with creative writing, new media pieces, and book reviews. The first edition (1 May 2010) is available, with content based on the theme "Rethinking Contemporary Australian Fiction." The inaugural issue contains poetry by John Kinsella and an essay on Alexis Wright's first novel, *Plains of Promise* (St. Lucia: University of Queensland Press, 1997).

Colonial Australian Popular Fiction is an online bibliography and digital archive that offers a wide selection of popular colonial publications, many of which are out of print and previously difficult to obtain. The archive consists of 439 authors, with references to more than 2,000 published materials and an additional 1,500 images. Texts are presented in their original format to highlight physical and visual characteristics common to books published during the late nineteenth century and early twentieth century. Many of the works digitized were best sellers at the time of publication but are no longer read or studied by scholars. *Colonial Australian Popular Fiction* is part of a larger project funded by the Australian Research Council and the University of Melbourne's department of English and e-Scholarship Research Centre. The goal of the project is to produce a complete critical history of Australian popular or genre fiction from the early to late colonial period. Texts are categorized by six different genres, including adventure, bush melodrama, crime, gothic, romance, and science fiction. Users may browse the collection by genre, alphabetically by author or publisher, or elect to perform a keyword search on the full-text content.

The *New Zealand Electronic Poetry Centre* is a project based at the University of Auckland. The site is designed to be a comprehensive discovery tool for poetry resources in Aotearoa / New Zealand and the Pacific region as a whole. One of the goals of the *New Zealand Electronic Poetry Centre* is to collect current and archival publishing information by poets, and to present full-text poetry and critical commentary in consultation with authors and their publishers. Established in 2001, the site contains links to information on approximately thirty-two poets from New Zealand and the Pacific region. Each page in the "authors" section offers a photo, a bibliography of works, online poems and prose by the poet, and selected critical and audiovisual materials. In most cases you can access poems by major authors like Albert Wendt, as well as hear him read from his own poetry through attached audio clips. There is a selection of full-text commentary, criticism, and reviews by poets and critics, with selected links to online materials. Additional full-text poems are listed under the "poems online" category and include poetry by authors such as Fleur Adcock and Allen Curnow. "Soundnz" is a list of additional audio files of poets (not included in the "authors" section) reading from their poetry. The final category, "tapa notebooks," is a guide to poetry-related materials in the libraries and manuscript collections of Aotearoa / New Zealand and the Pacific region. Currently, nine different authors are featured in this section. The *New Zealand Electronic Poetry Centre* also promotes live poetry events and hosts an online journal, *Ka Mate Ka Ora: A New Zealand Journal of Poetry and Poetics*. More information about the journal may be found in chapter 5.

Sponsored by the National Library of Australia, **Open Scholar** is dedicated to the publication of freely accessible electronic books written by academics. At the present time, *Open Scholar* contains five books, all devoted to the study of Australian writing. These books are part of the *ASAL Literary Series*, published by the Association for the Study of Australian Literature. More information about the association may be found later in this chapter under "Current Awareness Resources."

SETIS (*Sydney Electronic Text and Image Service*) provides access to a large number of networked and in-house full-text databases pertaining to areas within the humanities, including literature, language, philosophy, and religion. Many of the projects are commercially licensed and available only to users at the University of Sydney, but a number of materials are freely accessible on the Web. Of particular note are the ten full-text and image collections listed under "Australian Studies Resources." Those studying literature should examine "Australian Literary and Historical Texts," a collection of more than three hundred works of fiction, poetry, drama, and nonfiction. Examples from this category are comprehensive collections of the poems of Banjo Paterson, Henry Kendall, Adam Lindsay Gordon, and Ada Cambridge. The collection also includes the stories of Henry Lawson, most of the novels of Henry Handel Richardson, and canonical novels such as Marcus Clarke's *For the Term of His Natural Life*, Rolf Boldrewood's *Robbery under Arms*, and Joseph Furphy's *Such Is Life*. Among the nonfictional works are Watkin Tench's accounts of the first years of English settlement in Sydney. Users can identify texts alphabetically by author's name, or browse by broad subject categories such as "convicts" or "women writers." There is also the option of browsing content by thirteen different genres. For instance, forty matches appear for the genre "short fiction." In addition to the primary sources in *SETIS*, users may expect to find critical articles, reviews, and surveys relating to important Australian authors, their works, and other literary subjects. These materials have been selected to accompany specific texts in the "Australian Literary and Historical Texts" collection. Only *AustLit* subscribers have access to these articles.

Another section of interest within "Australian Studies Resources" in *SETIS* is "Australian Poets," a digitized collection of poetry by three major twentieth-century Australian poets: Christopher Brennan, Lesbia Harford, and Kenneth Slessor. Introductions to the poets are written by John Tranter, an important poet in his own right. In addition to being able to read the poems, users can search the texts for keywords. For instance, the term "bush" appears twelve times in the archive: ten times in Slessor's poetry, and twice in Hartford's poems.

AUTHOR SITES

AustLit, at www.austlit.edu.au/browse (accessed 13 January 2010).

Australian Poetry Resources Internet Library (APRIL), at april.edu.au (accessed 21 January 2010).

Contemporary Writers, at www.contemporarywriters.com/ (accessed 13 January 2010).

Katherine Mansfield Society, at www.katherinemansfieldsociety.org/ (accessed 27 January 2010).
Middlemiss, Perry. *Australian Literature*, at www.middlemiss.org/lit/lit.html#authors (accessed 7 March 2010).
New Zealand Book Council, at www.bookcouncil.org.nz/ (accessed 5 January 2010).
Peter Carey, at www.petercareybooks.com/ (accessed 20 January 2010).

The advantage of a website devoted to a particular author or group of authors is that it can link to additional sources, such as biographies, interviews, and bibliographies of both primary and secondary literature. In some cases you can even locate multimedia materials, such as an author reading a poem or an interview discussing a particular literary work. More resources of this type may be discovered through some of the gateways mentioned earlier, or through a focused Internet search. As is the case with all sites on the Web, the tools are useful only if they link to quality information and are maintained on a regular basis. Be sure to evaluate all sites before you include materials from them in your research project.

AustLit allows nonsubscribers access to brief biographical entries on approximately 6,600 Australian authors. Browsing alphabetically by name is the only means of searching content in this portion of the database. Place and date of birth and death are listed, along with a truncated biographical summary about each author. Those who subscribe to *AustLit* may view the full record, which includes details on the location of literary archives, and works by and about the author of interest. For more information on *AustLit* see the entry in chapter 4: "Print and Electronic Bibliographies, Indexes, and Annual Reviews."

The *Australian Poetry Resources Internet Library (APRIL)* project began in 2004 as an early website devoted to information on Australian literature. Designed and built by poet John Tranter, the site was actively developed through 2006, when it was awarded a four-year grant from the Australian Research Council. Professor Elizabeth Webby and Creagh Cole from the University of Sydney were chosen to coordinate a team of researchers charged with building a permanent and wide-ranging library of poetry resources on the Web. The primary goal of *APRIL* is to feature original literary content from Australian poets. It will also include biographical material on the poets, as well as bibliographical and critical materials on their works. As it expands, *APRIL* will feature original texts and basic background information on thousands of Australian poets who have been selected by an advisory committee composed of writers, scholars, reviewers, librarians, and publishers. Because one of its goals is to make texts more accessible for teachers and students of Australian poetry, *APRIL* will eventually offer print-on-demand books and anthologies of poetry. A similar project at *SETIS*, "Australian Classic

Works," currently offers print-on-demand versions of classic Australian books. *APRIL* is scheduled to launch soon.

Contemporary Writers is a database of current profiles of selected writers from the United Kingdom, the British Commonwealth, and the Republic of Ireland. The site is sponsored by the British Council, the United Kingdom's international organization for educational opportunities and cultural relations. Profiles are searchable by author, genre, nationality, publisher, and book title. A search on "Australian" as a nationality produces seven individuals— Richard Flanagan, Kate Grenville, Sonya Hartnett, Shirley Hazzard, David Malouf, Peter Porter, and Tim Winton. There is also a category for "British: Australian" that produces one author, Morris Gleitzman. Oddly missing from either category is Peter Carey, whose profile is featured in the resource. Only one author, Lloyd Jones, appears under the nationality "New Zealander." Entries are substantial for each author, listing biographical information, a bibliography of writings, lists of prizes/awards received, and in most cases a lengthy entry titled "critical perspective." Photographs are also present for all authors represented.

The **Katherine Mansfield Society** hosts an informative and well-organized website on one of New Zealand's most important authors. Because the site exists in part for its membership, much of the content is designed to inform constituents of upcoming society events and news, as well as post current tables of contents of the society's affiliated journal, *Katherine Mansfield Studies*. However, there are other sections of considerable value to members and nonmembers alike. Of particular interest is the category "Resources." Here, users will find a variety of useful tools on Mansfield, such as an interactive timeline of the author's life, a seventy-eight-page chronology spanning the years 1888 to 1923, links to image collections of Mansfield documenting her life both in New Zealand and elsewhere, bibliographies of primary materials by the author (with links to full-text versions online when available), and bibliographies of creative works written about Mansfield. There is also a comprehensive bibliography of secondary sources including biographies, journal articles, books, book chapters, and special issues of journals devoted to Mansfield studies. Similar lists for materials in French, German, Spanish, Italian, Portuguese, Catalan, and various eastern European languages are noted separately. In addition to these research tools, the society hosts a blog, encouraging the exchange of knowledge among Mansfield enthusiasts. The Mansfield Society succeeds in its goal to present the most comprehensive source of information on Katherine Mansfield in existence.

Australian Literature, one of the oldest websites devoted to the subject, has been in existence since 1996. It presents information on Australian authors, major literary prizes, descriptions of selected fictional and nonfictional works, and a blog called "Matilda," which offers opinions and summaries of works since 2004. At present, there are links to approximately sixty-seven Australian authors. As is the case with all information on the website, author biographies are written and posted by its creator, Perry Middlemiss. Each author entry contains a brief biographical sketch and a bibliography of writings. A separate section is devoted to websites maintained by the authors themselves. Currently, twenty-two links are available, including one for contemporary fiction writer Nicholas Jose (www.nicholasjose.com.au/). As more and more authors are creating their own presence online, tools like *Australian Authors* are becoming less useful. However, for information on earlier authors, or as a guide to locating links to author-maintained sites, this resource is still beneficial to consult.

The core mission of the **New Zealand Book Council** is to inspire New Zealanders to read more by promoting reading in general, but particularly to promote New Zealand writing and writers. The council publishes a quarterly newsletter, *Booknotes*, designed to encourage New Zealanders' interest in reading by featuring a mix of news and views on books, writers, and writing. One of the most impressive features of the New Zealand Book Council's website is the "Writers Files." Approximately 150 biographical entries reprinted from the *Oxford Companion to New Zealand Literature* may be found here. For more information on the *Oxford Companion*, see the entry in chapter 2. The "Writers Files" is perhaps the most comprehensive collection of information about New Zealand writers on the Internet today. In addition to the material taken from the *Oxford Companion*, links to updated content are available, such as bibliographies of new works by and about individual authors, interviews, and media clips.

Peter Carey is the official website of one of Australia's most popular and internationally acclaimed authors. To date, Carey has won more than twenty-eight awards, including five Miles Franklin awards for best Australian fiction, two Booker Prize Winners (*Oscar and Lucinda*, 1988, and *True History of the Kelly Gang*, 2001), and one Commonwealth Writers Prize, also for *True History of the Kelly Gang*. All his awards are listed, along with a humorous biographical sketch that could only have been written by Carey himself. Links to numerous interviews, both in print and audio files, are also available. Descriptive information on the books written by Carey is featured on the website. For each title there are links to reviews, a plot synopsis, and a lovely collection of digital images of the dust-jacket covers produced by publishers from around the world. Finally, researchers will find an extensive bibliography of primary and secondary materials, which includes unpublished works, essays, screenplays, reviews, and scholarly criticism on all of Carey's published works.

CURRENT AWARENESS RESOURCES

American Association of Australian Literary Studies (*AAALS*), at www.australianliterature.org/ (accessed 1 January 2010).

Association for Commonwealth Literature and Language Studies (*ACLALS*), at www.aclals.ulg.ac.be/index.html (accessed 7 January 2010).

Association for the Study of Australian Literature (*ASAL*), at asaliterature.com/ (accessed 15 February 2010).

Australian Institute of Aboriginal and Torres Strait Islander Studies (*AIATSIS*), at www.aiatsis.gov.au/index.html (accessed 27 January 2010).

Australian Poetry Centre, at www.australianpoetrycentre.org.au/ (accessed 31 January 2010).

New Zealand Poetry Society / Te Hunga Tito Ruri o Aotearoa, at www.poetrysociety.org.nz/ (accessed 5 January 2010).

New Zealand Studies Association (*NZSA*), at www.nzsa.co.uk/index.htm (accessed 31 January 2010).

The websites described in this section are all sponsored by groups involved in the study and promotion of Australian and New Zealand literature, history, and culture. Because associations are often dedicated to furthering scholarship and fostering communication among people interested in a specific discipline/area of study, their websites can offer a variety of valuable resources. Most of the groups described in this section publish a peer-reviewed journal, convene a regularly scheduled conference, and produce a newsletter or e-mail list announcing recent publications and other news of interest to their membership. In addition, some of the sites feature specialized bibliographies and links to related websites that may prove useful to your research. Along with scholarly gateways and other available Web tools, scanning association websites is a viable strategy to discovering information on a particular topic.

Established in 1986, the *American Association of Australian Literary Studies* (*AAALS*) is a professional organization with members in North America, Australasia, Europe, and Asia. Those interested in Australian literature and culture as well as postcolonial studies are encouraged to join. *AAALS* holds an annual Australian literary and cultural studies conference that offers a forum for the presentation of scholarly work and social interaction with other members of the academic community. Because the association is an allied organization of the Modern Language Association, members are encouraged to attend and speak at sessions organized for the annual Modern Language

Association convention. *AAALS* sponsors *Antipodes*, a fully refereed North American journal of Australian literature and culture. More information about *Antipodes* is available in chapter 5. Members and nonmembers alike may view the association's newsletter on the *AAALS* website, which features current information on new publications and upcoming conferences on Australian literature.

The objectives of the ***Association for Commonwealth Literature and Language Studies*** (***ACLALS***) are to promote and coordinate Commonwealth literature studies, organize seminars and workshops, arrange lectures by writers and scholars, publish a newsletter featuring activities in the field of Commonwealth literature, and convene a conference every three years. Membership in *ACLALS* is offered through ten different local branches in Commonwealth countries. The branch that focuses on literatures from Australia and New Zealand is the South Pacific Association for Commonwealth Language and Literary Studies (SPACLALS), which sponsors a scholarly journal entitled *SPAN*. Similarly, the European Association of Commonwealth Language and Literary Studies (EACLALS) also publishes a journal that often features articles on Australian and New Zealand literature, *Kunapipi*. More detailed information on *SPAN* and *Kunapipi* is located in chapter 5. *ACLALS* encourages conversation among its members through the association's electronic discussion list at Yahoo. The discussion list often posts announcements, such as conference alerts and calls for papers, and allows members to submit photos and other items from conferences. The *ACLALS* website is an amazing resource for those interested in Commonwealth literary studies. Not only does it feature journals sponsored by its local branches, but it also contains an impressive list of other scholarly journals (both subscription and open-access), associations, research groups, and institutes that promote the study of Commonwealth literatures and cultural studies (www.aclals.ulg.ac.be/links.html#aclalsjournals). Finally, the site hosts a small list of bibliographies on selected authors, as well as the major publishers of Commonwealth literature and studies.

The ***Association for the Study of Australian Literature*** (***ASAL***) promotes the study, discussion, and creation of Australian writing. It also seeks to increase awareness of Australian writing within Australia and throughout the world. *ASAL* holds an annual conference and maintains a directory of postgraduate research on its website. The association publishes a peer-reviewed journal, the *Journal of the Association for the Study of Australian Literature* (*JASAL*), which is published twice a year. More information on *JASAL* may be viewed in chapter 5. *ASAL* also sponsors a series of monographs, the *ASAL Literary Series*, designed to meet the need for specialist monographs on Australian writing. The series publishes small print-runs of books on Australian writing designed to promote scholarly debate on Australian literary culture. A list of these publications may be found on the website. The full text may be viewed free of charge via the National Library of Australia's *Open Scholar* Web page (www.nla.gov.au/openscholar.html).

The *Australian Institute of Aboriginal and Torres Strait Islander Studies* (*AIATSIS*) is situated within the Australian government's Department of Innovation, Industry, Science and Research. It serves as the primary body for providing information and research about the cultures and lifestyles of Aboriginal and Torres Strait Islander peoples. All activities of the institute are designed to affirm and raise awareness of the richness and diversity of Australian indigenous cultures and histories. The institute encourages research by maintaining a comprehensive collection of films, photographs, videos, and audio recordings, as well as printed materials on Australian indigenous studies. *AIATSIS* also has its own publishing house, Aboriginal Studies Press, which is one of the most important contributors to monographs by and about Aboriginal Australia (www.aiatsis.gov.au/asp/about.html). In addition to these resources, the institute sponsors the primary journal devoted to scholarly research on indigenous Australia, *Australian Aboriginal Studies*. The journal is interdisciplinary in scope, with a focus on the humanities and social sciences. More information about *Australian Aboriginal Studies* may be found in chapter 5. For those interested in Aboriginal Australia, familiarity with *AIATSIS* and its wealth of resources is essential.

The *Australian Poetry Centre* is an association established in 2007 to strengthen the presence and profile of Australian poetry within Australia and overseas and foster the writing, reading, and appreciation of poetry in general. The *Australian Poetry Centre* offers a variety of services, such as organizing workshops and competitions, creating educational and promotional materials, and marketing and distributing small-press publications. It also publishes a national journal, *Blue Dog: Australian Poetry*, which features poetry as well as reviews and critical essays on poetry. On the center's website users can find poetry blogs, cultural organizations involved in poetry (both Australian and international), an impressive list of poetry organizations and serial publications, book publishers, and multimedia resources devoted to poetry. Not yet developed but coming soon is a comprehensive directory of Australian poets working today. A similar but more limited resource is the *Poets Union* website (www.poetsunion .com/). The primary purpose of the *Poets Union* is to encourage and develop opportunities for poets and contemporary poetry in Australia by organizing readings, workshops, tours, and festivals. Information on these activities is posted on the website, along with links to small poetry journals, poetry publishers, and other resources of interest to those researching Australian poetry. Clips of poets reading poetry is an added feature of the *Poets Union* website.

The *New Zealand Poetry Society / Te Hunga Tito Ruri o Aotearoa* was founded in 1973 by Wellington writer Irene Adcock. It has been a registered incorporated society since 1981, with its stated goal to advance education by promoting, developing, and supporting poetry and poets in New Zealand. The society provides news on recent publications, upcoming readings, national and international competitions, and awards or prizes won by New Zealand poets. In addition to current awareness information, the website contains a "links" page, featuring a selection of resources devoted to poetry from New Zealand and elsewhere. Categories include international websites on poetry, born-digital poetry, and small-press poetry magazines pertaining to New Zealand poets. Sample magazine titles are *Best New Zealand Poetry* online from 2001 to 2007 (www.vuw.ac.nz/modernletters/bnzp/index.html), and *Deep South*, Otago University's online poetry journal (www.otago.ac.nz/ DeepSouth/). Finally, the *New Zealand Poetry Society* site offers links to Web pages on individual poets, as well as funding opportunities and poetry organizations for the support of their craft.

The primary goal of the **New Zealand Studies Association** (**NZSA**) is to encourage the study of New Zealand, both within the United Kingdom and overseas. The association serves as a forum for the artistic, social, cultural, political, scientific, and economic study of New Zealand / Aotearoa. Since its beginning in 1994, the *NZSA* has organized an annual conference, which has taken place at various locations throughout Europe. The association website features a variety of useful resources on New Zealand, including recent publications, news and upcoming events, and an interactive map of researchers within the field of New Zealand studies working in a particular country. Currently, more than 115 educational institutions from nineteen countries are represented on the map. The *NZSA* sponsors a publisher, Kakapo Books, which supports and promotes new and original research seeking to examine, question, and communicate developments in New Zealand culture. It also sponsors a fully refereed journal, the *CNZS Bulletin of New Zealand Studies*. More information about the journal may be found in chapter 5. Unfortunately, the Centre for New Zealand Studies closed in late 2009. Hopefully, the wealth of information linked to the association's website will remain available for future researchers to explore.

CULTURAL AND HISTORICAL RESOURCES

Austanthrop, at www.ausanthrop.net/resources/ausanthrop_db/ (accessed 5 February 2010).

Australian Screen, at aso.gov.au/ (accessed 5 January 2010).

Documenting a Democracy, at www.foundingdocs.gov.au/default.asp (accessed 1 March 2010).

New Zealand History Online, at www.nzhistory.net.nz/ (accessed 1 March 2010).

As mentioned in previous chapters, it can be important to consider the environment in which a particular author lived to establish context for his or her writing. For instance, knowledge about the political, social, and economic climate of nineteenth-century Britain and details about its criminal justice system during that time is vital to an understanding of Marcus Clarke's *For the Term of His Natural Life.* Some of the gateways and electronic text archives we have covered thus far include links to both historical and cultural resources on the Web. The following sites are additional examples of online resources that might supplement your research on Australian and New Zealand literature.

Austanthrop is an online database devoted to Australian Aboriginal tribes, nations, languages, and dialectal groups. Originally, the database was based on Norman B. Tindale's *Aboriginal Tribes of Australia: Their Terrain, Environmental Controls, Distribution, Limits, and Proper Names* (Canberra, A.C.T.: Australian National University Press, 1974). The creator of *Austanthrop* added alternative names of tribes and their places of location. The database is designed to assist students and scholars trying to locate a tribe or a language from the many alternative names and spellings used throughout the literature on Aboriginal Australia. In addition to the alternative names and locations, the author includes brief bibliographies, links to archival files at the South Australian Museum, and linguistic classifications used by the Summer Institute of Linguistics and the Australian Institute for Aboriginal and Torres Strait Islander Studies. Currently, more than six hundred Australian Aboriginal tribes make up the body of the database.

Australian Screen is one of the many outreach programs operated by the National Film and Sound Archive, the government body responsible for collecting, preserving, and sharing Australia's moving image and recorded sound heritage. *Australian Screen* is a promotional and educational resource designed to provide worldwide access to information about the Australian film and television industry. Excerpts from a wide selection of Australian feature films, documentaries, television programs, newsreels, short films, animations, and home movies produced over the past one hundred years are featured on the site. *Australian Screen* also contains biographical portraits of people involved in the industry, including directors, producers, writers, composers, and cast members. Of interest to those researching Australian literature is the incorporation of information on authors like Thomas Keneally, whose works have been made into feature films.

The National Archives of Australia offers a free, online tool that allows you to identify and view 110 key documents that constitute the founding sources of the nation. Users can search *Documenting a Democracy* by region, time line, and four basic themes in Australian history—"Foundation," "Building," "Freedoms," and "Land." In all cases, researchers can link to primary documents associated with each area, such as early Aboriginal land rights and the text of the famous Mabo case of 1992, which inserted the legal doctrine of native title into Australian law. This court decision determined that native title existed for all Aboriginal people in Australia prior to the establishment of the British colonies in 1788. The decision changed the foundation of land law in Australia, as it replaced the seventeenth-century doctrine of *terra nullius*, on which the British claimed total possession of Australian soil. The original materials in *Documenting a Democracy* have all been scanned and include descriptions with explanations of their significance in Australian history.

New Zealand History Online features information and resources on New Zealand history. Content is organized by three categories: culture and society, politics and government, and war and society. A section devoted to writing is available under the culture and society page and includes a seven-page article on the history of New Zealand literature. A media gallery showcases images of major authors. *New Zealand History Online* is sponsored by the History Group of the New Zealand government's Ministry for Culture and Heritage. Another facet to note is "Hands-on history," which offers links to guides, external websites, and other materials of interest to those researching New Zealand history. Finally, the New Zealand history calendar is a regularly updated chronology of key events, complete with images and links to additional information for each occurrence.

CONCLUSION

Resources on the Web are constantly changing. New sites appear while others disappear on a regular basis. The websites described in this chapter represent a sample of the various types of information that can be discovered on the World Wide Web. Because most of the primary texts and secondary materials on Australian and New Zealand literature are under copyright protection, freely accessible Internet content can only complement the other tools used throughout the course of your research process. Print materials and online subscription databases are still essential to a thorough investigation of an Australian or New Zealand author and his or her works. For scholars outside these two countries, the ability to access digitized content through the Web constitutes a significant advancement in access to information, as it eliminates the necessity of traveling great distances in order to conduct basic-level research. Hopefully, the trend toward open access will result in more quality content posted online, further expediting the process of studying Australian and New Zealand literature for scholars in other parts of the world.

Chapter Eleven

Researching a Thorny Problem

Writing about Literature from a Foreign Culture

This final chapter is designed to take you through some of the steps of a research problem. At this point, you have been introduced to a wide variety of reference tools and research practices that will be important when undertaking a literary research project. This chapter will not present a problem and follow it through to its completion, but rather it will illustrate how you can use the expansive compilation of sources discussed in the previous chapters and in the appendix to bring together a logical research plan. Here you will see how to synthesize the types of tools covered and to reach your goal of a well-planned and thoroughly researched product. You can evaluate which tools you wish to use from the titles suggested in the rest of this book, keeping in mind that not every resource will be useful for every project. Similarly, there are resources that will be singularly helpful for this arena of research. Remember, regardless of the research problem, the steps that begin your endeavor should be similar.

We are cognizant of the importance of developing content that runs from the general to the specific, that covers both countries as they are proportionately represented in academic publishing, that is open to a range of theories and approaches, and that evenly embodies the diversity inherent in these separate national literatures in genre, gender, and race. Throughout this text we have paid particular attention, when possible, to works that deal with writing from the Aboriginal and Torres Strait Islander populations of Australia and the Māori population of New Zealand. Certain sensitivities and care are necessary in discussing these groups of writers, and as such the problem of writing about authors or works that derive from these cultures will serve as an appropriate example of how to work through the research process, starting from a point of distinct unfamiliarity.

The research problem treated in this chapter will center on the large concept of Aboriginal Australian literature, but it could just as easily be Māori literature. The processes will follow analogous patterns, and for both topics you will find the resources covered so far will be of immense help. Regardless of your level of experience, the initial research steps for a new project will be similar. For a researcher who has developed an interest in Aboriginal writing but who has no real experience in the subject, a bit of creative curiosity can be an advantage. Some of the general resources in the appendix, such as *The Dictionary of New Zealand Biography*, *The Encyclopedia of Aboriginal Australia: Aboriginal and Torres Strait Islander History, Society and Culture*, and *The Oxford Companion to Aboriginal Art and Culture*, will help to familiarize you with the cultures in a broad sense. Similarly, some of the general literary resources in chapter 2, such as Ali Gumillya Baker and Gus Worby's "Aboriginality since Mabo: Writing, Politics, and Art" and Anita Heiss's "Writing Aboriginality: Authors on 'Being Aboriginal'" in the *Companion to Australian Literature Since 1900* and Jane McRae's "Māori Literature: A Survey" in *The Oxford History of New Zealand Literatures in English*, can help transform an idea to a more defined concept. Soon, an overarching interest in Aboriginal Australian literature can become more focused on the use of myth in the literature.

Before moving too far along in the process, it is important to be able to define the parameters of your topic as discussed in chapter 1. It is also imperative to be able to define the terminology that you use to describe your topic. When dealing with the indigenous literature of Australia, you have two distinct populations, although they are often discussed as one: the Australian Aboriginal tribes and the Torres Strait Islanders. In New Zealand, the Māori population is often erroneously assumed by foreigners to be an indigenous population. Obviously, definitions are important, and your research should start here.

In *Te Ara—The Encyclopedia of New Zealand*, discussed in the appendix following this chapter, you can find an extensive explanation of the culture and history of the Māori people. The *Encyclopedia* explains that the Māori make up more than 16 percent of the New Zealand population and that more than half of them live in urban areas, while some still live in tribal homes. Along with English, the Māori language is an official New Zealand language. The Māori are socially and politically active, encouraging the continued use of the language, supporting Māori radio and television, leveraging tribal assets in the New Zealand economy, and representing the culture with sixteen members of Parliament as of 2004. The Māori were living in New Zealand by 1300 AD, arriving possibly from what are now the Cook Islands and the Society Islands. The Māori was an oral culture, so there is little in writing from the years before European exploration found the islands that are now New Zealand. They were also a tribal culture that emphasized their connection with nature, which was held sacred. White European (Pākehā) settlement took hold in the early 1800s, and this encroachment had an impact on the Māori, particularly the influence of Christian missionaries and the Treaty of Waitangi in 1840. The treaty in English gives power to the Queen of England, while in the Māori language, rule over the country belongs to the Māori. The Māori resisted European control throughout the nineteenth century, and several wars were the result. The Treaty of Waitangi remains contentious into the twenty-first century. In the early twentieth century, the Māori found a strong social and political voice, and into the later decades protestors asserted Māori rights and questioned the Treaty of Waitangi through the Waitangi Tribunal.[1]

More complicated are the Aboriginal Australians, and for this reason it is a good idea to develop a basic and broad familiarity with the history of a diverse tribal population. For a concise and clear explanation, the *Encyclopaedia Britannica* will provide a solid and necessary starting point. After grounding yourself with a general introduction, you will likely want to move into resources that provide more detailed and nuanced treatments, such as *The Encyclopaedia of Aboriginal Australia: Aboriginal and Torres Strait Islander History, Society and Culture.* Broadly, an Aboriginal Australian is indigenous to the country, from any of several tribes that have been in Australia for forty-five thousand years. Likely they arrived in Australia from Asia and from the Torres Strait Islands to the north of Queensland and south of Papua New Guinea. The Torres Strait Islanders differentiate themselves from Aboriginal Australians as a result of their differing geographic origins. As such, you will sometimes see the combined groups referred to as Aboriginal and Torres Strait Islander people or population. Characterized as nomadic hunter-gatherers, the many tribes, more accurately called language groups, at one time spoke more than two hundred languages, and individuals could easily be fluent in several languages, which were loosely geographically centered. Nomadic movement was usually based on getting to water sources, and individuals owned little beyond tools and rarely had established dwellings.

The Dreaming or the Dreamtime is an elaborate spirituality that runs through the beliefs and practices of the Aboriginal people, and it is something that you will want to incorporate into your research if you decide to pursue Aboriginal myth and spirituality in your project. The Dreaming bestowed upon the Aboriginal Australian population the responsibility to care for their land, and much of this was accomplished through ritual. Land belonged to groups based on messages from the Dreaming, and its sacred places were cared for by the males. The details of the Aboriginal society, class, and familial roles are complex. If you want, you can find monographic explorations of Aboriginal culture through your online catalog or through *WorldCat*.

European settlement had a destructive impact on the Aboriginal population. European cultural concepts of land ownership were alien, and British expansion appropriated lands used by the Aboriginal peoples. The population was diminished through a combination of battles and the Aboriginal inability to withstand European disease. By the middle of the nineteenth century, the British settlers enacted laws to care for the Aboriginal population. Aboriginal people were placed on reserves in the early decades of the twentieth century, much like American Indians, and virtually removed from their former way of life. The Australian government and missionaries removed children of mixed heritage from their families starting in the late nineteenth century, a practice that officially ended in 1969, roughly one hundred years after it started. Precise dates for this system are difficult, as it was practiced before it became policy in the early twentieth century and lasted beyond its stated end. In 2008 the Australian government officially apologized to the "Stolen Generations" and the Aboriginal population as a whole for the treatment suffered under the government. By and large, the Aboriginal population still lives in considerable poverty, caught between the new society that is Australia and the culture that was theirs for thousands of years.[2] Take note that sensitivity surrounds the tradition in which names and images of recently deceased Aboriginal people are not to be used for a period of a few months to a few years. You will often see, at the beginning of books, entrances to museums, on online products, and so on, a caveat warning people that they may encounter such names or images. *AustLit*, for example, clearly posts this message on its front page: "Users are advised that *AustLit* contains names and images of people who have died."[3] Regardless of the level of research you have undertaken previously, you may find this area now a nascent interest, with little background knowledge. For a literary researcher this endeavor presents difficulties, because it brings with it areas that fall beyond the traditional purview of literature. Entering into a project like this, you should naturally understand that you are treading on new territory not only in terms of previous interests, but also in regard to your research experience. The Aboriginal Australian culture has been predominantly oral for thousands of years, and undertaking research in this area will require considerable time for discovery and even more time for dedicated reading and conscientious effort to understand a cultural heritage new to you. Using some general encyclopedias and looking at the Internet in order to educate yourself about this new area can provide insight that could lead you to develop a tentative and broad topic statement such as: "I want to explore Aboriginal Australian myth in literature." Obviously this is a huge topic, but when starting on a new area, sometimes your initial inquiry needs to be that broad. A frequent instinct of the literary researcher is to search the *MLA International Bibliography*, so trying a search for *aborigin* and australia* and myth** is not a bad way to start. This search, as stated, is a fairly far-reaching one, designed to retrieve records that include Aboriginal or Aborigine, Australia or Australian, and myth or mythology, but the results list is only seventy-one items. While this is certainly not an overwhelming number of citations, close examination reveals that many are inappropriate for the research project at hand.

Figure 11.1 provides a representative example of *MLA International Bibliography* results for this search. It is important to look closely at these results for a couple major reasons and benefits. First, because the *MLA International Bibliography* indexes folklore resources, you will notice that quite a few titles border on the sociological rather than literary study. For example, item nine in figure 11.1 appears to lean more toward a sociological approach than may be appropriate for your interests. Second, by examining this list carefully, you should notice that some of the articles (numbers four, five, and eight) narrow the focus

1. Indigenous Spirit and Ghost Folklore of 'Settled' *Australia By:* Clarke, Philip A.; Folklore, 2007 Aug; 118 (2): 141-61. (journal article) Subjects: ghost; spirits; myth; British colonialism
2. Pickerdar: The Black One *By:* Lore, Tereetee McPherson, Kaye; Australian Folklore: A Yearly Journal of Folklore Studies, 2005 Nov; 20: 107-20. (journal article) Subjects: swan; beliefs; Anglo-Australians
3. Patricia Wrightson and *Aboriginal Myth By:* Attebery, Brian; Extrapolation: A Journal of Science Fiction and Fantasy, 2005 Fall; 46 (3): 327-37. (journal article) Subjects: narrative technique; myth; Australian aborigines; Australian landscape; Australian landscape; Wrightson, Patricia
4. Rêver pour chanter: Apprentissage et création onirique dans le désert australien *By:* Glowczewski, Barbara; Cahiers de Littérature Orale, 2002; 51: 153-68. (journal article) Subjects: dream; **myth**
5. The Dreaming, Human Agency and Inscriptive Practice *By:* Rumsey, Alan; Oceania, 1994 Dec; 65 (2): 116-30. (journal article) Subjects: history
6. Narratives of Survival in the Post-Colonial North *By:* Merlan, Francesca; Oceania, 1994 Dec; 65 (2): 151-74. (journal article) Subjects: history; myth; Australian aborigines; Raymond, Elsie
7. The Dog and the *Myth* Maker: Macassans and *Aborigines* in North-East Arnhem Land *By:* MacIntosh, Ian; Australian Folklore: A Yearly Journal of Folklore Studies, 1994 July; 9: 77-81. (journal article) Subjects: Djuranydjura; Makassarese
8. Algebra Dreaming: An *Aboriginal* Sequence *By:* Lucich, Peter; Australian Folklore: A Yearly Journal of Folklore Studies, 1994 July; 9: 128-31. (journal article) Subjects: dream; structuralist approach
9. Tracks, Traces, and Links to Land in *Aboriginal Australia*, New Guinea, and Beyond *By:* Rumsey, Alan. pp. 19-42 *IN:* Rumsey, Alan (ed.); Weiner, James (ed.) Emplaced *Myth*: Space, Narrative, and Knowledge in *Aboriginal Australia* and Papua New Guinea. Honolulu, HI: U of Hawaii P; 2001. vii, 281 pp. (book article) Subjects: rhizome; land ownership

Figure 11.1. Modified *MLA International Bibliography* **search results for** *aborigin* and australia* and myth**. **Source:** *MLA International Bibliography* **via EBSCO.**

aborigin* and australia and dream*

1. A Politics of the *Dreamtime*: Destructive and Regenerative Rainbows in Alexis Wrights's Carpentaria. *By:* Devlin-Glass, Francis; Australian Literary Studies, 2008; 23 (4): 392-407. (journal article) Subjects: magic realism; folk narrative; aborigines
2. Looter of the *Dreamings*: Xavier Herbert and the Taking of Kaijek's Newsong Story. Sansom, Basil; Oceania, 2006 Mar; 76 (1): 83-104. (journal article) Subjects: folk narrative; Australian aborigines
3. Songs, *Dreamings*, and Ghosts: The Wangga of North *Australia*. *By:* Marett, Allan. Middletown, CT: Wesleyan UP; 2005. xxiii, 292 pp. (book)
4. Ambrymese *Dreams* and the Mardu *Dreaming*. *By:* Tonkinson, Robert. pp. 87-105 *IN:* Lohmann, Roger Ivar (ed. and introd.); Kracke, Waud (afterword) *Dream* Travellers: Sleep Experiences and Culture in the Western Pacific. New York, NY: Palgrave Macmillan; 2003. x, 246 pp. (book article)
5. 'This Is Good Country. We Are Good *Dreamers*': *Dreams* and *Dreaming* in the Australian Western Desert. Citation Only Available *By:* Poirier, Sylvie. pp. 107-25 *IN:* Lohmann, Roger Ivar (ed. and introd.); Kracke, Waud (afterword) *Dream* Travellers: Sleep Experiences and Culture in the Western Pacific. New York, NY: Palgrave Macmillan; 2003. x, 246 pp. (book article) Subjects: dream
6. Defending the *Dreamtime*. *By:* Gallant, Mike; Language Magazine, 2002 Aug; 1 (12): 19-22. (journal article) Subjects: oral tradition
7. Irruptions of the *Dreamings* in Post-Colonial *Australia*. *By:* Sansom, Basil; Oceania, 2001 Sept; 72 (1): 1-32. (journal article) Subjects: metamorphosis; dreaming; postcolonialism
8. Clocktime and *Dreamtime*: A Reading of Mudrooroo's Master of the Ghost *Dreaming By:* Knudsen, Eva Rask. pp. 111-20 *IN:* Riemenschneider, Dieter (ed.); Davis, Geoffrey V. (ed. and introd.) Aratjara: *Aboriginal* Culture and Literature in *Australia*. Amsterdam, Netherlands: Rodopi; 1997. xvi, 234 pp. (book article) Subjects: magic realism; aboriginal experience; colonialism; dreaming; nomadism
9. Algebra *Dreaming*: An *Aboriginal* Sequence. *By:* Lucich, Peter; Australian Folklore: A Yearly Journal of Folklore Studies, 1994 July; 9: 128-31. (journal article) Subjects: dream; structuralist approach

Figure 11.2. Modified *MLA International Bibliography* search results for *aborigin* and australia* and dream**. Source: *MLA International Bibliography* via EBSCO.

from the large concept of myth to a narrower cultural theme of the Dreaming or Dreamtime. Often, following a lead that you detect in an otherwise too-broad topic will be exactly the thing you need in order to guide research on a new concentration. Look carefully at your results lists, because even if they seem far too broad, you can use them to provide clues and suggestions for new directions that your searches may take. Altering the search based on the discovery in the initial attempt produces a more direct and precise list of citations and is a welcome result. Figure 11.2 represents a part of the thirty-three-item list that a search for *aborigin* and australia* and dream** returns.

This list is useful not only for the citations for articles that will move you along in your research, but also because it includes names of particular Aboriginal tribes. The third and fourth citations use tribal names rather than the broad descriptor "Aboriginal Australians" in their titles. Depending on how far you are planning to proceed with your interest in this topic, looking at specific tribes may be an approach you want to take. Look back at chapter 3 for the Library of Congress Subject Headings (LCSH) that have been developed for Australia and New Zealand. Tribe names are included, but remember that the lists in chapter 3 are selected as representative examples and not the complete headings lists, so if you are interested you will want to look at the complete list. It is also important to understand that a subject heading such as "Aboriginal Australians in literature" does not necessarily indicate literature by Aboriginal Australians but also encompasses characters in the literature, while "folk tale of Australian aborigines" indicates that the literature comes from, rather than is written about, the Aboriginal population.

Remember also that individual records provide more extensive subject headings than you see on the brief records in figure 11.2. If you were to look at the full record for item number seven, for example, you might find other concepts that would be fitting for your interests. Figure 11.3 reveals that ideas

Title: *Irruptions of the Dreamings in* Post-Colonial *Australia*

Authors: Sansom, Basil

Source: Oceania 2001 Sept; 72 (1): 1-32.

Peer Reviewed: Yes

ISSN: 0029-8077

General Subject Areas:

> *Genre:* folk literature
> *Folklore Topic:* folk narrative; folk tale; *of* Australian aborigines
> *Location: Australia*

Subject Terms:

> treatment *of* metamorphosis; *dreaming*; relationship to postcolonialism

Document Information:

> *Publication Type:* journal article
> *Language of Publication:* English

Figure 11.3. Modified *MLA International Bibliography* record for "Irruptions of the Dreamings in Post-Colonial Australia." Source: *MLA International Bibliography* via EBSCO.

such as "metamorphosis" or "postcolonialism" are potentially appropriate for your research. If this article looks to be of interest, you could try searching for *folk literature*, *folk tale*, or *metamorphosis* as subject or keyword terms in the *MLA International Bibliography*.

Locating stories of the Dreaming will also be something you will need to do in order to fully conduct research on this topic. If you have access to *AustLit*, discussed in chapter 4, you can use the guided search option to look for "all languages" of writing, "all genders" of authors, writers of "Aboriginal heritage," and the "Dreaming story" as genre. Such a search will yield sources in English as well as Aboriginal languages. Limiting to the genre of "Dreaming story" will yield 730 hits for Aboriginal Dreaming stories. Figure 11.4 represents this search, and within the *AustLit* record for the individual titles there will often be a link to an external online version of the story. Also within *AustLit* you can search for secondary resources such as criticism. The guided search option will let you look for "all cultural heritages," "criticism" as the form (in other words, the type of article you are looking for), and "all genres," with Dreaming as the subject. This strategy returns fifty-six citations

Austlit guided search in all languages, all genders, Aboriginal heritage, and dreaming story as genre yields 730 hits.

1. Ballawinne (Red Ochre). PROSE. DREAMING STORY. Unknown date. Pura-lia Meenamatla (a.k.a. Everette, Jim)

2. Bangarra Blue Tongue Lizard Story. PROSE. DREAMING STORY. Unknown date. Palmer, Alf

3. Budadji. PROSE. DREAMING STORY. Unknown date.

   Coleman, Ashley (a.k.a. Galgam)

4. The Coming of a Warrior. PROSE. DREAMING STORY. Unknown date. Hanson, Elaine

5. Djet PROSE. DREAMING STORY. Unknown date. Gunumunga, Shirley

6. The Goori Goori Bird. PROSE. DREAMING STORY. Unknown date. Fraser, Reg; Saylor, Betty; Wymen, Betty; Lawton, Joyce; Robinson, Nell Muriel

7. How the Mopoke Came To Be. PROSE. DREAMING STORY. Unknown date. Boyle, Josie

8. Manala the Monster Cod. PROSE. DREAMING STORY. Unknown date. McLeod, Pauline E.

9. Ngarntipi (Spinifex Pigeon). PROSE. DREAMING STORY. Unknown date. Nagamarra, Janet

Figure 11.4.   Modified *AustLit* guided search results in all languages, all genders, authors of Aboriginal heritage, and Dreaming story as genre. Source: *AustLit*.

for critical explorations of the Dreaming story. In this database, you can also find Dreamtime as a subject. Once in a record, by following a subject link you will enter into a hierarchical list of broader and narrower topics, including concepts such as magical realism, Aboriginal Dreamtime, Aboriginal oral tradition, and so on. Look back to chapter 4 for a more thorough explanation of the helpful but potentially confusing guided search.

Keep in mind that there are other bibliographies that also provide information about Aboriginal Australian literature, and these resources can be particularly useful if you do not have access to *AustLit*. *Black Australian Literature: A Bibliography of Fiction, Poetry, Drama, Oral Traditions and Non-Fiction, Including Critical Commentary, 1900–1991*, covered in chapter 4, is a thorough although somewhat dated bibliography of primary and secondary works by and about Aboriginal authors and literature. *Modern Australian Prose, 1901–1975: A Guide to Information Sources*, also discussed in chapter 4, has a section on Aboriginal themes in literature. Note, however, that this book was published in 1980, and it at once reflects a different approach to the topic than you will find with today's scholarship and lacks several years of coverage.

While this is a good start for a new research project, think now about what other types of documents you might like to use in such an undertaking. As your research progresses, it will reach the point where you have several directions in which you can take it. You may want to look at a particular state or geographical region, a particular language group, or a specific Dreaming theme, to name a few examples. The *Australian Indigenous Index*, discussed in chapter 7, indexes the *Koori Mail* and several other publications for and by Aboriginal peoples. This will be a good place to look for commentary from the Aboriginal and Torres Strait Islander populations about the Dreaming or literature in general. *Intute*, covered in chapter 10, is a solid resource for locating Internet resources in your research. Searching *Intute* broadly for websites about Aboriginal Australians retrieves links to and descriptions of high-quality resources that cover Aboriginal art, literature, social justice, history, reaction to white settlement, and more. For detailed and authoritative information on the culture, historical and current, of the Aboriginal population, the *Australian Institute of Aboriginal and Torres Strait Islander Studies* (see chapter 10 for details) contains a wealth of material in a variety of formats, including archival materials. One of the institute's primary goals is "to develop, maintain and preserve well-documented archives and collections, and to maximise access to these materials," so you will be well served by exploring their Web page.[4]

Also revisit the biographical resources covered in chapter 2. The *Dictionary of Literary Biography* (particularly volume 325, *Australian Writers,*

1975–2000; volume 289, *Australian Writers, 1950–1975*; and volume 230, *Australian Literature, 1788–1914*) includes bio-bibliographic essays on authors of Aboriginal heritage. Similarly, *Australian Literary Pseudonyms: An Index with Selected New Zealand References* can be of potential benefit because, as mentioned in chapter 2, some white authors have co-opted or created Aboriginal identities in order to sell their books.

As you pursue this project, also remember to take note of those resources that do not seem to cover the literary traditions of Aboriginal Australians. Is there a trend in coverage, or lack thereof? Are certain publishers more likely than others to include commentary on Aboriginal authors? Is there a developing tendency throughout time toward acknowledgment and acceptance? These issues are all important to consider when in the midst of a research project, and one such as this is particularly sensitive to trends and perceptions. *Australian Newspapers, 1803–1954* and *Australian Periodical Publications 1840–1845*, from chapter 7, are excellent places for contemporary commentary on the Aboriginal population from the point of view of white Australia, representing a broad temporal coverage. Review chapter 7 for other period publications. If you want to look at reviews of books by Aboriginal authors, take another look at the copious resources treated in chapter 6. Similarly, once you have made a decision about a topical direction, use your library catalog and *WorldCat* to locate monographic treatments of Aboriginal literature. Also remember, research that involves a culture unfamiliar to you, a culture surrounded in a difficult and increasingly sensitive history and future, warrants respect and sincerity of intention. In recent years there have been several academic treatments of Aboriginal and Māori writings. Penelope Van Toorn's *Writing Never Arrives Naked: Early Aboriginal Cultures of Writing in Australia*, for example, explores Aboriginal reading and writing, colonial impact on literacy, appropriation of writing systems among colonists and the indigenous population, women's writings, and contemporary Aboriginal writing. Anita Heiss's *Dhuuluu-yala—To Talk Straight: Publishing Indigenous Literature* provides a historical overview of Aboriginal writing and authors, editing, publishing, and reading, and closes with a lengthy bibliography of primary and secondary resources. *The Circle and the Spiral: A Study of Australian Aboriginal and New Zealand Māori Literature* by Eva Rask Knudsen treats the developments toward the end of the twentieth century in Māori and Aboriginal literatures. These books, and others, offer a wealth of information, much of which is based on extensive research. They also are prefaced by important introductory material that discusses the difficulty in writing about the literature of the Aboriginal Australians. If these books are promising for your research, you can use the subject headings in catalog records to help you find other similar titles.

This is only one example of an area that is at once of interest and potential but also a difficult area. If you find yourself in a situation like this, one that is greatly interesting but also complicated and potentially loaded, remember that your reference librarians are a willing resource who can be of immense help. They will be able to point you in directions to propel your research toward a successful end. If you approach a reference desk with your research at a point where you do not know where to go next, you are really asking a network of colleagues who share an interest in helping researchers and who know where to turn when they may not know how to handle your specific request. Reference librarians enjoy challenges, so take advantage.

CONCLUSION

When we started this book, we did so with a realization that many students and scholars who would use it would likely not be overly familiar with the literatures of Australia and New Zealand. This final chapter also reflects that assumption. As the academic community becomes an increasingly global one, the traditional English literary canon is expanding to embrace Anglophone literatures like those from Australia and New Zealand, as well as from Canada, the West Indies, Africa, South Asia, and so on. For these areas, you and your eventual project will benefit from familiarizing yourself with the country and the culture in addition to the specific work or author that you find interesting. Regardless of the research problem, the works covered in this book should help move your project through to completion.

Research is not necessarily a linear process, in spite of the fact that this book takes you on a neat, step-by-step walk through research resources. At any point, you may have to jump ahead or return to a book or database that you thought you were through with long ago. Although we have made every attempt to provide the most current information in this book, circumstances can change quickly. New titles supersede older ones, sometimes with little change and sometimes with important new information. Formats are also fluid. With the proliferation of online resources available, it can be hard to stay on top of the newest resources, while high-quality, open-access resources can disappear overnight or languish unattended due to funding issues. Use this book to help you navigate your research, but also use it as a starting point. The methodologies and processes discussed should also lead you to areas and tools that are not covered here but that will nevertheless serve you well in your research. The literatures of Australia and New Zealand offer challenges and opportunities that are unique and exciting, and ideally this book will help you develop a lasting interest in these areas.

NOTES

1. Te Ahukaramū Charles Royal, "Māori—People and Culture Today," in *Te Ara—the Encyclopedia of New Zealand*, 2009 (www.TeAra.govt.nz/en/maori/1).

2. *Encyclopædia Britannica Online*, s.v. "Australian Aborigine," search.eb.com/eb/article-9394920 (accessed 11 April 2010).

3. *AustLit: The Australian Literature Resource* (Canberra, A.C.T.: University of New South Wales at Australian Defense Force Academy, 1999–), www.austlit.edu.au (accessed 15 April 2010).

4. Australian Institute of Aboriginal and Torres Strait Islander Studies, www.aiatsis.gov.au/collections/overview.html (accessed 15 April 2010).

Appendix

Selected Resources in Related Disciplines

The final section of this book is devoted to a selective list of resources that supplement the materials discussed throughout previous chapters. Most of the items featured are reference tools, such as encyclopedias or dictionaries that may be used to locate definitions or brief articles on a variety of topics pertaining to Australia and New Zealand. Knowledge about a specific person, place, or event in Australian or New Zealand history can contribute to the understanding of a work of literature. For example, having a sense of the historical and cultural importance of Ned Kelly is extremely valuable when reading Peter Carey's *True History of the Kelly Gang*. Not as critical as the Ned Kelly example but still pertinent to appreciating Carey's later novel, *My Life as a Fake*, is background information on the Ern Malley hoax. Specialized dictionaries and encyclopedias devoted to Australia furnish facts and data in a brief essay, alleviating the need to read an entire book on a topic. Australians and New Zealanders are noted for their colorful slang and abbreviated expressions. Thus, you may find it beneficial to consult a dictionary as you read a particular text. If you find that the typical overview of an encyclopedia is not enough information for your needs, consider using an index or a subject-specific bibliography to identify additional resources. Selected indexes and bibliographies are listed in the following sections, along with details on their coverage and scope.

The first category is devoted to guides and bibliographies that outline and describe reference materials on a variety of topics. The remaining sections are arranged alphabetically and profile encyclopedias, dictionaries, and indexes devoted to a particular subject area. An emphasis on materials in the humanities and social sciences disciplines is deliberate. As noted in chapter 2, the research guides by Michael Marcuse and James Harner remain the best option for literary studies. Remember to consult a librarian if you have questions about these or other reference materials that might augment your research in Australian and New Zealand literature. Some of the online tools mentioned in this chapter are available only through commercial subscriptions, and licensing agreements for their use will vary among institutions. Check your local library catalog to determine if you have access to these restricted databases.

GENERAL

Dictionaries, Encyclopedias, and Handbooks

MacDougall, Tony, ed. *The Australian Encyclopaedia*. 6th ed. 8 vols. Terrey Hills, N.S.W.: Australian Geographic Society, 1996.

This encyclopedia bills itself as the oldest and the newest of authoritative general reference works on Australia. As typical of most multivolume encyclopedias, content is arranged alphabetically within the first seven volumes, and the final volume serves as an index to the entire set. Volume 8 also contains an appendix of useful facts on population, government, and literary and art award winners, as well as Australian sporting records. Many entries contain illustrations or photographs, and bibliographies are available for those interested in learning more about a specific topic.

Te Ara—The Encyclopedia of New Zealand. Available online at www.teara.govt.nz/.

This website incorporates and updates the content in A. H. McLintock's *An Encyclopaedia of New Zealand* (3 vols. Wellington: R. E. Owen, Government Printer, 1966), serving as a comprehensive guide to New Zealand's people, culture, history, environment, economy, and society. The online version is a work in progress but eventually will consist of nine major themes: New Zealanders—the arrival and settlement of the people; Earth, Sea, and Sky—marine life, natural resources, geology, and climate; The Bush—New Zealand's landforms, fauna, and flora; The Settled Landscape—farming, rural life, and people's impact on the land; Trade and Exchange—the economy, business, and city life; Connections—social groups, families, and communities; Nation—systems of government and symbols of national identity; Daily Life—the customs, leisure activities, and beliefs unique to New Zealand; and Creativity—arts, culture, and invention. "New Zealand in Brief" lists current facts about the country and its people.

Guides

Balay, Robert, ed. *Guide to Reference Books*. 11th ed. Chicago: American Library Association, 1996.

Balay's guide is a standard tool for locating reference books in all disciplines. Works are arranged by broad subject areas, such as general reference works, humanities, social and behavioral sciences, history and area studies, and science, technology, and medicine. Resources devoted to Australia and Oceania are located under the history and area studies section. Entries are annotated, featuring tables of contents and a description of the source. *Guide to Reference Books* is a good place to begin research; however, it is advisable to consult the index to locate resources specific to Australia and New Zealand.

Blazek, Ron, and Elizabeth Aversa. *The Humanities: A Selective Guide to Information Resources.* 5th ed. Englewood, Colo.: Libraries Unlimited, 2000.
Blazek and Aversa's guide highlights core reference tools in the humanities. Chapters are devoted to areas such as general humanities, philosophy, religion, visual arts, performing arts, and language and literature. Sections present an overview of the discipline, followed by annotated entries on major bibliographies, guides, dictionaries, encyclopedias, handbooks, histories, directories, Internet sites, and other tools available in each area. For literature, materials are arranged by genre and by language. A subject/keyword index provides additional access to content. An alternative source that describes reference materials specific to the study of religion, language, literature, performing arts, and fine arts in Australia is Wilma Radford's *Guide to Australian Reference Books: Humanities* (Sydney: Library Association of Australia, 1983).

Borchardt, D. H. *Australian Bibliography: A Guide to Printed Sources of Information.* Rushcutters Bay, N.S.W.: Pergamon, 1976.
Even if a bit outdated, this bibliography is still a useful tool for guiding researchers to important resources on Australia. Rather than providing long lists of annotated items, Borchardt opted for descriptive essays on core materials by subject area, and in doing so created a very readable overview of disciplines covered. Most of the content is devoted to bibliographies in the social sciences, humanities, and pure and applied sciences. The final chapter lists all works mentioned in the text of the book. A subject index allows quick access to titles by topic.

Walford's Guide to Reference Material. 8th ed. 3 vols. London: Library Association, 1999—.
Similar to Balay's guide, *Walford's* is designed to identify and evaluate the widest possible range of reference materials available on a given subject area. The three volumes are divided into broad subject areas: volume 3 pertains to language, literature, and the arts; volume 2 is devoted to sociology, history, philosophy, and religion; and volume 1 covers science, technology, and medicine. Materials in each section are arranged by type, such as bibliographies, indexes, encyclopedias, dictionaries, histories, and periodicals. Note that volume 3 contains a section on "Australasian Literature," which may be useful, though most of the items have been mentioned in previous chapters of this book.

Wood, G. A. *Studying New Zealand: A Guide to Sources.* Otago: University of Otago Press, 1999.
Wood's book is indispensable to those seeking guidance on the discovery of resources about New Zealand. Historical overviews of the standard tools are included, as well as descriptions of updated versions that may have replaced them. Chapters are devoted

to major reference works, subject bibliographies, periodicals, official government documents, theses, and archives and manuscripts. Chapter 10 concentrates on locating Māori-specific information. Finally, an index to content allows quick access to specific tools by title, author, and subject.

Indexes and Bibliographies

A Bibliography of New Zealand Bibliographies. Wellington: New Zealand Library Association, 1967.
While increasingly outdated, this bibliography is still useful for identifying information within the humanities, social sciences, and sciences disciplines in New Zealand. Approximately twenty entries are devoted to literary studies (literature, poetry, drama, and fiction).

Ferguson, John Alexander. *Bibliography of Australia*. 7 vols. Sydney: Angus and Robertson, 1941–1969.
Each volume in this bibliography covers a specific time period: 1. 1784–1830; 2. 1831–1838; 3. 1839–1845; 4. 1846–1850; 5. 1851–1900 (A–G); 6. 1851–1900 (H–P); 7. 1851–1900 (Q–Z). Entries are arranged chronologically and include books, pamphlets, broadsides, and periodicals. Maps, charts, and prints, as well as specific articles in periodicals, have been excluded. Materials featured may be published anywhere, but the content must relate to Australia. Descriptions of content with selected tables of contents are available for most items. Ferguson's work is modeled on the standard bibliographic tool for early New Zealand publishing, Thomas Hocken's *Bibliography of the Literature Relating to New Zealand* (Wellington: J. Mackay, Government Printer, 1909).

Kepars, I., comp. *Australia*. 2nd ed. Santa Barbara, Calif.: ABC-CLIO, 1994.
Volume 46 of *The World Bibliographical Series*, this bibliography contains annotated entries for works dealing with all aspects of Australia—history, geography, economy, and politics. Materials on the Australian people, their culture, customs, religion, and social structures are featured, along with the environment, immigration, ethnic groups, performing arts, literature, and language studies. Of particular note are the sections devoted to film and Aboriginal studies. The section on Aboriginal Australia is divided into the subcategories of general works, black viewpoints (which includes autobiographies by Aboriginal authors), and race relations. For more detailed information on Tasmania, see Kepars's companion volume in the same series (volume 194, Santa Barbara, Calif.: ABC-CLIO, 1987).

Patterson, Brad, and Kathryn Patterson, comps. *New Zealand*. Santa Barbara, Calif.: ABC-CLIO, 1998.
Volume 18 in the *World Bibliographical Series*, this work contains annotated lists of materials focusing on all aspects of New Zealand studies. Categories include history, geography, economics, politics, New Zealand culture, customs, and religion. Other sections are devoted to geography, flora and fauna, Māori history, language,

environment, education, literature, visual arts, performing arts, and printing history. Of particular note is the section on media, which lists major newspapers and journals published in New Zealand. Within each section, categories subdivide topics in more detail. For example, within "Literature" are "General," "Literary History & Criticism," "Māori Writing," "Anthologies," and "Humor" sections. Annotations are particularly helpful for understanding the scope of each item. Three indexes assist in the identification of a particular resource by author, title, and subject.

ART

Dictionaries, Encyclopedias, and Handbooks

Dictionary of Australian Artists Online (DAAO). Available online at www.daao.org .au/main.
The *DAAO* is an open-access, scholarly reference work. Currently, more than 7,026 biographies written by more than four hundred people are available. Scholars and others who are interested in art history can create new biographies, comment or revise existing biographies, and write interpretations on artists already in the database. Information submitted is subject to editorial protocols before it is published. The *DAAO* is a work in progress, and new content is constantly being added.

Kerr, Joan, ed. *The Dictionary of Australian Artists: Painters, Sketchers, Photographers and Engravers to 1870*. Melbourne: Oxford University Press, 1992.
Kerr's work examines all known artists in Australia during the first one hundred years of European settlement. A criterion for inclusion is that an artist must have arrived in Australia before 1870 and made at least one painting, sketch, photograph, or pictorial print while there. Beautiful illustrations are prevalent throughout the work, and most entries contain a brief list of references for additional reading. A chronological list of major exhibitions to 1870 is available.

Kleinert, Sylvia, and Margo Neale, eds. *The Oxford Companion to Aboriginal Art and Culture*. Melbourne: Oxford University Press, 2000.
Anyone interested in Aboriginal art and culture must take a look at this volume, which contains four hundred color and black-and-white photographs of Aboriginal arts in all manifestations. Content is drawn from a broad field of indigenous contributors—artists, poets, oral historians, tribal elders, and scholars. Emphasis is on the influence of Aboriginal cultures on Australian history and society, and the scope is not limited to any single period or artistic medium. The book is divided into two parts. Section 1 features material on all aspects of Aboriginal and Torres Strait Islander culture, including religion, sacred sites, kinship, rock art, urban art, literature, music, performance, and popular reception of Aboriginal art. An index to content by topic is available. Section 2 resembles a dictionary, with alphabetical entries on major artists, institutions, key issues, concepts, and events that pertain to Aboriginal art. Approximately three thousand biographies of individual artists are present in this section.

McCulloch, Alan. *The New McCulloch's Encyclopedia of Australian Art*. 4th ed. Fitzroy, Vic.: AUS Art Editions, 2006.

McCulloch's *Encyclopedia of Australian Art* (Hawthorn, Vic.: Hutchinson of Australia, 1984) is known as Australia's leading art reference work. This new edition contains up-to-date information on topics of current interest, such as Australian Aboriginal art. It also presents facts on artists, community art centers, and regional art. More than eight thousand entries on Australian art and artists, art movements, groups, prizes and awards, exhibitions and galleries are featured in the updated edition, as well as 1,500 new entries on contemporary artists, essays on artistic mediums, and links to online galleries and other informative sites.

Platts, Una. *Nineteenth Century New Zealand Artists: A Guide & Handbook*. Christchurch: Avon Fine Prints, 1980. Available online at the New Zealand Electronic Text Centre, www.nzetc.org/tm/scholarly/tei-PlaNine.html.

Platts admits to using the term "nineteenth century" in a very liberal sense, as her goal was to include anyone who made a pictorial record of the country or the people of New Zealand in its earliest days of European settlement. In cases where information on the artist is limited, only a brief entry with the name of a drawing or watercolor is provided. In other cases, biographical information, along with exhibition notes and the location of individual works of art, accompanies each listing. Illustrations are limited, and the online version contains links to the *Dictionary of New Zealand Biography* for the more prolific artists. A bibliography on New Zealand art is also available.

Turner, Jane, ed. *The Dictionary of Art*. New York: Grove, 1996. Available as *Grove Art Online* at www.oxfordartonline.com/public/book/oao_gao.

Grove Art Online is a core tool for the study of art history. Biographical information on individual artists, surveys of topics and movements, links to images, and bibliographies of additional resources accompany each entry. Coverage of Australian and New Zealand art is adequate, but you may need to consult other sources for information on minor artists from Oceania. To supplement information on New Zealand artists, refer to the *Dictionary of New Zealand Biography* (see entry in chapter 2) and Barrow's *Illustrated Guide to Māori Art* (Honolulu: University of Hawaii Press, 1984) for images and brief histories on Māori art.

Guides

Choate, Ray. *A Guide to Sources of Information on the Arts in Australia*. Sydney: Pergamon Press, 1983.

Choate's book is one of three in a series designed to update information in Borchardt's *Australian Bibliography: A Guide to Printed Sources of Information*, last issued in 1979. This guide focuses specifically on reference tools important to the study of the arts. Content is divided into categories such as painting, drawing, prints, sculpture, Aboriginal art, decorative arts, architecture, and music. Along with detailed descriptions, a bibliography of additional resources is available for each item. Materials excluded are those on individual artists, musicians, and architects. A name index and subject index allows quick access to relevant content in the guide.

Jones, Lois Swan. *Art Information: Research Methods and Resources*. 3rd ed. Dubuque, Iowa: Kendall/Hunt, 1990.
Designed to help students develop efficient art research techniques, this work also attempts to identify a wide variety of materials pertaining to art and art history. Approximately nineteen thousand citations, with an emphasis on research methodology, are listed. Sections simulate the research process, beginning with how to define a thesis, reviewing general resources, then delving into more specific tools within a discipline. Materials are organized chronologically by period as well as by geographic location. One section is devoted to "Pacific Studies, Including Australia and New Zealand."

Marmor, Max, and Alex Ross. *Guide to the Literature of Art History 2*. Chicago: American Library Association, 2005.
This highly organized and comprehensive work is designed for the serious researcher of art history. Selection of titles reflects a critical examination of almost all the literature of art history published since 1977. Contents are organized by type of source, including bibliographies, directories, visual resources, dictionaries and encyclopedias, histories and handbooks, and sources and documents. Each section is broken down further by medium, such as sculpture, drawings, painting, and photography. The best approach to locating materials on Australia and New Zealand is to consult the index.

Indexes and Bibliographies

Art Abstracts. New York: H. W. Wilson. Available online via multiple vendors.
Art Abstracts offers abstracts from 1994 and indexing from 1984 of an international array of scholarly publications on all aspects of art. In addition to articles, *Art Abstracts* indexes reproductions of works of art that appear in indexed periodicals. Some of the subjects covered include architecture and architectural history, art history, folk art, graphic arts, motion pictures, painting, photography, sculpture, and textiles.

ARTbibliographies Modern (ABM). Santa Barbara, Calif.: Clio Press, 1969—. Available online at www.csa.com/factsheets/artbm-set-c.php.
ABM provides abstracts of journal articles, books, exhibition catalogs, reviews, and dissertations on all forms of modern and contemporary art. As the premier source of information on modern and contemporary arts, content covers the late nineteenth century forward. English and foreign-language materials are available. Topics in *ABM* are performance art, video art, body art, graffiti, theater arts, crafts, ceramic and glass art, ethnic arts, and traditional media such as illustration, painting, printmaking, sculpture, and drawing. A nice complement to *ABM* is the *Bibliography of the History of Art*, which covers European and American art from late antiquity to the present, indexing art-related books, conference proceedings, dissertations, exhibition and dealer's catalogs, and articles from more than 2,500 periodicals. Unfortunately, the *Bibliography of the History of Art* ceased publication in March 2010, so no new content will be added after that date. However, the database is available to search for free through the Getty Center website (www.getty.edu/research/conducting_research/bha/).

AustArt: Australian Art Journals Index. Available online at austart.library.unsw.edu
.au/AustArt.
AustArt is an online index to approximately one hundred Australian art journals held
in the College of Fine Arts Library at the University of New South Wales. Coverage
begins in 1987. Subject indexing is minimal, so be careful when creating your search
strategies. Since there are sources in this tool that are not available in the two databases mentioned previously, *AustArt* is worth consulting.

FILM STUDIES

Dictionaries, Encyclopedias, and Handbooks

Martin, Helen, and Sam Edwards. *New Zealand Film, 1912–1995.* Auckland; New
York: Oxford University Press, 1996.
Chronicles all New Zealand feature films made domestically, or externally, when
the content pertains to New Zealand. Entries record major production information,
technical and cast credits, awards, a brief synopsis, and history and reception, when
pertinent. Descriptions are typically one page in length, and for those films based on
a work of literature (such as *An Angel at My Table* and *Once Were Warriors*), notations
are added to the commentary. Additional features include a chronology of important
dates in New Zealand cinema history, a list of feature films by date (1913 to 1996),
a list of international films associated with New Zealand by date (1947 to 1994), and
a three-page bibliography of additional resources. An index to content completes this
essential reference work on New Zealand film.

McFarlane, Brian, Geoff Mayer, and Ina Bertrand. *The Oxford Companion to Australian Film.* South Melbourne; New York: Oxford University Press, 1999.
Most of the alphabetically arranged content in this work is devoted to people or individual films. Sample subjects covered are "mateship," "Aboriginality and film," and
places in film (Tasmania, Queensland). Entries vary from a small paragraph to several
pages in length. Two appendixes add important facts about Australian cinema history,
including the Australian Film Institute first-prize award winners from 1976 to 1998
(best film, director, leading actor/actress, supporting actor/actress, cinematography,
screenplay, music score). A bibliography and a subject index are also available.

Moran, Albert, and Errol Vieth. *Historical Dictionary of Australian and New Zealand
Cinema.* Lanham, Md.: Scarecrow Press, 2005.
As a recent reference work on Australian and New Zealand cinema, this dictionary
presents information on both historical and more recent films, directors, producers, and
actors/actresses. Content is divided into two parts, one featuring Australian cinema, the
other, New Zealand. Sections include a chronology of important dates and a historical
overview of each national film. A lengthy bibliography (sixty-plus pages) divided into
helpful subcategories (genres, film criticism, and topics such as "Aborigines and Film")
makes this a highly useful tool for those researching down-under cinema studies.

Murray, Scott. *Australian Film 1978–1994: A Survey of Theatrical Features.* Melbourne: Oxford University Press, 1995.
A companion volume to *New Zealand Film, 1912–1995*, Murray's work records information on Australian feature films. Entries are one page in length and arranged chronologically by year of release. Seven appendixes to additional information are available, including a section on the animated feature films of Yoram Gross and a selected bibliography of resources on Australian cinema studies. Finally, the index allows users to locate films based on works of literature, such as Thomas Keneally's *Chant of Jimmie Blacksmith*, which became a feature film in 1978. For a similar guide that examines earlier films, see Pike and Cooper's *Australian Film 1900–1977* (Oxford University Press, 1980). If a simple fact book without critical commentary is preferable, refer to Stewart's *An Encyclopaedia of Australian Film* (Frenchs Forest, N.S.W.: Reed, 1984), which also devotes two pages of content to major novels made into feature films.

Indexes and Bibliographies

Film Literature Index. Albany, N.Y.: Filmdex. webapp1.dlib.indiana.edu/fli/index.jsp.
From 1971 to 2004 the *Film Literature Index* served as the primary index for cinema studies, covering more than 350 film and television periodicals from thirty different countries. In 2002 Indiana University converted the print version of *Film Literature Index* to electronic form. This freely available online database contains citations to articles, film reviews, and book reviews published from 1976 to 2001. Periodicals are a mix of scholarly and popular sources. For more current periodical literature on film-related topics, consult the *International Index to Film Periodicals*.

Hall, Sandra. *Australian Film Index: A Guide to Australian Feature Films since 1900.* Port Melbourne, Vic.: Thorpe, 1992.
This single volume indexes more than one thousand four hundred films that were released from 1900 to 1992. Films were either produced in Australia or produced elsewhere by an Australian director. Documentaries, "telemovies," television miniseries, and short films have been omitted. Each listing notes whether the film was based on a novel, play, comic strip, or work of nonfiction. Thus, the entry for *Picnic at Hanging Rock* refers to the novel by the same name written by Joan Lindsay. Numerous indexes list important actors, directors, producers, editors, composers, scriptwriters, cinematographers, and production designers. A chronological list of films that received Australian Film Institute awards from 1976 to 1992 is available in the back of the volume.

International Index to Film Periodicals. New York: R. R. Bowker. 1972—. Available online via ProQuest at www.proquest.com/en-US/catalogs/databases/detail/fiaf.shtml.
Created by the International Federation of Film Archives (FIAF), this database offers in-depth coverage of 340 of the world's most important academic journals and popular magazines devoted to cinema studies, from 1972 to present. *International Index to Film Periodicals* also incorporates the *International Index to TV Periodicals* and the *International Directory of Film/TV Documentation Collections.*

HISTORICAL ATLASES AND
GEOGRAPHICAL RESOURCES

There are many free online gazetteers devoted to Australia. Since most are sponsored by local territory or state governments, the Australian National Library created a list for easy access (www.nla.gov.au/app/eresources/browse). Look under "Browse a Category," "Social Sciences," and then "Place Names." Print copies of atlases on Australia and New Zealand may be located by searching your library catalog or browsing the collection by the call number range G2740 to G2799.

Appleton, Richard. *The Cambridge Dictionary of Australian Places*. New York: Cambridge University Press, 1992.
Virtually every population center in Australia, down to townships with a population of two hundred or less, is listed in alphabetical order. Government areas and important geographical features are also included. A pronunciation guide is available for most names.

Camm, J. C. R., and John McQuilton. *Australians, a Historical Atlas*. Broadway, N.S.W.: Fairfax, Syme & Weldon Associates, 1987.
The first historical atlas of Australia is part of Tony MacDougall's *Australians: A Historical Library*, mentioned earlier in this appendix. The atlas attempts to re-create the experience of people living in Australia since 1788. Content is divided into three major sections: "Place" examines the environment, land use, and economic activity; "People" examines Australia's social history; and "Landscapes" demonstrates the impact of European settlement on both city and rural landscapes. Maps and graphs are abundant. A subject index promotes access to topics such as Aboriginal languages and population settlements by ethnic groups. For a similar and more up-to-date atlas, see Johnson's *AUSMAP Atlas of Australia* (New York: Cambridge University Press, 1992).

McKinnon, Malcolm, Barry Bradley, and Russell Kirkpatrick, eds. *Bateman New Zealand Historical Atlas / Ko Papatuanuku e Takoto Nei*. Auckland: David Bateman in Association with the Historical Branch, Department of Internal Affairs, 1997.
As the first historical atlas published in New Zealand about New Zealand, this source uses maps and other graphics to illustrate the country's history. The main section consists of one hundred plates focusing on broad subjects such as the settlement of the early Polynesians, the arrival of the Europeans, industry, population, key events, and the environment. A subject index promotes access to more specific subjects featured in the atlas.

Reed, A. W. *The Reed Dictionary of New Zealand Place Names*. Auckland: Reed, 2002.
Reed's dictionary is the most comprehensive record of the origin and meaning of New Zealand place names. Use of the dictionary can be important to those studying New Zealand, as much of the country's history, both European and Māori, is reflected in the names of the towns, cities, and natural features of the landscape.

HISTORY

Dictionaries, Encyclopedias, and Handbooks

Barwick, Diane, Michael Mace, and Tom Stannage, eds. *Handbook for Aboriginal Islander History.* Canberra, A.C.T.: Aboriginal History, 1979.
This handbook was designed to help Aborigines locate information on family history, but it also benefits students interested in researching the history of Australia's original inhabitants. Traditional written sources used by historians, combined with primary sources from state and Commonwealth government departments, mission authorities, parliamentary reports/debates on Aboriginal affairs, and information gathered by anthropologists, linguists, and archaeologists, comprise the tools featured in the handbook. Separate chapters on land rights, oral histories, music, film, and women in Aboriginal society are included.

Crowley, Frank, Peter Spearritt, Alan D. Gilbert, and K. S. Inglis, eds. *Australians: A Historical Library.* 11 vols. Broadway, N.S.W.: Fairfax, Syme & Weldon Associates; New York: Cambridge University Press, 1987.
Published in honor of Australia's bicentennial, this eleven-volume set is a wealth of information for anyone interested in Australian history and culture. Each of the first five volumes examines Australia's history in fifty-year intervals and features an amazing number of photographs and illustrations. The last five volumes focus on specific types of resources, such as *Historical Statistics*, featuring facts about population, economics and trade, education, health, religion, and public opinion. *Events and Places* combines a chronology of important dates and a gazetteer. *The Historical Dictionary* has more than one thousand entries on people, movements, ideas, and institutions that have shaped Australia. Of particular note is *A Guide to Sources.* This volume is edited by D. H. Borchardt, an important scholar in bibliographical studies of Australia. References are divided into categories such as environment, Aborigines, colonization, politics, economy, society, and culture. The final volume serves as a single access point to content in the other ten volumes.

Davison, Graeme. *The Oxford Companion to Australian History.* Melbourne: Oxford University Press, 1998.
Davison's work represents a comprehensive and authoritative guide to all aspects and periods of Australian history. Summaries are written for a general readership and point to additional sources for those interested in learning more about a particular subject. Broad topics featured are the people, institutions, and events that shaped Australian culture and society.

Docherty, J. C. *Historical Dictionary of Australia.* 3rd ed. Lanham, Md.: Scarecrow Press, 2007.
Docherty's work is an introduction to modern Australia and its history. An up-to-date bibliography arranged by subject and type of source is available for those seeking additional information on a particular topic. Various appendixes and a chronology of key events present important statistics, facts, and dates, which lead to a better understanding of the history and people of Australia.

Emerson, Arthur. *Historical Dictionary of Sydney*. Lanham, Md.: Scarecrow Press, 2001.
Entries in this specialized dictionary cover a wide variety of subjects, including famous people from the present and past, major geographic features, notable institutions, and interesting architectural works. A chronology of the city's history and several specialized appendixes present useful statistics and facts about Sydney. A bibliography of books and scholarly journal articles on the history of Sydney, its suburbs and neighborhoods, multiculturalism, social conditions, the literary scene, graphic arts, performing arts, and sports compose a portion of the references. Emerson's book is an invaluable tool for researching Sydney or subjects pertaining to the city and its importance in the history and establishment of Australia.

Horton, David. *The Encyclopaedia of Aboriginal Australia: Aboriginal and Torres Strait Islander History, Society and Culture*. 2 vols. Canberra, A.C.T.: Aboriginal Studies Press for the Australian Institute of Aboriginal and Torres Strait Islander Studies, 1994.
This encyclopedia is the first authoritative and comprehensive resource covering all aspects of Australian Aboriginal and Torres Strait Islander history, society, and culture. Containing approximately two thousand essays and one thousand photographs, maps, and drawings, the *Encyclopaedia* has entries covering subjects such as art, music, language, and land rights. More than five hundred profiles of important indigenous people are also available. A comprehensive bibliography and several appendixes of statistics and other useful information about Aboriginal Australia is located in volume 2.

Jackson, Keith, and Alan McRobie. *Historical Dictionary of New Zealand*. Lanham, Md.: Scarecrow Press, 1996.
The goal of this dictionary is to demonstrate how New Zealand was shaped during early European settlement and how it became the country it is today. Alphabetically arranged entries focus on recent events and individuals, rather than the nineteenth century. A chronology from ca. 200 AD to 1995 offers an overview of New Zealand history and key events that shaped it. Another useful component of this source is the extensive bibliography, which concentrates mostly on history, international relations, politics, and the economy, but also contains sections on literature, fiction, women's writing, New Zealand culture, and Māori society.

Jupp, James. *The Australian People: An Encyclopedia of the Nation, Its People and Their Origins*. 2nd ed. Cambridge: Cambridge University Press, 2001.
Originally published in 1988 as part of the bicentennial, this work was meant to celebrate the ethnic diversity of Australia. Content is organized in four parts: the early history and settlement of the country; indigenous Australians and their society and culture; ethnic groups from around the world who settled in Australia (these entries are arranged alphabetically); and the final section, "Building a Nation," which focuses on issues and themes associated with assimilation, nationhood, diversity, and identity. Color plates and photographs are prominent throughout, and a useful chronology

offers an overview of important historical facts and events. A bibliography of additional sources on the cultures and ethnic groups represented is available, along with a subject index.

Guides

Fritze, Ronald H., Brian E. Coutts, and Louis A. Vyhnanek. *Reference Sources in History: An Introductory Guide.* 2nd ed. Santa Barbara, Calif.: ABC-CLIO, 2004.
This is a useful guide for locating core reference tools in all areas of historical research. Chapters are arranged by type of resource, such as guides, handbooks and manuals, bibliographies, book reviews, indexes to periodicals, dissertations, and government publications. Because the subcategories are broad and tend to focus on the United States, Canada, and Europe, it is advisable to use the index for locating tools specific to Australia and New Zealand. All entries are annotated.

Indexes and Bibliographies

Annual Bibliography. Canberra, A.C.T.: Australian Institute of Aboriginal and Torres Strait Islander Studies, 1989–1995. ISSN: 1320-1158. Former Titles: Australian Institute of Aboriginal Studies, *Annual Bibliography* 0156-1553 (1975/76–1988); *Current Bibliography*, ISSN: 1320-1174 (1967–1975); *Bibliography Series A: Selected Periods*, ISSN: 0572-1059 (1961–1966).
The print form of this bibliography ceased in 1995, but content is indexed in the *Australian Public Affairs Information Service* (see entry in chapter 4) from 1996 forward. Especially for years 1961 to 1995, this is the best bibliography available on Aboriginal studies. Types of materials covered are books, book chapters, magazine and journal articles, conference papers, manuscripts, theses, sound recordings, and photographs. Main entries in the *Annual Bibliography* are arranged by author or contributor, but a separate title index and a subject index enable the discovery of content by broad categories like Aboriginal studies, art, anthropology, health, religion, education, linguistics, history, and land rights. For more current information on Aboriginal studies consult *APAIS*. For earlier resources, use Greenway's *Bibliography of the Australian Aborigines* (see following).

Greenway, John. *Bibliography of the Australian Aborigines and the Native Peoples of Torres Strait to 1959.* Sydney: Angus and Robertson, 1963.
Greenway's bibliography is the first comprehensive list produced on the Australian Aborigines. More than ten thousand entries from books and periodical literature are numbered and arranged alphabetically by author. Content is identified by using the subject index in the back of the volume. This listing can be a bit tricky to use, as there are larger categories with many subcategories through which to wade. The scope of coverage is broad, but categories of interest to humanities researchers are "Fiction Dealing with the Aborigines," "Language: Linguistic Studies," "Literature of the Aborigines," "Mythology and Legend," "Art," "Material Culture," "Music,"

and "Religion." A map of Aboriginal tribes with a corresponding alphabetical list identifies where each group is located geographically. An attempt to update Greenway's bibliography is the book by John Thawley and Sarah Gauci, *Bibliographies of the Australian Aborigine: An Annotated Listing* (Bundorra, Vic.: La Trobe University Press, 1987). All entries are bibliographies arranged alphabetically by author. A subject index and geographic index promotes identification of items by subjects, such as Aboriginal literature, Aborigines in film, languages, culture, music, and song.

Historical Abstracts Online. 1954—present. Santa Barbara, Calif.: ABC-CLIO. Available online at www.abc-clio.com/products/serials_ha.aspx.
Historical Abstracts is the core indexing tool for scholarly research in world history (excluding the United States and Canada) from 1450 to the present. Abstracts for more than one thousand seven hundred academic historical journals from 1955 to the present are featured in the database. Book reviews, book chapters, and dissertations are also indexed in *Historical Abstracts*.

Taylor, C. R. H. *A Bibliography of Publications on the New Zealand Māori and the Moriori of the Chatham Islands.* Oxford: Clarendon Press, 1972.
Sections are divided into forty-two areas, including race relations, economic and social aspects, education, religion, language studies (dictionaries and grammars), folklore, music, traditional arts, and history. Entries within each section are arranged alphabetically. Abstracts are not available. The author has made an attempt to be as inclusive as possible, as reflected in the variety of resources listed (journal articles, books, book chapters, reports, and newsletters). An index by author promotes the location of pertinent information in the body of the work, as well as the identification of prevalent scholars in all areas of Māori studies.

LANGUAGE AND LINGUISTICS

Dictionaries, Encyclopedias, and Handbooks

Baker, Sidney. *A Dictionary of Australian Slang.* South Yarra, Vic.: Currey O'Neil, 1982.
Baker's goal is to offer definitions for several hundred Australian terms, reflecting the variety of colloquialisms used in Australia today. The dictionary represents approximately one-third of the slang currently used. Obsolete slang is not included, but older terms and phrases that readers of Australian literature may encounter are available. Terms covered reflect the developing nature of the Australian character, as recent slang derives from urban areas, rather than the outback, which constituted most of the earlier colloquialisms. The *Macquarie Australian Slang Dictionary: Complete and Unabridged* (Macquarie University, N.S.W.: Macquarie Library, 2004) is a more comprehensive guide to Australian slang and should be consulted if a term is not listed in Baker. Unfortunately, the Macquarie slang dictionary is not widely available outside Australian libraries.

Macquarie Dictionary. North Ryde, N.S.W.: Macquarie Library, 2005. Available online at www.macquariedictionary.com.au/.
The *Macquarie Dictionary* is the standard for Australian English. The most recent edition is the fourth since the first edition appeared in 1981. Many words added to the new edition reflect areas pertaining to popular culture. Definitions and etymologies indicate the historical development of specific words. While recent scholarship on problematic etymologies is available as part of the dictionary, the overall emphasis is on information of interest to the general reader. The dictionary offers a guide to pronunciation, as well as phrases and sentences to illustrate the use of each word. For those interested in words specific to Tasmania, see Brooks and Ritchie's *Tassie Terms: A Glossary of Tasmanian Terms* (Melbourne: Oxford University Press, 1995).

McGill, David. *The Reed Dictionary of New Zealand Slang.* Auckland: Reed, 2003.
New Zealand slang can be very different from Australian slang. Thus, if researching New Zealand language or reading creative works from the area, this dictionary may prove indispensable to understanding Kiwi terminology.

Moorfield, John C. *Te Aka: Māori-English, English-Māori Dictionary and Index.* Auckland: Pearson, 2005.
This is a newer dictionary of Māori that features a basic introduction to grammar and a guide to pronunciation. For a more traditional dictionary see Herbert Williams's *A Dictionary of the Māori Language* (Wellington: R. E. Owen, 1957), which is available online through the New Zealand Electronic Text Centre (www.nzetc.org/tm/scholarly/tei-WillDict.html). For more information on early Māori dictionaries, see Parkinson and Griffith's *Books in Māori 1815–1900: An Annotated Bibliography* (Auckland: Reed, 2004).

Orsman, H. W. *The Dictionary of New Zealand English: A Dictionary of New Zealandisms on Historical Principles.* Auckland: Oxford University Press, 1997.
Orsman's dictionary attempts to record the history of words that are distinctively New Zealand in meaning or use. Featured are words that are important to a New Zealander's vocabulary, words originating in New Zealand, or words used elsewhere but with a significantly different meaning or use in New Zealand. Entries are arranged chronologically from earliest to latest, and each term is accompanied by supporting quotations, a guide to pronunciation, variant spellings, and a brief etymology.

Papps, E. H. *Aboriginal Words of Australia.* Sydney: A. H. and A. W. Reed, 1965.
This dictionary is not comprehensive but attempts to list a representative selection of Aboriginal words from all regions of the Australian continent. Words are arranged in alphabetical order, both in English and the original Aboriginal language. A selection of phrases and sentences is added to reflect context, as well as a brief description of the origin of each word.

Indexes and Bibliographies

Carrington, Lois, and Geraldine Triffitt. *OZBIB: A Linguistic Bibliography of Aboriginal Australia and the Torres Strait Islands*. Canberra, A.C.T.: Pacific Linguistics; Research School of Pacific and Asian Studies, Australian National University, 1999. *OZBIB* is a list of published works and theses about Australian indigenous languages. Entries can be examples of languages recorded as vocabulary, texts or songs, linguistic analysis and comparisons, dictionaries, grammars, language surveys, and other works pertaining to theoretical and applied linguistics. Items are enumerated and arranged alphabetically by author. A separate languages index and topic index allows further identification of content. *OZBIB* is available online for free on the Australian Institute of Aboriginal and Torres Strait Islander Studies website (ozbib.aiatsis.gov .au/ozbib_main.php).

Linguistics & Language Behavior Abstracts (*LLBA*). Bethesda, Md.: Cambridge Scientific Abstracts. Available online at www.csa.com/factsheets/llba-set-c.php. *LLBA* is the premier resource for identifying scholarship on linguistics and related disciplines in the language sciences. All aspects of the study of language are covered, such as phonetics, phonology, morphology, syntax, and semantics. Various fields of linguistics are included as well, such as descriptive, historical, comparative, theoretical, and geographical. *LLBA* features abstracts of journal articles and citations to book reviews published in more than one thousand five hundred periodicals, as well as abstracts of books, book chapters, and dissertations from 1973 to the present.

MUSIC

Dictionaries, Encyclopedias, and Handbooks

Bebbington, Warren Arthur. *Oxford Companion to Australian Music*. Melbourne: Oxford University Press, 1997. This single volume features information on all music from every culture within Australia. Entries on individual composers, performers, lyricists, critics, and scholars make up most of the content. The rest is devoted to articles on musical works, institutions, genres, instruments, and terminology. An alternative source is Bebbington's *Dictionary of Australian Music* (Melbourne: Oxford University Press, 1998), designed to be a more compact version of the *Oxford Companion*. For more in-depth information on a selection of important composers in Australia, see James Murdoch's *Australia's Contemporary Composers* (Melbourne: Macmillan, 1972). For a more comprehensive resource on music worldwide, consult Stanley Sadie's *New Grove Dictionary of Music and Musicians*. Available online at www.oxfordmusiconline.com/public/book/omo_gmo.

Murdoch, James. *A Handbook of Australian Music*. Melbourne: Sun Books, 1983. Considered the first guide to Australian music, Murdoch's work contains more than one thousand alphabetically arranged entries on all aspects of music, such as composers and their works, performers, music companies and associations, music publications and publishers, critics, and major awards and festivals. All genres of music are covered, including folk, orchestral, jazz, country, and Aboriginal.

MusicAustralia. Available online at www.musicaustralia.org/.
MusicAustralia is designed to help researchers access and navigate a rich store of information on Australian music, musicians, organizations, and services. Music scores, sound recordings, websites, and a wide range of other materials held by Australian institutions are featured in this database. All formats, styles, and genres of music are covered. Information about people and organizations essential to Australian music is also listed.

Thomson, John Mansfield. *The Oxford History of New Zealand Music.* Auckland: Oxford University Press, 1991.
Unfortunately, no single-volume encyclopedia or dictionary to New Zealand music exists to date. Thus, this history is a valuable source of information for those interested in learning more about topics such as music from the first settlements, themes and genres of New Zealand music, individual performers, and music of the Māori. Illustrations and photographs accompany content, and a sixteen-page bibliography may be of use for locating additional materials. For more information on New Zealand composers from the nineteenth century to the late 1980s, see John M. Thomson's *Biographical Dictionary of New Zealand Composers* (Wellington: Victoria University Press, 1990).

Guides

Duckles, Vincent H., and Ida Reed. *Music Reference and Resource Materials: Annotated Bibliography.* 5th ed. New York: Schirmer Books, 1997.
Designed for the more advanced researcher, this is a selective list of reference materials devoted to music. Sections are arranged by type of resource—dictionaries and encyclopedias, histories and chronologies, guides to musicology, bibliographies of music literature, bibliographies of music, works on individual composers, catalogs of music libraries, catalogs of musical instrument collections, histories of music printing, discographies, yearbooks, and electronic information. Within the chapter on dictionaries and encyclopedias, items are grouped by nationality and genre of music. Entries on Australia and New Zealand are available here, but use the subject index to locate additional resources in other sections of the work. Although some annotations are brief, this is an indispensable tool for locating information on music.

Indexes and Bibliographies

Music Index Online. Ipswich, Ma.: EBSCO. Available online at www.ebscohost.com/.
The *Music Index* is the most comprehensive subject-author guide to periodical literature on music. More than 850 music periodicals from more than forty countries are indexed. While the print version begins its coverage in 1949, the online version

does not start until 1973. Book reviews, obituaries, news, and scholarly articles about music, musicians, and the music industry are all featured in the database. The thoroughness of indexing and the comprehensive coverage of the music field make *Music Index Online* an indispensable tool for music research.

RILM Abstracts of Music Literature. New York: RILM. Available online at www .rilm.org.
RILM is a comprehensive guide to music publications from around the world. All areas of musical endeavor are covered, and a wide variety of document types, such as scholarly articles, books, bibliographies, catalogs, dissertations, ethnographic recordings, and conference proceedings, are indexed in *RILM*.

RELIGION

Dictionaries, Encyclopedias, and Handbooks

Eliade, Mircea, ed. *Encyclopedia of Religion*. 16 vols. 2nd ed. New York: Macmillan, 2005.
A core work for the study of religion, this tool provides in-depth essays on every aspect of religion—history of religious traditions (Western and non-Western), symbols, legends, rituals, beliefs, doctrines, and institutions and organizations, as well as leading figures, theories, and concepts. Volume 16 is the index to the set and includes a number of entries on Australia and New Zealand. Of special note is a section devoted to indigenous religions in Australia. Each article contains a lengthy bibliography of additional resources for further research.

Orbell, Margaret. *The Illustrated Encyclopedia of Māori Myth and Legend*. Sydney: University of New South Wales Press, 1996.
Complete with extensive illustrations and photos, this is an excellent guide to the myths, legends, and cultural history of New Zealand's Māori population. A list of references for additional information is available, as well as an index to subjects covered in the encyclopedia.

Guides

Marsden, Lucy E. *Guide to New Zealand Information Sources. Part IV: Religion*. 4th ed. Palmerston North: Department of History, Massey University, 1993.
This guide features some two thousand four hundred items pertaining to religion in New Zealand. Categories featured are Māori religion and missions, churches and historical developments by period, religion by regions, Christian denominational histories, non-Christian religions, ethnicity and religion, social and public issues/attitudes, religious movements, and historical theology. Brief annotations describe each item, and a classified index allows subject access to the content, which is arranged alphabetically by author. For a more comprehensive bibliography of religious history in New Zealand see Peter Lineham's *Religious History of New Zealand: A Bibliography* (Palmerston North: Department of History, Massey University, 1993).

SCIENCES AND MEDICINE

Dictionaries, Encyclopedias, and Handbooks

Heilbron, J. L., ed. *The Oxford Companion to the History of Modern Science*. New York: Oxford University Press, 2003.

This work presents a history of modern science that features information on the technology, ideas, discoveries, and institutions that have helped shape the world over the past five centuries. Coverage is international in scope, beginning with the Renaissance in Europe and ending with the early twenty-first century. One hundred biographies of the most iconic figures in the world of science are included.

Guides

Hessenbruch, Arne, ed. *Reader's Guide to the History of Science*. Chicago: Fitzroy Dearborn Publishers, 2000.

The goal of this tool is to offer guidance to those with varying levels of scientific knowledge who wish to explore the vast array of information available on the history of science. It presents a series of essays that attempt to describe and assess books on approximately five hundred topics relating to all areas of science. The three main categories featured are individuals, disciplines, and institutions. A bibliography accompanies each essay. A separate subject index allows access to more specific topics within the broad categories, such as information on Australia and New Zealand.

Indexes and Bibliographies

Web of Science. Philadelphia: Institute for Scientific Information. wokinfo.com/products_tools/multidisciplinary/webofscience/.

This database can search more than ten thousand journals in more than forty-five different languages across the sciences, social sciences, and, to a lesser degree, arts and humanities. Dates of journal coverage will vary by subscription, so check your library for more information.

SOCIAL SCIENCES

Dictionaries, Encyclopedias, and Handbooks

Scott, John, and Gordon Marshall. *A Dictionary of Sociology*. 3rd ed. New York: Oxford University Press, 2005.

Written by a team of distinguished sociologists, this dictionary is intended for those who are relatively new to sociology as a discipline. It serves as a guide to the content and terminology of the discipline and only mentions people when they are sociological subjects themselves. A list of useful websites devoted to sociology is featured in the introduction (viii–ix.).

Smelser, N. J., and P. B. Baltes. *International Encyclopedia of the Social and Behavioral Sciences*. 26 vols. New York: Elsevier, 2001.
This set is designed to offer comprehensive, well-organized presentations on all areas pertaining to the social sciences. It seeks to document established knowledge, while also highlighting current thinking about all disciplines. Each entry defines a specific topic, notes changes in scholarship emphasis over time, discusses current theory and research and specific methodological issues or problems, and concludes with a bibliography of additional resources. The final volume is a subject index and a classified list of entries to the entire set.

Guides

Herron, Nancy L. *The Social Sciences: A Cross-Disciplinary Guide to Selected Sources*. 3rd ed. Englewood, Colo.: Libraries Unlimited, 2002.
This important tool serves as a textbook for students wanting to learn more about the most important reference sources in the social sciences, both in print and electronic. Chapters focus on the following areas: general social sciences, political science, economics, business, history, law and justice, anthropology, sociology, education, psychology, geography, and communication. Within each section are annotated lists of core guides and handbooks, bibliographies, indexes and abstracts, dictionaries and encyclopedias, directories, core journals, and Internet resources. A title index and a subject index allow additional means of accessing content.

Indexes and Bibliographies

Web of Science. Philadelphia: Institute for Scientific Information. wokinfo.com/products_tools/multidisciplinary/webofscience/.
This database can search more than ten thousand journals in more than forty-five different languages across the sciences, social sciences, and, to a lesser degree, arts and humanities. Dates of journal coverage will vary by subscription, so check your library for more information.

THEATER AND PERFORMING ARTS

Dictionaries, Encyclopedias, and Handbooks

Atkinson, Ann. *The Dictionary of Performing Arts in Australia*. 2 vols. St. Leonards, N.S.W.: Allen & Unwin, 1996.
Atkinson's dictionary attempts to cover all areas of the performing arts in Australia, from the colonial times to the present. Volume 1 concentrates on theater, film, television, and radio and features more than eight hundred entries on actors, directors, producers, writers, designers, specific works, companies, festivals, and awards. Volume 2 contains more than seven hundred alphabetically arranged entries on opera, dance,

and music, with short entries on performers, composers, conductors, choreographers, individual works, set designers, companies, orchestras, festivals, and awards. Each volume contains a separate bibliography of sources used to compile the dictionary, as well as a subject index for access to content by topic.

Irvin, Eric. *Dictionary of the Australian Theatre, 1788–1914*. Sydney, N.S.W.: Hale & Iremonger, 1985.

This is an excellent source of information for those interested in nineteenth-century Australian theater. Entries are arranged alphabetically and cover a wide range of subjects—actors and actresses, performances, theater terminology, stagecraft, movements pertinent to the time period, and the role of groups, such as Aborigines and child actors. The dictionary is full of photographs and other illustrations to simulate a multidimensional perspective of theater life in nineteenth-century Australia. Entries vary in length from a few sentences to several pages. Of additional interest is the bibliography of books and journal articles on Australian theater.

Parsons, Philip, ed. *Companion to Theatre in Australia*. Sydney: Currency Press, in association with Cambridge University Press, 1995.

This work attempts to cover every major development and significant figure in Australian theater history. Information is available on all theatrical forms, including circus, mime, puppetry, vaudeville, and musical theater (except for opera and dance). Photographs are available for some entries. A subject index allows access to content by topic.

Guides

Simons, Linda Keir. *The Performing Arts: A Guide to the Reference Literature*. Englewood, Colo.: Libraries Unlimited, 1994.

As there are no entries specific to Australia or New Zealand, the value of this book is its guidance on general resources pertaining to the performing arts. The author attempts to describe, evaluate, and compare a variety of reference sources in the performing arts, concentrating on theater and dance, puppetry, mime, magic, circus, and musical comedy. Music, film, and television have been excluded, but all aspects of theater performance are represented, such as costume, lighting, makeup, and stage design.

Indexes and Bibliographies

Australia Dancing. Available online at www.australiadancing.org/.

This website features both current and historical information about dance in Australia. The directory of resources describes dance research materials held by the National Library of Australia, ScreenSound Australia, the National Screen and Sound Archive, and other selected institutions. The directory is supplemented by links to other relevant Internet sites, which enable the discovery of information about dance and the dance industry in Australia.

HAT—The History of Australian Theatre. Available online at www.hat-archive.com/index.html.
HAT is a nonprofit website that seeks to promote and encourage the study of Australian theater history and the people associated with the industry. It contains articles on theater, short biographies from various newspapers, autographs, and historic pictures of theaters and performers, as well as links to other websites that feature theater and performance history.

International Bibliography of Theatre & Dance with Full Text. (IBTD). Ipswich, Mass.: EBSCO. www.ebscohost.com/thisTopic.php?marketID=1&topicID=177
IBTD, the definitive research tool for the study of theater and the performing arts, is a joint project of the American Society for Theatre Research and the Theatre Research Data Center (TRDC) at Brooklyn College. The database contains annotated entries for more than sixty thousand journal articles, books, book articles, and dissertation abstracts on all aspects of theater and performance in 126 countries. As an alternative source, researchers may wish to use *International Index to Performing Arts (IIPA)*, available through ProQuest-Chadwyck-Healey (iipa.chadwyck.com/home.do).

McNaughton, Howard, comp. *New Zealand Drama: A Bibliographical Guide.* Christchurch: University of Canterbury, 1974.
Though a bit outdated, this source is still valuable to anyone interested in New Zealand drama. The guide attempts to list every play (published or unpublished) and record the details of each play's publication and first production. Location information for scripts within seven New Zealand libraries is available. Entries are listed alphabetically by author, but a separate title index is available, along with a subject index to children's and religious plays.

Bibliography

Adelaide, Debra. *Australian Women Writers: A Bibliographic Guide*. London: Pandora, 1988.

Altick, Richard D., and John J. Fenstermaker. *The Art of Literary Research*. 4th ed. New York: W. W. Norton & Co., 1993.

Atlas of New South Wales. Sydney: Central Mapping Authority, 1987.

Barrow, Terence. *An Illustrated Guide to Māori Art*. Honolulu: University of Hawaii Press, 1984.

Barzun, Jacques, and Henry F. Graff. *The Modern Researcher*. 6th ed. Belmont, Calif.: Thomson/Wadsworth Learning, 2004.

Bebbington, Warren Arthur. *A Dictionary of Australian Music*. Melbourne: Oxford University Press, 1998.

Bennett, Bruce, John Hay, and Susan Ashford. *Western Australian Literature: A Bibliography*. Melbourne: Longman Cheshire, 1981.

Billot, C. P. *Melbourne: An Annotated Bibliography to 1850*. Geelong, Vic.: Rippleside Press, 1970.

Booth, Wayne C., Gregory G. Colomb, and Joseph M. Williams. *The Craft of Research*. 2nd ed. Chicago: University of Chicago Press, 2003.

Brooks, Maureen, and Joan Ritchie. *Tassie Terms: A Glossary of Tasmanian Terms*. Melbourne: Oxford University Press, 2005.

Burns, James. *A Century of New Zealand Novels: A Bibliography of the Period 1861–1960*. Auckland: Whitcombe & Tombs, 1961.

Cameron, J. M. R. *Atlas of Northern Australia*. Darwin: Northern Territory Department of Education, 1982.

Carter, David, and Anne Galligan. *Making Books: Contemporary Australian Publishing*. St. Lucia: University of Queensland Press, 2007.

Curnow, Jennifer, Ngapare Hopa, and Jane McRae. *Rere Atu Taku Manu! Discovering History, Language & Politics in the Māori Language Newspapers*. Auckland: Auckland University Press, 2002.

247

Dampier, William. *Voyage to New Holland: The English Voyage of Discovery to the South Seas in 1699*. London: James Knapton, 1703.

Darling, Keith. *Guidelines to Australian Short Stories: An Index to Australian Short Stories Published in Anthologies and in Certain Periodicals*. Mount Waverley, Vic.: Bibliographic Services, 1978.

Davies, John Lloyd. *Atlas of Tasmania*. Hobart: Lands and Surveys Department, 1965.

Dixon, Robert M. W. *Handbook of Australian Languages*. 5 vols. Canberra, A.C.T.: Australian National University Press, 1979–.

Duncan, John Stuart. *Atlas of Victoria*. Melbourne: Victorian Government Printing Office, 1982.

Farber, Evan Ira. *Combined Retrospective Index to Book Reviews in Scholarly Journals, 1886–1974*. Woodbridge, Conn.: Carrollton Press/Research Publications, 1979–1982.

Fletcher, John. *Poetry Books and Poetry Broadsheets Published in New South Wales: A Catalogue*. Sydney: Book Collectors' Society of Australia, 1989.

Flinders, Matthew. *A Voyage to Terra Australis*. London: G. and W. Nicol, 1814.

Gaile, Andreas. *Fabulating Beauty: Perspectives on the Fiction of Peter Carey*. Amsterdam: Rodopi, 2005.

Greenop, Frank. *History of Magazine Publishing in Australia*. Sydney: K. G. Murray, 1947.

Greetham, D. C. *Textual Scholarship: An Introduction*. New York: Garland Publishing, 1994.

Griffin, Trevor, and Murray McCaskill. *Atlas of South Australia*. Adelaide: South Australian Government Printing Division, 1986.

Griffith, Penny, D. R. Harvey, and K. I. D. Maslen. *Book & Print in New Zealand: A Guide to Print Culture in Aotearoa*. Wellington: Victoria University Press, 1997.

Guide to New Zealand Information Sources. Palmerston North, 1975–1982.

Harner, James L. *On Compiling an Annotated Bibliography*. 2nd. ed. New York: Modern Language Association of America, 2000.

Hazell, Walter, and Howard Hodgkin. *The Australasian Colonies: Emigration and Colonization*. London: Edward Stanford, 1887.

Heiss, Anita. *Dhuuluu-yala = To Talk Straight: Publishing Literature*. Canberra: Aboriginal Studies Press, 2003.

Hocken, Thomas Morland. *Bibliography of the Literature Relating to New Zealand*. Wellington: J. Mackay, Government Printer, 1909.

Hornibrook, J. H. *Bibliography of Queensland Verse*. Melbourne: Longman Cheshire, 1981.

Houbein, Lolo. *Ethnic Writing in English from Australia: A Bibliography*. 3rd revised and extended ed. Adelaide: Department of English Language and Literature, University of Adelaide, 1984.

Hughes, Joan. *Australian Words and Their Origins*. Melbourne: Oxford University Press, 1989.

Jarvis, Neil. *Western Australia: An Atlas of Human Endeavour*. 2nd ed. Perth, W.A.: Department of Lands and Surveys, 1986.

Johnson, Ken. *AUSMAP Atlas of Australia*. New York: Cambridge University Press, 1992.

Johnson, Louis. *New Zealand Poetry Yearbook: An Annual Collection*. Wellington: A. H. and A. W. Reed, 1951–1964.

Karakostas-Seda, Alexandra. "Creative Writing in Languages Other than English in Australia 1945–1987." (M.A. thesis, Monash University, 1988).

Kepars, I. *Tasmania*. Santa Barbara, Calif.: ABC-CLIO, 1987.

Knudsen, Eva Rask. *The Circle and the Spiral: A Study of Australian Aboriginal and New Zealand Māori Literature*. Amsterdam, New York: Rodopi, 2004.

Lambert, James. *Macquarie Australian Slang Dictionary: Complete and Unabridged*. Macquarie University, N.S.W.: Macquarie Library, 2004.

Lineham, Peter. *Religious History of New Zealand: A Bibliography*. Palmerston North: Department of History, Massey University, 1993.

Loder, John, and Sally Batten. *Australian Crime Fiction: A Bibliography, 1857–1993*. Clayton, Vic.: Thorpe in association with the National Centre for Australian Studies, 1994.

Lumb, Peter, and Anne Hazell. *Diversity and Diversion: An Annotated Bibliography of Australian Ethnic Minority Literature*. Richmond, Vic.: Hodja Educational Resources Cooperative, 1983.

Mann, Thomas. *The Oxford Guide to Library Research*. 3rd ed. New York: Oxford University Press, 2005.

Mayer, Henry. *The Press in Australia*. Melbourne: Lansdowne Press, 1964.

McCooey, David. *Artful Histories: Modern Australian Autobiography*. Melbourne: Cambridge University Press, 1996.

McCulloch, Alan. *Encyclopedia of Australian Art*. Hawthorn, Vic.: Hutchinson of Australia, 1984.

McLauchlan, Gordon, ed. *Bateman New Zealand Encyclopedia*. Auckland: David Bateman, 1987.

McLintock, A. H. *An Encyclopaedia of New Zealand*. 3 vols. Wellington: R. E. Owen, Government Printer, 1966.

Murdoch, James. *Australia's Contemporary Composers*. Melbourne: Macmillan, 1972.

National Library Service Cumulative Book Review Index, 1905–1974. Princeton, N.J.: National Library Service Co., 1975.

Peacocke, Kathryn. *Newspaper Indexes in New Zealand: A Guide*. Hamilton: University of Waikato Library, 1994.

Pike, Andrew, and Ross Cooper. *Australian Film 1900–1977*. Melbourne: Oxford University Press, 1980.

Pitt, George Henry. *The Press in South Australia: 1836 to 1850*. Adelaide: Wakefield Press, 1946.

Radford, Wilma. *Guide to Australian Reference Books: Humanities*. Sydney: Library Association of Australia, 1983.

Ramson, W. S. *The Australian National Dictionary: A Dictionary of Australianisms on Historical Principles*. Melbourne: Oxford University Press, 1988.

Savery, Henry. *Quintus Servinton: A Tale Founded upon Incidents of Real Occurrence*. Hobart Town: Henry Melville, 1830.

Scott-Maxwell, Aline, and John Whiteoak. *Currency Companion to Music and Dance in Australia.* Sydney: Currency 2003.

Serles, Percival. *A Bibliography of Australasian Poetry and Verse: Australia and New Zealand.* Melbourne: Melbourne University Press, 1925.

Stewart, John. *An Encyclopaedia of Australian Film.* Frenchs Forest, N.S.W.: Reed, 1984.

Stone, Graham. *Australian Science Fiction Index 1925–1967.* Canberra, A.C.T: Australian Science Fiction Association, 1967.

Stuart, Charles. *Two Expeditions into the Interior of Southern Australia.* London: Smith, Elder and Co., 1833.

Stuart, Lurline. *Nineteenth Century Australian Periodicals: An Annotated Bibliography.* Sydney: Hale & Iremonger, 1979.

Tasman, Abel Janszoon. *Abel Janszoon Tasman's Journal of His Discovery of Van Diemens Land and New Zealand in 1642.* Amsterdam: F. Muller, 1898.

Tench, Watkin. *Narrative of the Expedition to Botany Bay.* London: J. Debrett, 1789.

Thawley, John, and Sarah Gauci. *Bibliographies of the Australian Aborigine: An Annotated Listing.* Bundorra, Vic.: La Trobe University Press, 1987.

Thomson, John M. *Biographical Dictionary of New Zealand Composers.* Wellington: Victoria University Press, 1990.

Tindale, Norman B. *Aboriginal Tribes of Australia: Their Terrain, Environmental Controls, Distribution, Limits, and Proper Names.* Canberra, A.C.T.: Australian National University Press, 1974.

Van Toorn, Penelope. *Writing Never Arrives Naked: Early Aboriginal Cultures of Writing in Australia.* Canberra: Aboriginal Studies Press, 2006.

Walker, R. B. *Yesterday's News: A History of the Newspaper Press in New South Wales from 1920 to 1945.* Sydney: Sydney University Press, 1980.

Wilkes, G. A. *A Dictionary of Australian Colloquialisms.* 4th ed. Oxford: Oxford University Press, 1996.

Williams, Herbert. *A Dictionary of the Māori Language.* Wellington: R. E. Owen, 1957.

Index

About the Authors

H. Faye Christenberry is the English studies librarian at the University of Washington Libraries in Seattle, Washington. She has compiled the annual *Antipodes* "Bibliography of Australian Literature and Criticism Published in North America" since 1992 and is a senior bibliographer for the *MLA International Bibliography*, responsible for indexing Australian and New Zealand literary journals since 1993. Her current projects include putting together a comprehensive bibliography of Aboriginal author Oodgeroo Noonuccal and finding time to add content to *AustLit*.

Angela Courtney is head of the Arts and Humanities Department at the Indiana University, Bloomington, Libraries, where she is also the English literature, film studies, theater and drama, communication and culture, and comparative literature librarian. She is the author of *Literary Research and the Era of American Nationalism and Romanticism*, part of Scarecrow Press's *Literary Research: Strategies and Sources* series. She also edited *Nineteenth-Century British Dramatists*, a volume in the *Dictionary of Literary Biography* series. Current research interests include the outdoor picture gardens of Western Australia, magic lantern slides, and the digital humanities.

Breinigsville, PA USA
15 November 2010
249408BV00001B/2/P